The Philosophy of Science Fiction

Also available from Bloomsbury

Henri Bergson: Key Writings, edited by
Keith Ansell Pearson and John Ó Maoilearca
Understanding Bergson, Understanding Modernism, edited
by Paul Ardoin, S. E. Gontarski and Laci Mattison
*I Am Alive and You Are Dead: A Journey into the
Mind of Philip K. Dick*, Emmanuel Carrère
A History of Light, by Junko Theresa Mikuriya
General Ecology, edited by Erich Hörl with James Burton

The Philosophy of Science Fiction

Henri Bergson and the Fabulations
of Philip K. Dick

James Burton

Bloomsbury Academic
An imprint of Bloomsbury Publishing Plc

B L O O M S B U R Y
LONDON • OXFORD • NEW YORK • NEW DELHI • SYDNEY

Bloomsbury Academic
An imprint of Bloomsbury Publishing Plc

50 Bedford Square	1385 Broadway
London	New York
WC1B 3DP	NY 10018
UK	USA

www.bloomsbury.com

BLOOMSBURY and the Diana logo are trademarks of Bloomsbury Publishing Plc

First published 2015
Paperback published 2017

© James Burton, 2015, 2017

James Burton has asserted his right under the Copyright, Designs and Patents Act, 1988, to be identified as Author of this work.

All rights reserved. No part of this publication may be reproduced or transmitted in any form or by any means, electronic or mechanical, including photocopying, recording, or any information storage or retrieval system, without prior permission in writing from the publishers.

No responsibility for loss caused to any individual or organization acting on or refraining from action as a result of the material in this publication can be accepted by Bloomsbury or the author.

British Library Cataloguing-in-Publication Data
A catalogue record for this book is available from the British Library.

ISBN: HB: 978-1-47422-766-7
       PB: 978-1-35002-827-2
       ePDF: 978-1-47422-767-4
       ePub: 978-1-47422-768-1

Library of Congress Cataloging-in-Publication Data
A catalog record for this book is available from the Library of Congress.

Typeset by Fakenham Prepress Solutions, Fakenham, Norfolk NR21 8NN

Contents

Acknowledgements		vii
Abbreviations		ix
Introduction		1
Philosophy and science fiction		3
Bergson and Dick at the edge of the known		11
The ethics of balking		17
Philip K. Dick studies		21
Note on terminology		26
1	Fabulation: Counteracting Reality	29
	Mechanization and the war-instinct	30
	The biological origins of society	35
	Countering the intellect	38
	The morality of violence	43
	Open morality and the misdirection of mechanism	46
	True mysticism: Immanent salvation	50
	An incomplete soteriology	53
	Fabulation for the open	57
	Conclusion	59
2	Fabulating Salvation in Four Early Novels	61
	Solar Lottery (1972 [1955])	63
	The World Jones Made (1993b [1956])	70
	Vulcan's Hammer (1976c [1960])	73
	Time Out of Joint (2003c [1959])	76
	Conclusion: Super-everyman to solar shoe salesman	81
3	The Empire that Never Ended	85
	A matter of life or (life under the sign of) death	88
	The open and the universal	89
	The life–death chiasmus	91
	The fictitious event	96
	The messianic tension	97

	The remnant and messianic time	99
	The magic of language	102
	Sci-fi: The genre of 'as not'	105
	Conclusion: Gnostic politics	107
4	Objects of Salvation: *The Man in the High Castle*	113
	The fabulation of history	113
	Mechanization and paralysis	118
	Worldly remains	120
	Openings between worlds	124
	The tyranny of the concrete	128
	Objects of salvation	131
	Conclusion: Reality fields	134
5	How We Became Post-Android	137
	The mechanization of pot-healing	138
	The alien god	141
	The saviour in need	144
	Robot theology	148
	Humans: The cosmic bourgeoisie	151
	Android and theoid	157
	Creative destruction	161
	Conclusion	164
6	The Reality of Valis	169
	Salvator salvandus	173
	The believer and the sceptic	178
	The pharmakonic god	183
	Reduplicative paramnesia (time becomes space)	186
	The fabulative cure	191
	Recursion: Valis as limitlessly iterative soteriology	195
	Befriending god	197
	Conclusion	201
Epilogue: Soter-ecologies		205
Notes		212
Bibliography		220
Index		231

Acknowledgements

The researching and writing of this book took place in several different contexts. Part of the final manuscript was produced during a fellowship at the Ruhr University, Bochum, generously funded by the Alexander von Humboldt Foundation. I am grateful to the Institute for Media Studies at Bochum, and in particular Erich Hörl and Maren Mayer-Schwieger, for providing great intellectual stimulation within a supportive working environment, and for helping me find time to work on this manuscript alongside other projects. The patient support and feedback of Leila Whitley was invaluable during this phase of the writing.

The book's main argument, along with earlier versions of several sections, was central to a doctoral thesis researched and produced at Goldsmiths, University of London, between 2003 and 2008. During that time I benefited greatly from the supervision and support of Scott Lash and Howard Caygill, each of whom made the extraordinary range of his intellectual and intuitive knowledge of cultural theory and philosophy available to me throughout (and has done since). I am also grateful to John Hutnyk for his comments on a late draft of that text, and to Andrew Benjamin and Josh Cohen for their careful engagement with the final version. Within the already vibrant interdisciplinary research community at Goldsmiths, I was lucky enough to be surrounded by an exceptional group of fellow students and staff, who provided endless opportunities for stimulating and open-minded discussion on a limitless range of topics: among many others, I would especially like to thank Laura Cull, Sean McKeown, Joel McKim, Theresa Mikuriya (to whom I am also indebted for generous feedback on several drafts), Susan Schuppli, Craig Smith, Daisy Tam, and everyone in the Contemporary Thought seminars.

Though too late to have any substantial effect on the text, a series of inspiring encounters and presentations in late 2012 at the Philip K. Dick Festival (San Francisco) and the 'Worlds Out of Joint' conference (Dortmund) – with, among others, Dilara Bilgisel, Erik Davis, Alexander Dunst, Daniel Gilbert, David Gill, Ted Hand, Pamela Jackson, Roger Luckhurst, Laurence Rickels, Lord Running-Clam (aka David Hyde) and Stefan Schlensag – offered much encouragement for the completion of my own project and the future of Philip K. Dick studies in general.

I am also indebted to the following for a range of contributions, some tangible, some intangible, some recent, some going a long way back: Jay Basu, Pete De Bolla, Laura Burton, D. F. Chang, Deirdre Daly, Robin Durie, Geoff Gilbert, James Gitsham, David Kleijwegt, Yari Lanci, Chris Manasseh, Joe McKee, Leo Mellor, John Ó Maoilearca (then Mullarkey), Sebastian Olma, Ian Patterson, Michael Williams, Tom Wills, David Wright and Nicky Zeeman.

Finally, this book would never have been completed without the constant love and support (and patience) of my parents, Janice and Gil.

Abbreviations

Where a work is cited for the first time in a chapter, the first date given is the edition used or cited, followed by the date of the work's original publication, if different, in square brackets; thereafter only the date of the edition consulted is given. Certain frequently cited works are abbreviated as follows:

CE   Bergson, Henri (1998), *Creative Evolution* (Toronto: Dover Publications) [1907]

MR   Bergson, Henri (1977), *The Two Sources of Morality and Religion* (Notre Dame, IN: University of Notre Dame Press) [1932]

TR   Agamben, Giorgio (2005), *The Time That Remains: A Commentary on the Letter to the Romans* (Stanford, CA: Stanford University Press) [2000]

SP   Badiou, Alain (2003), *Saint Paul: The Foundations of Universalism* (Stanford, CA: Stanford University Press) [1997]

E   Dick, Philip (2011), *The Exegesis of Philip K. Dick* (New York: Houghton Mifflin Harcourt), ed. Pamela Jackson and Jonathan Lethem

Where there are multiple references to a single novel, only the page number of the cited edition is given, except where this might lead to confusion.

Introduction

In his *Histories*, Herodotus tells of a battle interrupted – and a war ended – by what we would now think of as a natural event. The conflict between the Lydians and the Medes had been ongoing for more than five years, with neither side able to establish a decisive dominance. Then, during a battle in the sixth year,

> the day suddenly turned into night. The Ionians received a prediction of this eclipse from Thales of Miletus, who had determined that this was the year in which an eclipse would occur. The Lydians and the Medes, however, were astonished when they saw the onset of night during the day. They stopped fighting, and both sides became eager to have peace. (Herodotus 2007: 44–5 [1.74])

Why should a sudden, though short-lived, inversion of day and night be mirrored by the inversion of war and peace? It is not too hard to imagine how the unexpected descent of a shadow across the battlefield might have given rise to a spontaneous ceasefire. Even today, an eclipse will cause people to stop what they are doing. But in this case, Herodotus tells us, there was no resumption of normal activity when the sun re-emerged: instead, everything was different, and the two warring sides, having made peace, entered a lasting alliance.

Whether we consider Herodotus an inquiring historian or a storyteller, this account seems to invite us to speculate, to experiment with ways of filling in the absent details, just as Walter Benjamin responded to Herodotus' account of the grief of Psammenitus in 'The Storyteller' (1999: 89–90). How was this astronomical event able to have such a lasting effect on human affairs? Were the Lydians and the Medes already weary of the conflict, simply waiting for a legitimate pause in the fighting to open negotiations? Or did the turning of day into night have a more dramatic effect, being taken as the literal or symbolic herald of the end of the world – whose onset abated only when the fighting ceased? Or might the merging of the sun and the moon, two entities appearing equal in power and size, have been interpreted as a sign that the two equally matched peoples should align themselves into a single, superior force?

Missing from such speculations is the significance of the fact that Thales had predicted the eclipse. Does Herodotus include this merely as a tangential historical detail, to add context and corroboration to the main story? Or, conversely, might it have played a more active role in the alchemical transmutation of war into peace? Herodotus seems to imply that the soldiers might have reacted differently had they, like the Ionians, been forewarned of the eclipse. But what if they were astonished precisely because news of the prediction *had* reached them? The idea of being able to anticipate the occurrence of an eclipse based on natural observations was not established as it is today: indeed, Thales' reputed pioneering ability in such areas is among the reasons many have regarded him as the founder of Western philosophy – and some as the first scientist. Yet in that he was extrapolating from his contemporary scientific knowledge to tell of strange future events, in an era in which accurate predictions of this kind were virtually unknown, it would be tempting to add to these accolades the title of first science fiction storyteller.

I would like to posit the idea – somewhat outlandish perhaps, though no more so than foretelling the irruption of night within the day – that the account of an unheard-of, unbelievable event, whose status subsequently shifted, all of a sudden, from the realm of impossibility to reality with its first-hand experience, might have changed everything. Suddenly the impossible appeared possible, as the astronomical and the mundane spheres merged, and the most unlikely, ridiculous ideas about the future became realistic options. The boundaries between the fictional and the real, between war and peace, friend and enemy, dissolved as easily as the circular outlines of the sun and moon.

In fact, there is no first philosopher, no first scientist, though both philosophy and science, like (and perhaps through) storytelling, may have a new beginning at any moment. I chose to begin with an account of an eclipse not only because of its resonance with a series of other syzygies which appear in the course of this study and throughout Dick's work, but because it suggests to me, in an oblique yet compelling manner, a particular power of fictionalizing, of imaging or narrating the impossible, which is able to put an end to violence and warfare. My telescoped view of the eclipse is the product of pure speculation – in fact, it has been suggested that it was impossible for Thales to have predicted a solar eclipse based on the resources available to him, and that Herodotus may have misinterpreted reports of a lunar eclipse that possibly interrupted a night battle (Worthen 1997). Yet if my version of the story seems tenuous and far-fetched, this only serves to underscore how weak this power of fictionalizing is, how easily it may turn against and undermine itself, and thus how much care is required in both its examination and its application.

Philosophy and science fiction

This strange zone of the eclipse, in which the impossible and the possible begin to blur, or to reveal their secret affinity, and to point towards formerly unthinkable changes in human behaviour, such as a turning away from violence, may also serve poetically as an image of the meeting-point of the two central figures in this book, Henri Bergson and Philip K. Dick. One a philosopher, the other a writer of science fiction, as we superimpose each upon the other, like the sun and the moon during the eclipse, it becomes increasingly hard to see which is which.

Despite belonging to very different historical and cultural milieux, Bergson and Dick can each be seen to engage with the possibility of salvation – from violence, war and the mechanization of life – through the power of fictionalizing, or fabulation. Although this book is primarily concerned with their specific approaches to the problem of what I will term an immanent soteriology – that is, the search for a form of salvation that would be adequate for a post-industrialized, globalized society – their shared concern with the relationship between mechanization, salvation and fabulation is one that resonates with a number of strands in both philosophy and science fiction more generally. According to at least some ways of understanding philosophy and science fiction, there is a certain kind of experience and activity in which they may be said to share an origin – albeit an origin that can only be registered as a repeated, originating occurrence, rather than one that is historical and singular. It is thus worth exploring this activity a little at the outset, both as a means of highlighting the ways in which this book is and is not concerned with the (or a) philosophy of science fiction, and as the basic ground of the fabulative activity that I will posit as the heart of the soteriological enterprises of both Bergson and Dick.

The relationship between philosophy and science fiction has received an increasing amount of attention over the past three decades. Several monographs and edited collections are now available on the topic, some aimed at an academic and some at a more general readership, many seemingly intended to supplement the teaching of philosophy, and to a lesser extent science fiction.[1] Such texts frequently suggest or imply that science fiction makes philosophical ideas more accessible. Their increasing proliferation can also be taken as one indicator among others of the erosion, to a large degree, of formerly strong boundaries between the academic and popular spheres, at least with regard to areas of culture such as literature, media and philosophy, and the overcoming of certain prejudices regarding the intellectual value of science fiction, along with a relative easing of the genre's traditional inferiority complex. These trends are also reflected in the appearance, increasingly over the past decade, of a number of publications dealing with philosophy and particular works or figures from popular culture, many of which focus on science fiction. Blackwell's 'Philosophy and Pop Culture' series, for example, has titles dealing with philosophy and Batman, *Battlestar Galactica* (2004–2009) and *Inception* (2010), while Open Court's equivalent series includes volumes on philosophy and *The Matrix* (1999), *Doctor Who* and the *Star Wars* films, not to mention Philip K. Dick.

Whether for the purposes of marketing, pedagogy or research, such publications all suggest that there is value in bringing philosophy and science fiction together. What remains ambiguous is whether, as is sometimes implied, this value derives from the fact that each is able to supplement the other with something it has generally tended to lack; or whether it reflects a greater affinity between them, whereby despite surface differences, they share many basic activities, qualities and functions. It is the latter possibility that I want to pursue here. Drawing connections between philosophy and science fiction as conventionally, professionally understood, clearly *can* have the effect of giving colourful and lively illustration to long-standing philosophical questions and debates (which are often inaccessibly expressed in the philosophical vernacular), while simultaneously according to science fiction a level of academic respect which it struggled to attract through much of the twentieth century: yet we should not allow this to eclipse the less obvious, but potentially very illuminating ways in which key aspects of philosophical activity and science fiction storytelling might *already* be intertwined. I hope to give here a sense of why the strangest aspect of the relationship between philosophy and science fiction might lie not in their coming together, but in the idea of their easy separation.

At first glance, philosophy and science fiction may seem like two quite different creatures. A common general view is that (Western) philosophy dates back at least to the sixth century BCE, if not earlier, while science fiction is generally perceived as a predominantly modern phenomenon. Such conceptions, even when implicit or treated as according with common sense, can be seen as based on what we might call cultural-historical or sociological determinations. They more or less identify the emergence of a phenomenon with the entry into cultural usage of the name by which it has come to be known, that is, with the moment it began to be treated as having a specific cultural identity. Thales has often been viewed as the first Western philosopher because he is the earliest figure referred to as a philosopher by those whose contemporaries had come to view them as philosophers, such as Aristotle and his followers. In a parallel manner, many consider science fiction to have appeared only when the term entered common usage in the 1920s, when Hugo Gernsback employed it (initially in the variant 'scientifiction') to describe the stories published in his journals *Modern Electrics* and *Amazing Stories*, paving the way for its recognition by publishers as a discrete genre.[2] As with philosophy, such a conception allows the 'origins' of science fiction to be located a generation or two earlier, in the writers whose work figures like Gernsback were citing (and indeed republishing) as pioneering science fiction (H. G. Wells, Jules Verne, and Edgar Allan Poe and others).[3]

However, many have argued that science fiction long pre-dates its nineteenth- and twentieth-century forms, a notion which, once entertained, immediately diminishes the apparent historical gap between the respective origins of philosophy and science fiction. In fact, many of the texts cited as early works of science fiction turn out either to be overtly philosophical works or to have a strong philosophical dimension. When in 1752 Voltaire published an account of a visit to Earth by an alien from a planet in the Sirius star system, he referred to it as a 'philosophical story' [*histoire philosophique*]. While Brian Aldiss (1973) maintains that science fiction begins with Mary Shelley's *Frankenstein*, in the heart of the Romantic movement, Darko Suvin has prominently advocated a much older, pre-modern literary tradition of science fiction affiliated with the long history of writing on utopia (Suvin 1979), from Plato's *Republic* to works by Thomas More, Jonathan Swift and many other pre-nineteenth-century authors.

Alternatively, on the basis of Steve Clark's (1995) surprisingly compelling argument that immortality is the most definitive theme of science fiction, possible candidates for the earliest work might be found among the pre-Socratic philosophers, with Pythagoras precluded only by the lack of any extant material; perhaps Xenophanes' parodic 'story' of Pythagoras' belief that a howling dog contained the soul of an old friend would qualify, as having a narrative structure (however compact) and as the first overt reference to Pythagorean metempsychosis (Lesher 1992: 78). Or we might look yet further back, towards explorations of the theme of immortality in much earlier mythological sources, notably the Gilgamesh epic, with its hero's quest to find the secret of eternal life possessed by the legendary Ut-napishtim. There are also non-thematic definitions which would equally seem to produce an overlap between philosophy and science fiction. For example, Alexandra Aldridge's definition of science fiction as fiction which represents a 'cosmic point of view' where 'individual experience recedes into the background' (1983: 16), would seem to offer grounds for locating any philosophical text which deals poetically with cosmology, such as Lucretius' first-century BCE *De Rerum Natura*, within the bounds of science fiction.

It seems one can make a case with at least some merits for finding science fiction virtually anywhere one can find records of storytelling. Nevertheless, the common-sense or sociological view of science fiction as a modern phenomenon remains culturally dominant. It is worth taking a closer look at the presumptions on which this view is based. It seems that, at the core of this established common understanding is the idea that science fiction has an essential relationship to modern science and technology – whether this is understood in terms of its historical conditions of emergence, as discussed by Roger Luckhurst (2005: 15–29 and *passim*) and others, or in terms of the prescriptions and expectations of its founding and formative figures. Hugo Gernsback, mentioned above, one of the most instrumental figures in shaping US science fiction as a modern genre through his efforts as a pioneering editor, critic and author, promoted the binding of science fiction to modern science. As Gary Westfahl observes, Gernsback was explicit that in 'the process of writing science fiction, scientific knowledge comes first', and indeed that 'science fiction *must include scientific writing* (perhaps even taken from a textbook)' (1998: 42; original italics). William Wilson, who coined the term 'science-fiction' in the mid-nineteenth century (though apparently with little direct influence on the genre's subsequent emergence) had expressed a similar sentiment: 'Science-Fiction, in which the revealed truths of Science may be given interwoven with a pleasing story which may itself be poetical and *true* – thus circulating a knowledge of the Poetry of Science, clothed in a garb of the Poetry of Life' (Wilson 1851: 139–40). Meanwhile, the figure generally cited as the most influential science fiction editor following Gernsback, John W. Campbell, also emphasized the scientific dimension, suggesting that the aim of science fiction was 'to predict the future on the basis of known facts, culled largely from present-day laboratories' (quoted in Westfahl 1998: 181).[4]

Whether or not one accepts such prescriptions, it is hard to avoid the fact that science fiction as a modern genre arose within the socio-cultural context of the rise of modern industrial science and technology. However, we should remember that the modern conception of science itself evolved partly as a continuation of, and partly by distinguishing itself from what was previously termed 'natural philosophy'. The astronomer Johannes Kepler, in writing an account of a trip to the moon, titled *Somnium* (1634), '(a) Dream', distinguished his text from utopian fiction by stating that his intention was to 'remain in the pleasant, fresh green fields of philosophy' (quoted in Christianson 1976).

Broadly speaking, natural science distinguishes itself by narrowing the scope of natural philosophy through the exclusion of what it takes as its 'unscientific' or 'unnatural' aspects. Central to these developments, as detailed by twentieth-century historians and philosophers of science such as Edwin Burtt (2003 [1924]) and Alexandre Koyré (2008 [1957]), is the movement away from a view of the world as composed of substances and qualities towards an atomistic and mechanical worldview, in which mathematical and logical explanations are paramount. As this new outlook progressively becomes dominant, anything which is considered beyond its scope – that is, beyond nature – is discounted. Thus both God and the human soul, previously granted unproblematic metaphysical (literally super-natural) status, must, if they are to remain meaningful scientific entities worthy of discussion, either be naturalized, or abandoned (Burtt 2003: 300–2 and *passim*).

As post-Enlightenment science re-imagines and purifies its own history, it elides the fact that what have become its central principles, methods and concerns were not regarded as incompatible with so-called supernatural or metaphysical spheres of interest by those responsible for their formulation and development. Isaac Newton's interest in not only alchemy but religious prophecy and revelation, which has only recently become widely appreciated, would be a good example.[5] Indeed, as Paolo Rossi has argued, the supposedly defining characteristics of modern science as it emerged between the Renaissance and the Enlightenment – the rise of deductive reasoning, scepticism, and a mechanical approach to nature – emerged alongside an equally influential 'complex nexus of themes connecting the cabala, ideographic writing, the discovery of "real characters", the art of memory, the image of the "tree of the sciences", "mathesis", universal languages, "method" (understood as a miraculous key to the universe and a general science)' (2000: xvii). Only later would such areas be exorcized from the emerging model of science, along with 'the foolish, superstitious and impious pursuits of astrology, magic and alchemy – relics of medieval darkness, feebly persisting in the age of new science' (Rossi 2000: xvi). Kepler's *Somnium*, in combining technical details of lunar astronomy and scientifically informed speculations about the physical conditions of space travel, with a story of witchcraft and demons, would be a good illustration of Rossi's suggestion that pre-Enlightenment science had not yet – at least not universally – realized any strong split between a supposedly natural or materialist approach and what would subsequently be considered supernatural and metaphysical themes.

One way of characterizing this shift would be to suggest that modern science in its emergence (while still bound to philosophy) attempts to suppress or eliminate from its own constitution all those elements of the study of nature that from a (post-)Enlightenment perspective would be associated, overtly or not, with the *fictional* – with that which, though it may be speculatively described and discussed, is banned from inclusion in the real. Both rationalism and empiricism, whose rise in their modern forms can be said to be the two crucial driving forces in developing the dominance of this perspective, attempt to discern and specify the limits of knowledge, developing principles by which to separate the known and the knowable from what cannot be known. Anything discussed or considered in past or subsequent discourse which does not belong within the sphere of the knowable so defined, thus implicitly or explicitly acquires the status of what is commonly termed fiction: the contents of dreams, superstition, rumour, fancy and much of religion (though not yet God) are gradually relegated to this inferior, denigrated realm on the wrong side of the real, where they are increasingly viewed as not deserving of serious intellectual attention.

If modern science emerges in part by distancing itself from the fictional and from philosophy, this process is itself only enabled by a form of (hi)storytelling. Similar stories have been widely told of the way ancient philosophy emerged from mythological thinking. We have already seen that Thales' ability to predict eclipses, among other achievements, subsequently earned him the title of first philosopher, on the basis that those predictions were the result of rational and empirical investigations, using geometry, astronomical observation and logical reasoning. For those who celebrate these aspects of Thales' approach, not least Bertrand Russell (2004: 15), philosophy emerges when it becomes, effectively, scientific, eschewing formerly dominant mythological and superstitious ways of explaining and relating to the natural world.

A particularly influential version of this view of the emergence of philosophy as a shift from mythological to (proto-)scientific thinking was given by F. M. Cornford in *From Religion to Philosophy* (1957). As Drew Hyland has noted, Cornford's account presents a movement from 'a basically emotional reaction to a set of issues to a more rational reaction to essentially the same issues' – a movement whereby an older, non-rational approach is replaced by one of rationalist materialism (1973: 18). Hyland highlights several weaknesses in Cornford's position – not only in that it seems to ignore the extensive and often constitutive role played by mythology and storytelling throughout philosophy's history from (at least) Plato onwards, but also in that it implies an understanding of philosophy that would have to be located in human nature generally, rather than any cultural-historical moment, while still wanting to present philosophy as beginning (for the first time) with Thales and the pre-Socratic thinkers (1973: 22–3).

These two parallel views of the origins of ancient philosophy and modern science give two particular images of science and philosophy, based on the way they distance themselves from fiction. Recognizing this allows us to acknowledge the possibility of other images or conceptions of both that, in contrast, would bear a strong affinity with more or less the same category of the fictional. That is, this suppression or abolition of the fictional, which is the corollary of certain kinds of attempt to delineate what is known and knowable, may only occur in response to other ways of 'knowing' in which so-called fictional elements may be regarded as playing an essential part.

An often-cited conception of philosophy which would seem to allow a constitutive role for something other than the rational, found in both Aristotle and Plato, suggests that philosophy begins (wherever and however many times it begins) with an experience of wonder:

> It is through wonder that men now begin and originally began to philosophize; wondering in the first place at obvious perplexities, and then by gradual progression raising questions about the greater matters too, *e.g.* about the changes of the moon and of the sun, about the stars and the origin of the universe. (Aristotle 1933: 13; *Metaphysics* I.ii: 9)

Hyland (1973: 16) sets this Aristotelian notion of wonder as the non-historical origin of philosophy in direct opposition to the historicizing position (epitomized by Cornford) that philosophy begins at a certain time in ancient Greece. The word Aristotle uses for wonder is *thaumazein*, which gives its root to the word thaumaturgy, referring to the working of miracles or wonders by a saint – and which might equally serve as another alternative description of the activity of science fiction, a 'working with the miraculous'. Might it not be argued that this sense of wonder, in that it gives rise to speculation and narration about what *may* be, is the source of a kind of science fiction as much as it is of philosophy? In both contexts, a momentary glimpse of the possibility of the impossible casts a different light – or shadow – over the whole of reality, over what is taken as known. Is Plato's prisoner not a science fiction storyteller when he returns to the cave and begins to tell of the wondrous world he has seen – tales which, to his former cohabitants, seem fantastical and ridiculous? It does not seem too far-fetched to suggest that, whenever someone is inspired to begin telling stories about the hitherto unknown in contrast to the known, they enter the realm of science fiction, in an etymological sense if nothing else, that is, in the sense of fictionalizing knowledge (*scientia*).

There are modern counterparts to the classical sense of wonder as an inspiration for philosophizing. Kant seems to allude to the Aristotelian account of this experience when he concludes the *Critique of Practical Reason* (1997 [1788]) with a now famous reference to the amazement or awe generated by reflecting on the 'starry heavens'. This awe inspires Kant to contemplate 'a countless multitude of worlds' that 'as it were annihilates my importance as an animal creature, which after it has been for a short time provided with a vital force (one knows not how) must give back to the planet (a mere speck in the universe) the matter from whence it came' (1997: 133). Following his monumental *Critique of Pure Reason* (1978 [1781/87]), arguably the work most responsible for establishing the modern faith in the power and scope of reason, and the capacity of the rational human mind to comprehend the universe, here Kant suggests that this power of reason is itself dependent on an experience of the human's own cosmic insignificance. This anticipates his extension of the concept of the sublime in *Critique of Judgement* (1973 [1790]), where it comes to stand for the mind's experience of being faced with magnitudes and powers beyond its ability for comprehension or imagination.[6] The figure responsible for the Copernican Revolution that established a heliocentrism of the reasoning human, here reduces that same human figure to the level of the least significance by viewing it from a cosmic perspective. The human as the sun around which the world rotates, is eclipsed. Day becomes night and night becomes day, and for a brief moment, the illuminated realm of knowledge and the infinite dark expanse of the unknown give the impression of changing places.

It does not require much imagination to see how easily an experience of wonder may have been fostered by the key facets of the emergence of modern science, which even as it appeared to cast aside questions of transcendence and the imagination, in taking up Kant's cosmic perspective, exposed the figure of the human to the near-inconceivability of an infinite world. As Paolo Rossi neatly summarizes,

> Men in Hooke's times had a past of six thousand years; those of Kant's times were conscious of a past of millions of years. The difference lies not only between living at the center or at the margins of the universe, but also between

living in a present relatively close to the origins (and having at hand, what is more, a text that narrates the *entire* history of the world) or living instead in a present behind which stretches the 'dark abyss' (the term is Buffon's) of an almost infinite time. (1984: ix)

Considered from this perspective, a notion of science or philosophy *without* wonder, and without the capacity for fictionalizing, whether this means the explicit use of examples from myth or literature, or the constitutive role played by the thought of the unreal or unknown in theory, prediction and experimentation, would seem far stranger than the notion of a study of reality or nature which employs forms of fictionalizing.

What is salient in all this for the relationship between philosophy and science fiction, as well as for the affiliation between Bergson and Dick to which we will now turn, is the possibility that what come to appear, from a certain kind of scientific perspective, as modes of thought associated with knowledge, rationality and the real on the one hand, and the irrational and the fictional on the other, might at some other level, or at some other time, be or have been quite compatible, indeed, mutually conducive. In this light, it may make sense to consider the modern historical phenomenon of science fiction not as a bridge between two quite unconnected spheres – scientific rationalistism and the experience of wonder, the known and the unknown – but, rather, as the partial re(dis)covery of a far older and more fundamental relationship between them.

Bergson and Dick at the edge of the known

More than an archaeology, more than a genealogy, Bergson's anti-Platonism is an astronomy that looks for other forms of life.
(Lawlor 2003: 111)

In the 'Avant-propos' to *Difference and Repetition*, Deleuze avows that a book of philosophy should be part a crime thriller, and in part 'a kind of science fiction' (1994 [1968]: xx). Manola Antonioli (1999) provides a number of valuable insights into the significance of this comment in a text subtitled, 'on philosophy as science fiction'. With Deleuze, Antonioli suggests, 'one is before all else in the domain of *fiction*, one is in a possible world and not in the representation of the world "such as it is" or as it should be' (15).[7] Where the attempt to represent necessarily constitutes a deliberate reduction of the real, which may be considered a positive addition only in the limited sense of constructing a new object-text, science fiction makes additions of a qualitatively different order, supplying other possible worlds, multiplying the world itself. This description could equally be used to characterize that which makes Dick's science fiction philosophical. Antonioli suggests that

> philosophy is also close to science-fiction in that one can write only about that which one knows badly, 'at the edge of his knowledge' [*à la pointe de son savoir*], just as the science fiction writer always writes from the scientific knowledge of the present in the direction of a knowledge that we do not yet possess, or from this world in the direction of worlds that are possible but as yet unknown. (1999: 16)

Bergson and Dick can each in his own way be said to be writing 'at the edge of his knowledge' – where accepted reality, that which is taken as known, begins to break down, or simply reaches its limits: for both writers, although in different modes, one arrives at this point through the recognition of the artificiality of the conventional view of the world (the view provided by both science and everyday intellectual experience). Both collapse conventional notions of reality, and struggle with the consequences, the task of understanding what is beyond the artificial. Dick's characters, on breaking through one false version of reality, frequently find themselves lost in another, and only through prolonged striving against these artificial views may they occasionally – possibly – have a glimpse or a hint of underlying truth or reality. Likewise, the grasping of the processual, dynamic nature of time and matter described by Bergson requires a great effort of intuition, since all the exigencies of everyday social and physical human life work to push it aside. One of Dick's favourite pieces of philosophical terminology was the distinction between *idios kosmos* and *koinos kosmos*, Greek terms used by Heraclitus to differentiate between private and shared worlds (Dick 1995a [1965]; E: 243). In making the distinction, Heraclitus suggested that the waking share one common world while the sleeping turn away from this to worlds of their own: Bergson likewise, in writing about the nature of mind, theorized that in waking life memories tend to be oriented towards the exigencies of a shared social reality, with the unique, private aspects of our mental lives being filtered out, only to return while sleeping and dreaming, when 'the darkened images come forward into the full light' (1988 [1896]): 85). Both Dick and Bergson are deeply concerned with the way these two spheres of human existence function and dysfunction, how and why the shared reality of the *koinos kosmos* may emerge from so many *idioi kosmoi* that are in themselves mutually incompatible – and what different views of reality may be acquired on moving between them, or beyond the distinction.

Dick suggested in an interview that many science fiction writers, like himself, started off with a scientific desire for knowledge, yet coupled with a desire to speculate, to transcend the limits of the known and enter the imaginary realms that are generally prohibited for the scientist:

> It is first of all the true scientific curiosity, in fact, true wondering, dreaming curiosity in general, that motivates us [science fiction writers], plus a desire to fill in the missing pieces in the most startling or unusual way. To add to what is actually there, the concrete reality [...] my own 'glimpse' of another world. (Dick 1995b [1974]: 73)

While Dick's movement at or beyond the limits of the known immediately takes him into the realm of fiction and speculation, it would be difficult to maintain that with Bergson we are in the realm of fiction to the extent Antonioli regards this as true of Deleuze. Nevertheless, there are moments of fictionalizing in Bergson's philosophy that play a central role in its development, as Deleuze himself attested (1988: 25). *Matter and Memory*, for instance, begins neither with propositions nor questions about the nature of the world, but with a kind of story – an imagined scene depicting a universe of images surrounding the particular image of a body, which Bergson plays with freely: 'In this image I cut asunder, in thought, all the afferent nerves of the cerebro-spinal system [...] A few cuts with the scalpel [...]' (1988 [1896]): 21). Various concepts in Bergson could be interrogated as to the degree to which they involve fiction, or the extent to which they depend on a fictive mode in order to be adequately thought – among them, his notions of the virtual, of pure perception and pure memory. Yet we would not even need to delve into such examples to recognize that in challenging the scientific common sense of his era, such as confidence in the mechanistic nature of the material world and of biological evolution (the understanding epitomized by the work of Herbert Spencer, which Bergson himself had embraced in his youth), or the notion that memories are physically stored in the brain, Bergson can already be said to have been attempting to think 'at the edge of (his) knowledge'.

To an extent, the relationship between Bergson and Dick explored here can itself be considered something fabulated. Another way Antonioli develops the notion of philosophy as science fiction is by suggesting that Deleuze develops a kind of 'fictive genealogy' of philosophy, which receives its 'coherence from elsewhere' – that is, from Deleuze's own reworking and interrelating of his chosen thinkers' work in non-obvious ways. For the little 'fictive genealogy' I construct here between Bergson and Dick, the question of direct intellectual influence or affiliation is relatively inconsequential. There are some indications of direct historical connection, though they are subtle enough that one might do better to view them as resulting from an affinity between two thinkers, rather than indicating a strongly formative influence. For example, Dick mentions briefly in a late interview that as a student he read Bergson and Whitehead and became 'well grounded in process philosophy' (Bertrand 1995 [1980]: 46), and there are numerous references to both philosophers in the *Exegesis* – although generally as shorthand for a broadly conceived process ontology on which Dick does not elaborate. There are also many possible intellectual intermediaries, such as James Joyce, or Carl Jung, who could be seen as indirect channels by which some Bergsonian influence might have reached Dick's thought.[8] Nevertheless, it is the strong parallels rather than the weak historical connections between Bergson and Dick that form the basis for their consideration together here.

One important element that Bergson and Dick have in common is their refusal of any clear separation between materialism and spiritualism, or to use an opposition that has had much currency in European philosophy over the past few decades, between immanence and transcendence. This refusal manifests in various forms across the work of both thinkers, though is ultimately embedded in what for each amounts to an integrated relationship between ontology and ethics (a relationship which in turn, almost inevitably, grows to encompass a range of other dimensions of human thought and the thought of the human, such as psychology, epistemology and sociology). What often appears as dualistic thinking in both thinkers may in fact be understood as an unwillingness to choose between what for many others constitute binary alternatives between which it is relatively easy to decide. This is reflected in the ways the reception of each has been significantly shaped by a perceived contamination of the immanent or materialist aspects of their work by transcendental or mystical elements. In Bergson's case, this perception is evident in Deleuze's attempt to recuperate his thought for a philosophy of immanence, which played a decisive role in the still relatively recent revival of interest in Bergson, yet at the same time initiated a tendency to sideline his late work, *The Two Sources of Morality and Religion* (1977 [1932]): the subject-matter of *Two Sources* is mentioned only in the final two pages of Deleuze's *Bergsonism* (1991[1996]), with the title appearing only in a footnote. As Guerlac writes,

> it is as if, in *Le bergsonisme* (1966), Deleuze had carefully edited out all those features of Bergson's thought that might appear "metaphysical" (the soul, life,

value, memory choice), all those features that distinguish the human being from the machine, that suggest an appeal to experience and a phenomenological perspective. (2006: 179–80)

The mid-century decline of interest in Bergson's philosophy, following his immense popularity at the turn of the century, which culminated in his 1927 Nobel Prize (awarded in 1928) had largely resulted from the criticism of perceived metaphysical and irrational aspects of his thought, leading to his dismissal by influential early twentieth-century philosophers such as Bertrand Russell (1912). It is thus perhaps unsurprising that Deleuze, in attempting to reinstate Bergson as an important modern philosopher, would have been tentative in approaching a Bergsonian text dealing with religion and mysticism that appeared some twenty-five years after the works on which his philosophical reputation had originally been established. Though the task of restoring Bergson to the status of a major modern philosopher seems now to have been achieved, thanks to attentive readings of his work and its context by dedicated philosophers in France (Deleuze 1991 [1966]; Cariou 1976, 1990; Worms 1997) and the United Kingdom (Moore 1996; Mullarkey 1999; Pearson 2002; Lawlor 2003), *Two Sources* has continued to be relatively marginalized. Such marginalization is especially visible in works which have attempted to develop the socio-cultural and political dimensions of Bergson's philosophy, which has been used to engage with a range of areas of contemporary cultural theory and practice, including new media art (Hansen 2004), architecture (Kwinter 2002), politics and theories of affect (Adamson 2002; Massumi 2002; Grosz 2004), psychoanalysis (Campbell 2006) and the philosophy of science (Gunter 1969; Čapek 1971; Prigogine and Stengers 1984; Pearson 2002). *Two Sources*, Bergson's most directly ethical and arguably political work, which is concerned with the origins and nature of human culture and society, figures significantly in none of these texts.[9] While this imbalance is less prevalent in more strictly philosophical engagements (major recent Anglophone studies such as Mullarkey (1999) and Lawlor (2003) pay detailed attention to *Two Sources* and its ethics in their reconstructions of Bergson's thought), even within philosophy *Matter and Memory* and *Creative Evolution* (1998 [1907]) have received far more attention than Bergson's final work.

The efforts to elaborate a Bergson that would fit the prerequisites of a philosophy of immanence and a materialist politics have a parallel in the academic reception of Dick's work. Much early critical interest in Dick approached his work from a Marxist perspective, valuing his perceived critiques of capitalist society, yet found less value in his later work on the basis of its increasingly religious dimension.

The apparent causes of Dick's increased interest in religion were the events he experienced in February and March 1974, which he subsequently referred to using the shorthand cipher 2-3-74. A series of intense encounters with a godlike entity that he would come to refer to as Valis (among many other names), left him feeling irrevocably transformed: 'There have been more changes in me and more changes in my life [...] than in all the years before' (Dick 1991a: 4). These encounters took on a mind-boggling array of different forms, from the beam of pink light delivering information directly into his brain, to the visions of ancient Rome superimposed on twentieth-century California. For an extended period he believed he was sharing his mind with someone else, who he sometimes saw as a form of the same entity that he believed had contacted him through the pink light, and sometimes identified as another mind or spirit, theorizing at different times that it was an oppressed early Christian living in the time of Saint Paul, his recently deceased friend Bishop Jim Pike, Sophia the goddess of Wisdom, the Renaissance scholar Erasmus and the Greek god Dionysos.[10] From 2-3-74 until the end of his life in 1982, Dick's work was dominated by the attempt to understand these experiences, most explicitly in the pages of the journal he referred to as his 'Exegesis', and the late novel *VALIS* (1991d [1981]).

It would be tempting to think that 2-3-74 marked a religious turn in Dick's life and works, and some critics (notably Jameson 2005: 363) have gestured towards the separation of his later works from his previous writing as a distinct 'religious cycle'. Yet the approach I take here suggests that Dick's visionary experiences and his attempts to understand them may be considered a continuation of a quest for an adequate notion of salvation that can be traced throughout his work, and which culminates in the fabulations of Valis the entity, and the novel *VALIS*, as well as the *Exegesis*, as elaborated in the final chapter of this book.

Dick himself had averred, in 1966, that 'religion ought never to show up in SF except from a sociological basis' and denigrated his own novel *The Three Stigmata of Palmer Eldritch* (2003b [1964]) for this reason (1995: 58)[11] – anticipating Suvin's attempts to exclude all religious themes from science fiction (Suvin, 1979: 26).[12] The disparity between this statement and the frequency with which gods, saviours and other quasi-divine figures do appear in his work (even, as we will see, in the 1950s, long before the events of 2-3-74) may be taken as indicative of the strange combination of a need for salvation and the dissatisfaction with transcendent solutions that runs throughout Dick's oeuvre. My reading here is oriented by this disparity, which fuels a search for a notion of salvation that would address the fundamentally immanent exigencies of modern life.

What sometimes seems to have been neglected by those readers and critics of both Bergson and Dick who want to maintain the viability of their work for a philosophy of immanence or materialism and the critique of capitalism is that Bergson and Dick largely share these concerns: if this is not always obvious, it is because they have unconventional views regarding what is and is not compatible with these interests. Though Bergson, in *Two Sources*, discerned a continuing ethical and political role for a form of mysticism in modern human culture, he was centrally concerned with how the salient features of this mysticism may have arisen within the immanent biological development of the human, and the ways they could be used (or redirected) in order to target the very material effects of mechanization manifest in global warfare and exploitation. The transformation which is required, according to Bergson's account, to overcome the critical threats of mechanization in the modern era, is virtually impossible to conceive or address without some element or intimation of transcendence. Yet the question of how to match this requirement with the exigencies of an immanent worldview, one in which, for example, it is not deemed an effective strategy to depend on divine intervention, can be seen as one of the central problems of *Two Sources*. In a parallel though not identical manner, Dick's search for salvation was fuelled, I will suggest, by an irreducible need for an experience of transcendence or revelation that would make sense of the bafflingly cruel and inexplicable universe in which he found himself; yet this need was coupled with an equally deep-seated desire for verification, resulting in an extreme refusal to accept that anything was necessarily as it appeared to be. It is on the basis of this shared search for a salvation that would be in some sense transcendent, while at the same time able to fulfil the pragmatic, worldly function of overcoming material, social, political and psychological crises, that I view both Bergson and Dick as engaged in the work of immanent soteriology.

The ethics of balking

The shared element that perhaps most encapsulates the soteriological (and ethical) affinity between Dick and Bergson is their resistance to what Bergson calls mechanization. As elaborated in some detail in the following chapter, Bergson's use of this term to refer to the socio-historical rise of industrialization and modern technology can be understood as drawing on a much broader range of ethical and ontological associations, revolving around notions of the restriction of freedom, creativity and life, and their reduction to the status of the mechanical or non-living. The same combination is implicit in Dick's concern with what he sometimes refers to as 'androidization': 'Becoming what I call [...] an android, means [...] to allow oneself to become a means, or to be pounded down, manipulated [...] Androidization requires obedience. And, most of all, *predictability*' (1995c: 191). As for Bergson's mechanization, the technological or industrial face of androidization reveals in Dick's writing a deep affinity with a range of forces that tend to reduce life to the status of the material or mechanistic across different registers, from the physical (entropy) to the political (empire and law) to the metaphysical (death, non-existence).

Another Dickian figure in which this range of associations is embedded, again marking a seemingly fundamental indistinction between ethics and ontology, is the 'Black Iron Prison'. This term was a kind of shorthand for Dick's experience of the Roman Empire as infusing his contemporary world. This first took the form of a literal hallucinatory or mystical experience of a superimposed alternative reality, but Dick subsequently developed the broader conceptual, political and soteriological implications of the vision in the *Exegesis* and the novel *VALIS*, where he summarizes it as follows:

> during the interval in which he had experienced the two-world superimposition, he had seen not only California, USA, of the year 1974 but also ancient Rome, he had discerned within the superimposition of a Gestalt shared by both space-time continua, their common element: the Black Iron Prison. This is what the dream referred to as 'the Empire.' He knew it because, upon seeing the Black Iron Prison, he had recognized it. Everyone dwelt in it without realizing it. The Black Iron Prison was their world. (48)

The symbolism of the Black Iron Prison is both ancient and modern, recalling on the one hand the Iron Age and the advanced military technology of Rome, and on the other the machines and metallurgy of modern industrialization. In terms of modernity, in its capacity for imprisoning people while remaining invisible to them, it resembles Marx's alienation and commodity fetishism, and Foucault's panoptic society. It also seems to echo Weber's 'iron cage' [*stahlartes Gehäuse*] or 'shell as hard as steel' (Baehr 2001); the Orwellian-Kafkaesque integration of oppressive surveillance and dysfunctional but soul-crushingly incomprehensible bureaucracy is found in many of Dick's novels. For now we need only note that Dick, like Bergson, draws no strict boundaries between all these different kinds of mechanization – and that it is from this range of effects or processes that humanity requires saving.

Critical engagements with Dick's work have often focused on the two themes that he repeatedly acknowledged as his fundamental concerns: the human and the real. In the notion of androidization these two themes converge in a manner that is influentially prefigured in one of the most famous passages of Saint Paul. Dick frequently refers to the 'glass, darkly' passage from 1 Corinthians when referring to the illusory veil that occludes reality: 'For now we see through a glass, darkly; but then face to face: now I know in part; but then shall I know even as also I am known' (1 Cor. 13.12, KJV).[13] Yet this statement appears within a longer discussion of the importance of *caritas*, for which the chapter is equally well known: 'And though I have the gift of prophecy, and understand all mysteries, and all knowledge; and though I have all faith, so that I could remove mountains, and have not charity, I am nothing' (1 Cor. 13.2, KJV). Or, as Dick once paraphrased it, 'if I have not love then I am jack shit' (Dick, in Apel 1987: 35). It is in this property of *caritas*, or love, empathy, charity, that Dick locates the human, making this quality its only essential definition. Paul's intertwined comments on love and the obscured nature of the reality we perceive are frequently cited as though belonging to separate discussions, just as Dick's core questions 'what is reality?' and 'what is human?', though recognized as related, are often viewed as two separate concerns. Paul's suggestion that we can know the world and its future only 'in part', and that everything fades except love, corresponds to the underlying continuity between ethics and ontology that is found in Dick (and, though differently expressed, in Bergson): the only permanent, enduring aspect of reality, as well as the only characteristic of the human that does not fail, is *caritas*.

The struggle to make the perceived, temporary state of reality, and the outlook and behaviour of any given human, correspond to this unfailing form, however, is another matter. There is an underlying affinity between Dick's relative satisfaction with *caritas* as the defining characteristic of the human, and his dissatisfaction with (or distrust of) any given appearance or explanation of the nature of reality. The confusion and horror that can be generated by what Umberto Rossi (2011) terms the 'ontological uncertainty' expressed in Dick's novels have parallels in his dismay at the extent to which so-called humans can fail to demonstrate the *caritas* that supposedly defines them – that is, the ease with which they are 'androidized', able to act mechanically with regard to the lives of others. This is stated particularly effectively in an interview in which Dick recalls early on in his writing career reading some German SS files in a University of California (Berkeley) archive:

> the SS wrote to all the firms in Germany which had built ovens to make bread, and informed them that they wanted to build ovens to burn up human bodies,

and what were the bids on this project, like any commercial project. They got competitive bids. Not one firm wrote back and said, 'We don't build ovens to burn bodies. [...]'

It simply cannot be that such is the case and yet indeed it was the case. They actually – Jesus! – bid for that contract. I find this to be the most extraordinary thing I have ever heard. (Rickman 1988a: 143)

The firms' readiness to bid for the contracts is not simply immoral or condemnable – in Dick's eyes, it is impossible; it 'simply cannot be'. The impersonal, machinic reaction to the business-like invitation for bids characterizes androidization as the absolute opposite of *caritas*. Here the essence of mechanization is highlighted in the way the tendency to treat other humans as machines or things, and the tendency to *become* mechanical, thing-like, are mutually enhancing. McKee refers to a similar statement by Dick in which the Holocaust is invoked as the ultimate outcome of a mechanizing process 'in which the value of other human beings is disregarded' (McKee 2004: 17). Here again, the devaluation of the other comes about in tandem with a process by which those who are mechanizing others (in this case, concentration camp prisoners participating in the bureaucratic organization of daily extermination) themselves become mechanical instruments.

Dick often uses a particular word to describe the moment when someone resists the imperative or pressure of androidization – that is, refuses to respond mechanically to a mechanical (android, inhuman) demand: *balking*. To 'balk' against a pressure to become mechanizing is a refusal of the world in which this pressure arises: an act of ethical or political resistance is always likely to become an act of ontological resistance; in this case the effect is either to reveal apparent reality as a fake, or to posit it as such in contrast to an alternative world whose germinal or microcosmic form is the act of balking itself. In the *Exegesis*, Dick writes:

[Balking] is a refusal to cooperate with a harmful world, which, once one has balked against it, reveals its ersatz quality. [...] It is probably of extraordinary significance that repudiation of the mundane reality and acknowledgement of the transmundane is a single event or act, rather than two. The two realities cannot both exist, evidently. They are counter-realities. (E: 271)

The act of balking, of resisting or hesitating before the pressure to become an instrument of mechanization, already implies, for Dick, at least incipiently, the capacity to conceive of a world other than the mundane reality before one's eyes. To produce a counter-reality in the face of one whose existence one simply cannot accept, is, as we will see in the following chapter, the basic function of Bergsonian fabulation.

Philip K. Dick studies

I have already touched on some of the dominant concerns of existing critical engagements with Dick's work, yet it is worth giving a little further indication of where this study situates itself in relation to past and present Dick scholarship. From its relatively marginal status in the late 1970s and 1980s, as the pursuit of a small but dedicated assortment of researchers and fans, the study of Dick's life and work has gradually over the past decade begun to take on the appearance of an international research field. The journal *Science Fiction Studies* (founded in 1973) has paid consistent attention to Dick's writing since the 1970s, dedicating two special issues to his work (in 1975 and 1988). As noted above, several of the more influential early readings of Dick in *SFS* were produced by thinkers working within a broadly (or narrowly) Marxist framework, such as Darko Suvin, Fredric Jameson and Peter Fitting. The emphasis such scholars placed on reading Dick's work as a critique of capitalism was formative for the development of academic interest in his work in Europe (and France in particular), where the praise of Polish science fiction author Stanislaw Lem (1986; 1992 [1975]) was also pivotal. Since the early 1980s, Dick's work has been the subject of a growing number of monograph studies broadly within the field of literary criticism, including Robinson (1984), Warrick (1987), Mackey (1988), Palmer (2003), Barlow (2005), Vest (2009) and Rossi (2011). Several of these works (especially those produced in the 1980s) are concerned with establishing an overview of Dick's oeuvre, examining his key themes and stylistic tropes, and establishing his work as a legitimate object of literary-critical study. That this aim of several early studies of Dick had largely been achieved by the end of the century may be reflected in the appearance more recently of critical guides to his work (e.g. Butler 2000; Link 2009). Several of the literary monographs pursue particular theses regarding the interpretation or significance of Dick's work, in most cases associating it with one or many psychological, social and ontological aspects of the experience of postmodernism.

One way my approach differs from the major trends in past Dick scholarship is in its treatment of the religious dimension of his work. With the important exceptions of Davis (1998) and McKee (2004), and more recently Lash's account of Dick's 'information theology' (2010), none of them taking a literary-critical approach, most academic critics of Dick have either downplayed or struggled to integrate this aspect, which may initially seem quite incompatible with either a Marxist or a postmodernist framework. Through the paradigm of fabulation, I take Dick's interest in religious questions of salvation, theodicy and the nature of existence to be contiguous with his critiques of capitalism, Empire[14] and all other worldly manifestations of violence: nor does this entail ascribing to Dick any particular adherence to a given religious faith, though he may display strong leanings in certain directions at different times. If Dick is religious, I will argue, it is ultimately in the mode of what Bergson terms 'dynamic religion', which, as we will see in the following chapter, consists in the manifestation at the level of mind and society of a biological tendency towards openness that opposes all closed forms: in other words, a transformative, creative impulse that undermines static, exclusive forms of religion, along with all other mechanizing technologies of social power.

Dick has also been taken up by a diverse range of thinkers who can be located broadly within the transdisciplinary field of cultural theory, such as Jean Baudrillard, N. Katherine Hayles, Erik Davis, Steven Shaviro, and most recently, Laurence Rickels. In referring to Dick's work in *Simulacra and Simulations* (1994 [1981]), Baudrillard reflected and added early impetus to the tendency to associate Dick with postmodernism, with a world in which old distinctions between reality and fiction, the possible and the impossible, have been exploded, leaving behind only a hyperreal universe of simulations (1994 [1981]: 82–3 and *passim*). Hayles (1999) drew on Dick's mid-1960s novels in exploring the rise of cybernetic technology and thinking in contemporary culture, attending to the ways Dick's humans and androids reflect and respond to widespread (post) modern concerns with the destabilizing of boundaries between self and world, living and non-living subjects. These and other engagements with a postmodernist and posthumanist Dick share a tendency to move beyond the Marxist framework which shaped much early literary-critical work, by locating in his fictions a post-Marxist subject who continues to grapple with the alienating effects of late capitalism, but must also struggle to cope with the collapse of the old humanist subject which 'he' (dis)embodies.

As with more strictly literary-critical readings, an effect of these broad trends is that the religious and theological concerns of Dick's work, especially as pursued in his late novels and the *Exegesis*, have tended to be subsumed within other frameworks which downplay their significance. Concerns that are centrally associated with postmodernism and posthumanism certainly run through much of Dick's work, and his interest in religion and salvation surely cannot be isolated from such contexts. However, nor is the significance of these interests, it seems to me, fully engaged by such approaches: they may be 'explained' within a postmodernist paradigm, but at the risk of failing to realize their potential. Such potential is simultaneously the site of the soteriological and the political or emancipatory force of Dick's work. For example, where Palmer rightly recognizes that 'transformation is the engine, the pulsion of his fiction' (2003: 7), he nevertheless seems ultimately to tie this transformative power to the extent of Dick's 'anticipation of the condition of postmodernity' (2003: 9) – that is, to his engagement in critical activities (with regard, for example, to ideological constructions of reality and the human subject) whose full force and effects are located elsewhere. While literary-critical scholars like Palmer and Vest (2009), or theorists like Baudrillard and Hayles, continue to find much socio-political significance in Dick's fiction, their engagements tend to leave us with an idea of Dick as *representing* (albeit in both active and passive senses) rather than engaging in the *transformation* of an era: perhaps because of the originality and incisiveness of his insights and fictional creations, an image emerges of a writer with a great talent for depicting, reflecting, describing, exploring, elaborating a number of important cultural developments that were perhaps not yet widely apparent, but which have become increasingly visible since his death. While I value this dimension of past Dick scholarship (and of Dick's work), here I want to emphasize and pursue the ways in which he is not just a documenter or even investigator of his worlds and times, but is attempting, through his writing, to change them.

These attempts at transformation do not follow a coherent programme or a clear set of goals, but work upon a wide variety of targets, including the conventions of science fiction and literature, Dick's own personal circumstances and psychological states, his contemporary political culture, our understanding of the human, the perception of history, and even the fundamental nature of reality. In attempting to transform these aspects of his world, Dick is sometimes powerfully effective, often deluded, occasionally conventional, but consistently attentive to the ways subjective knowledge and objective reality cannot be separated from one another – and always perseveres, with a determination fuelled by both desperation and hope, in the quest to find, or to construct, a path to salvation.

Among those works which do pay attention to Dick's religious dimension without attempting to subsume it within a Marxist, postmodernist or other established paradigm of literary criticism are Erik Davis' *TechGnosis* (1998) and Gabriel McKee's *Pink Beams of Light from God in the Gutter* (2004). In McKee's short book, he conducts an excellent reading of Dick as speculative theologian, drawing on the late works and the relatively limited selection of the *Exegesis* writings that was available prior to the appearance of the 2011 edition, offering a valuable counter-balance to the downplaying of the religious dimension elsewhere (McKee 2004: 27). Ultimately, McKee's attempts to recuperate Dick's religious outlook for a broadly Christian framework may go too far in the other direction, flattening out some of the eclectic range of Dick's religious interests (for example, in relation to gnostic thought), and neglecting the compatibility of his religious and ethical concerns with the interests of revolutionary politics and critical theory. Nevertheless, McKee provides many valuable insights into Dick's relationship to salvation and religion, and, particularly for my own study, to the writing of Saint Paul. Davis, in contrast, situates Dick's gnostic and other mystical interests within the contemporary context of information culture. Though only a relatively small portion of *TechGnosis* focuses directly on Dick, the book as a whole tunes into a theme which is crucial to the connection between Bergson and Dick I pursue here – that of the relationship between technology and mysticism as always-already intertwined, mutually enhancing, though often opposed dimensions of human existence. Davis has been a key advocate of the significance of Dick's religious interests and the *Exegesis* in particular, playing a central role in the publication of the 2011 edition. A further significant recent intervention is found in Scott Lash's development of Dick's relevance to global information culture and what he calls 'intensive culture', using Dick's experimentation with notions of transubstantiation to develop parallels and convergences between the becoming substantial of the divine in religious thought, and the way 'substance enters the commodity itself' in informational capitalism (2010: 185).

The most recent attempt at developing an overall reading of Dick's oeuvre is Umberto Rossi's *Twisted Worlds* (2011). Rossi attempts to provide a key and framework for understanding Dick's work which he elucidates and affirms through readings of a large number of Dick's novels, suggesting that his approach may also be applied to those works he is not able to explore in depth. Although in the present book I do not engage in close readings of as many of Dick's works as Rossi, I would likewise suggest that the framework of fabulation as a mode of immanent soteriology developed here may similarly be considered an 'organic plan' (Rossi 2011: 3) that could productively be used to examine most areas of Dick's work. Rossi's central thesis – that Dick can be understood through the principle of 'ontological uncertainty', resulting from the author's continual struggle to maintain both subjective *and* objective modes of accounting for reality, the *idios* and the *koinos kosmos* (Rossi 2011: 7) – seems to me entirely apt. In his clear formulation, he makes a coherent interpretive framework out of a range of past critical engagements with the ontological questions raised by Dick's writing, while producing many valuable insights in his analyses of particular novels. What my engagement attempts to do is to set this aspect of Dick's approach not only to writing, but to fabulating reality in any register, within what I take to be its (immanently) soteriological context. This necessarily means operating partially outside of the paradigm of literary criticism within which Rossi situates his study.

Thus where I part with Rossi to an extent is in his conception of a strong boundary between philosophy and literary criticism (and thus, implicitly, between philosophy and fiction/storytelling). Rossi states that, despite his focus on ontological uncertainty, his is not a philosophical analysis, but a literary criticism monograph, because a novel 'aims at telling a story, after all – which is not the main purpose of philosophy' (10). The boundary between philosophizing and telling stories is one which Dick as much as any writer, it seems to me, challenges us to call into question. As I tried to suggest above, for me it is not at all certain that philosophy does not have the telling of stories as a central aim or function. Conversely, the function of Dick's writing is surely not exhausted by the fact that it aims to tell stories (though, of course, an explicitly literary-critical approach is at liberty to use this as a way of delimiting its scope). Even if we were to allow that Dick does little other than tell stories – which I find perfectly plausible – this would still leave open the question of what it means to engage in this activity, to fictionalize, to produce and multiply counter-realities, not to mention the functions and dynamics of such activity, of what storytelling *does*. Through both the Bergsonian theory of fabulation, and Dick's employment of fictionalizing in a range of modes that refuse to be restricted to the literary, the philosophical, the psychological, the political, or any other register, this book attempts to address such questions, locating the ontological and biological origins of storytelling at the point where survival and salvation converge in the fundamental indistinction of the impossible and the real.

Hence, just as Rossi argues that the co-presence of objective and subjective explanations 'should be preserved in the interpretive discourse, not explained away' (2011: 7), I would suggest that Dick's fluid ability to traverse literary, philosophical, theological, political and other modes of thought and creativity ought also to be preserved in our academic and critical engagements with him, or if unavoidably forgotten at times, attentively remembered wherever possible. A recent work which, more than most, follows Dick in moving freely across such disciplinary and discursive boundaries is Laurence Rickels' *I Think I Am: Philip K. Dick* (2010). Rickels not only reflects the creative relationship with death that Dick pursues (and which pursues him) through his writing, but explores the ways this simultaneously becomes a relationship with academic and popular psychology, philosophy and religion. The processes of mechanization and salvation which I focus on here could be understood respectively as processes of becoming-inanimate and becoming-animate – of dying and living (or coming back to life). Salvation as the escape from mechanization/androidization is escape from death, an impossible escape, in terms of both immediate and immanent experiences of mortality, and one which therefore requires the power of fabulation, of a potential for transforming or transmuting impossibility into the realm of experience and life. Yet Rickels, with Dick, reminds us that what we take to be a line of flight from death may turn out to be a short-cut passage straight into the heart of darkness – and that, by the same ferryman's token, embarking on a quest for life may well require deliberately stepping into the fantastic realm of the dead. Above all, *I Think I Am* reminds us of the incalculable value of serious playfulness – of madness, punning, irreverence – in any effective strategy for dealing with death: such devices for twisting free of the apparent constraints upon what one may or may not do might ultimately be the central element of Dick's great capacity for fabulation.

Note on terminology

Before concluding this introduction, it is worth giving one or two clarifications regarding the term 'fabulation', which is used in both technical and everyday contexts, but is not entirely commonplace in either. One general use of the term associates it with storytelling as the production of fables. It is also sometimes used as though synonymous with 'telling stories' in the related though less culturally sanctioned sense of lying or (dis)simulating. Bergson's employment of the term encompasses these senses, but is formally broader, in that it may refer to any act of fictionalizing, in virtually any register – mythological, literary, dramatic, spoken, gestural, hallucinatory. At the same time, it is functionally more specific, in associating such fictionalizing activity with a potentially saving function. Moreover, in contrast to the usual connotations of the term, for Bergson fabulating need not entail being aware or conscious that one is engaged in the activity of fictionalizing. Indeed, it is the very possibility of concealing the fact of fabulation from one's own intellect that gives it this saving potential.

Bergson's fabulation function is a faculty humans have evolved for reasons relating to survival, as we will see in the following chapter, but which, having been evolved, can be put to countless different uses, some of which may seem very far from such a function.

It is also worth noting that Bergsonian fabulation has little to do with the distinction made in Russian formalism between *fabula* and *siuzhet*, where the *fabula* or story is determined as the events of a narrative in their linear, chronological occurrence, and the *siuzhet* or plot refers to the order in which they are arranged in the story's telling (Kolesnikoff 1993: 631–2). It may be possible to make some case for relating this distinction to the one I will make here between static and dynamic fabulation, with the latter conceived as something like the *process* of inventing the unreal, and static fabulation as the contents or results of that process. However, even this parallel would be limited, not least because fabulation is a process that is not restricted to the context of narration – e.g. seeing a ghost is just as much a fabulation as telling a ghost story.

Furthermore, we should distinguish Bergson's 'fabulation' from Robert Scholes' (1979) use of the same term in relation to metafiction. Though Scholes does not appear to be drawing on Bergson, there are some parallels between the two usages – though these are again limited by the extent to which Scholes is operating within an explicitly literary-critical paradigm. Scholes uses the term 'fabulator' to refer to writers who share certain characteristics such as 'delight in design' and a 'concurrent emphasis on the art of the designer' (1979: 3). Such writers' work has since perhaps become more commonly associated with terms like 'postmodernism' and 'metafiction'. While this stylistic use of the term has little to do with Bergsonian fabulation, there is some resonance in Scholes' suggestion that fabulation turns away from realism and representation towards 'actual human life, by way of ethically controlled fantasy' (1979: 3). This could certainly apply to Dick's work, which, as we have begun to see, has an irreducible ethical dimension that is directly associated with the erosion of any stable boundary between fiction and reality – or, as Scholes puts it, the development of 'subtle correspondences between the reality which is fiction and the fiction which is reality' (1979: 8). Indeed, Scholes names Dick in the epilogue to *Fabulation and Metafiction* (1979) as one of a number of new writers from the realm of science fiction who are 'emerging to join the ranks of literary fabulators, bringing both a concern for the traditional values of story-telling and a fresh vision of human problems and aspirations' (1979: 218).

However, Dick is a fabulator in the Bergsonian sense first of all, meaning that he fabulates before (and regardless of whether) he produces literature; and most importantly, in that his fabulations maintain a crucial relationship, as I will argue throughout this book, to an ongoing search for salvation. In connection with this search, whatever elements of artifice and metafiction may be found in Dick can be considered to arise to a large extent organically or dynamically, rather than primarily out of an intellectual 'delight in design' or an abstract interest in self-referentiality, even if these are also at work.

Finally, it is worth noting, especially in light of the foregoing introduction, that it is only through a long history of accidents of naming that we have ended up with the Latinate term 'science fiction'. If we were to attempt to retrofit the term into a Greek form (forgetting, just for a moment, the great revisions to the history of thought that this would imply) we might find the best alternative to *scientia*, 'knowledge', to be *gnosis* or indeed *philosophia*. 'Fiction', meanwhile, would perhaps give way to *mythos*, or, given its roots in the Latin verb *fingere*, meaning 'to mould or shape' (e.g. out of clay), might be replaced by *poiesis*. Meanwhile, there is no reason we should not invert the traditionally cited etymology of 'philosophy' itself, such that, rather than 'the love of wisdom', its first and proper meaning is understood, following Luce Irigaray, to be 'the wisdom of love' (2004: 1–12). Taking all this into account, and briefly turning away from what Dick terms, as we will see in Chapter 4, 'The tyranny of the concrete', the whole phrase 'the philosophy of science fiction' may be transmuted into 'the wisdom of mythopoetic love'. Such might be the title of this book in an alternative universe.

1

Fabulation: Counteracting Reality

What's to be gotten over is the false idea that an hallucination is a private matter.

(Dick, E: 337)

One of the central achievements of Bergson's *The Two Sources of Morality and Religion* (1932) is to provide a convincing argument for the fundamental evolutionary, social and psychological reasons for our ability and tendency to fictionalize. The activity or process of fictionalizing, considered within such functional contexts, is what Bergson terms *fabulation*. It is easy to overlook the full significance of this concept in Bergson's argument, embedded as it is within his broader investigation of the nature of society, morality and religion. Furthermore, while Bergson pursues through this investigation the question of the past and future survival of humanity, addressing the socio-biological development of religion both in general and in relation to the ethico-political context of industrial, global modernity, the idea of a contemporary emancipatory role of fabulation as I will argue for it here, remains implicit within his project. For these reasons, this chapter focuses almost exclusively on elaborating the role of fabulation in *Two Sources*, and deriving a Bergsonian understanding of the role fabulation may play in the task of humanity's (self-)salvation from mechanization in the modern era. This is the task which, I argue across this book as a whole, Dick's oeuvre likewise undertakes, in ways that can be understood as enacting, exploring and developing a relationship between the general socio-cultural roles of fabulation as Bergson understands them, and the special significance it takes on in the industrial and post-industrial eras.

I will suggest that what Bergson offers in *Two Sources* may be considered an immanent soteriology: a theory or logic of salvation (as opposed to a theological contribution to the study of existing doctrine) stripped of any necessary ontologically transcendent aspects, which is nevertheless unthinkable without some concept, image or intimation of the transcendent. This strange hybrid of immanent and transcendent paradigms is conceived as a necessary response to the set of modern conditions in which the mechanization of human life – its reduction to the literal or symbolic status of the non-living – demands to be addressed as a fundamentally material, real threat, yet which in its near-infinite reach, almost unavoidably, in thought and image, takes on a sublime or quasi-divine dimension. Further, I will argue that, deliberately or not, Bergson's soteriology is left crucially incomplete, open to and perhaps inviting supplementation by something or someone that, from its own perspective, remains as yet unknown: in Dickian vocabulary, a divine invasion.

Mechanization and the war-instinct

Bergson's *Two Sources* is a work of urgency, despite or because of its late appearance in his life and career. Like several of his contemporaries who had attempted to investigate the origins of religion, Bergson was motivated by a concern for the plight of contemporary and future humanity. Thus, like Freud's *The Future of an Illusion* (2004 [1927]) and *Civilization and its Discontents* (2008 [1930]), *Two Sources* can to a large extent be read as an attempt, in the wake of the advent of global warfare, to diagnose where and how humanity had gone wrong: to discern how it had set itself on a course that was seemingly directed towards its own self-destruction, while asking what it would take to change this course.

While all of Bergson's philosophy may have profound ethical and social significance, in most of his writing this remains largely implicit. In the years leading up to the First World War, when he was at the height of his fame following the publication of his two best-known works, *Matter and Memory* (1896) and *Creative Evolution* (1907), several of Bergson's contemporaries urged him to turn his attention towards developing the socio-political dimension of his work – among them, Charles Péguy, Edouard Berth, and Georges Sorel, whose five articles drawing on Bergson in the journal *Mouvement socialiste* were the basis for his *Reflections on Violence* (2004 [1908]).[1] Though certainly conscious that his philosophy had potential ethical and political implications, Bergson seems initially to have been cautious about making this dimension overt. However, whatever reservations he may have had about engaging in politics were set aside when, following the outbreak of war, he accepted a duty to perform whatever roles he could in support of the war effort as a public intellectual. Aside from delivering speeches and lectures on the war and German imperialism, he was engaged in a significant diplomatic mission. Called on by the French government to serve as an unofficial diplomat in the USA, according to his biographer Philippe Soulez, Bergson was instrumental in conducting secret negotiations that played a key role in convincing President Woodrow Wilson to lead his country into the war against Germany. Following the end of the conflict, Bergson accepted a nomination to the International Committee on Intellectual Cooperation, an advisory group for the League of Nations, where he worked with other well-known cultural figures such as Thomas Mann, Paul Valéry and Albert Einstein to lay the foundations for what would eventually become UNESCO (Soulez and Worms 2002: 184–7). Only once illness had forced him to retire from public duties did Bergson finally undertake the extended philosophical engagement with social and political life that figures like Sorel and Péguy, now long dead, had asked him to undertake a quarter of a century earlier.

Two Sources carries out a philosophical investigation into the origins and evolution of social life, religion and morality, not as a disinterested analysis, but in the hope of contributing to the immense task of preventing future wars. It can be understood in this regard as continuous with his previous diplomatic efforts – though there is also much continuity with his earlier philosophical works. The investigation Bergson undertakes in *Two Sources* allows him to address simultaneously the crisis of modern humanity, with its apparently unprecedented capacity and will for self-destruction, and the question of human violence in general as an immanent self-destructive threat. At the core of both diagnoses is mechanization.

In its common usage as roughly equivalent to 'industrialization', the term 'mechanization' refers to the processes of using machinery to carry out work, and the hugely expanded role of such processes in modern society. Yet mechanization as a set of physical and social processes is also bound up with the epistemology of mechanism, a perspective underpinning or accompanying the beginnings of industrial modernity, which approaches the physical world as deterministic, as though composed of a set of machine parts which behave predictably according to fixed rules. A subtle, though no longer obscure set of connections ties this epistemological or scientific view to certain developments in the organization and modes of social life which have been critically analysed for their deleterious effects on physical and political freedom. Foucault's *Discipline and Punish* (1991 [1975]) can be read as an extended elaboration of these connections, showing how, for example, the mechanical view of the human body espoused by La Mettrie in *L'homme machine* ('Machine Man')

(2009 [1748]), becomes an image of the disciplined docile body of the modern factory worker, soldier or prisoner. Elsewhere Otto Mayr (1986) has exposed the direct and complex links between the so-called 'mechanical philosophy' and the modern discourses and practices of political liberty (and its restriction).

Mechanization in relation to such contexts can be understood as the reduction of the living to mechanical or non-living status. Yet while the accounts of Mayr, Foucault and others highlight how the discourses and disciplines of mechanization are specific to European modernity, it is also clear that the reduction of life to the status of the non-living, both in thought and practice, is virtually a permanent aspect of human social existence. We may consider any process by which the possible autonomy of one living being is restricted in order to render that being a resource or tool for the sustenance of another, as a form of mechanization. It is a human trait to instrumentalize other humans (and other life-forms). In fact, we can go further and suggest that the nonhuman, the technological, the mechanistic must already, in this and other senses, be considered a dimension of the human – a point that is made in diverse twentieth-century philosophical discourses, from Simondon's account of individuation and pre-individual being (1995 [1964]), to Heidegger's understanding of man as a being already 'claimed by a way of revealing' that is 'never a human handiwork' (1993 [1954]: 324), to Lyotard's conception of the 'inhuman' as both an effect of the modern technological condition, and as a repressed potential for becoming something other than human (1991 [1988]). Such examples parallel Bergson's approach to mechanization by unsettling a humanist ethics that would seek to restore an ideal or essential human against its corruption by mechanism. Acknowledging that the mechanical and mechanization are already deeply engrained in human existence before it is even possible to conceive of human essences and ideals is crucial to the possibility of overcoming the ethically and physically destructive dangers posed by mechanization, in the immanent soteriologies of both Bergson and Dick.

If Bergson uses the term 'mechanization' most frequently in the sense of industrialization, such usage is never easily separable from this range of ethical, physical and biological contexts, which run through the text as a whole. Indeed, to the extent that Bergson's philosophy repeatedly explores a conception of life in relation to the non-living, of the reduction of dynamic, living or creative processes to the status of the static and mechanistic, a concern with mechanization, in a variety of terminologies, can be seen as implicit in most of his philosophical work. At the core of both *Time and Free Will* (1960 [1889]) and *Matter and Memory* (1988 [1896]), for example, is the critical exposition of the ways in which duration, the enduring continuity forming the basis of our relation to time and memory, is reduced to the status of the mechanical and quantifiable. These works critique the mechanization of time (its treatment as though equivalent to spatial extension), freedom (the erosion of the capacity to behave non-deterministically) and mind (its reduction to the status of machine) – which are habitual in both everyday life and in dominant modes of scientific thinking.

To explain how it is possible to think beyond or against these habits, Bergson develops a dualistic understanding of the human mind, in which the intellect is conceived as the aspect which approaches phenomena practically by breaking them down into significant, analysable and quantifiable parts, while intuition is conceived as the aspect which, at least to some degree, is able to grasp things in their wholeness or continuity with the rest of the universe. This conception of intuition which, in refined form, becomes the basis of Bergson's philosophical method, requires one to attend constantly to the habits and presumptions of one's own intellect. This, he suggests, necessitates that the mind effectively do violence to itself, in order to 'reverse the direction of the operation by which it ordinarily thinks, continually upsetting its categories' and arriving at 'fluid concepts, capable of following reality in all its windings' (2002: 190). Thus from an early stage in his career Bergson critiques mechanization simultaneously at the level of the phenomena he sets out to investigate, *and* in the method of investigation – such that mind and reality, knowledge and world, cannot be considered to belong to separate realms.

When in *Creative Evolution* Bergson undertook a critical examination of the tendency to reduce biological life and its historical development to a mechanistic, determinate status, he was thus careful not to restrict his critique to contemporary scientific thinking: his study took account of the fact that both such thinking and his own re-examination of evolution were affected by that very evolution – in that human thought is one of its products. Thus in addition to his proposition of an original vital principle (which he famously termed the *élan vital*) as responsible for the creative transformation of life, he pursued the dualistic development of intellect and instinct as two dominating and divergent tendencies in the history of life. The first of these aspects of his approach – apprehending evolution as driven by a creative principle – requires one to overcome, to a degree, the habits of intellect whose long evolution is accounted for in the second aspect. This recognition of a necessary recursivity between the method and the thing studied anticipates Maturana and Varela's account of the biological origins of cognition, which is guided by the principle that the phenomenon of knowing cannot be taken as though there were 'facts' or objects out there that we grasp or store in our head. The experience of anything out there is validated in a special way by the human structure, which makes possible 'the thing' that arises in the description. (1987: 25–6)

For Maturana and Varela, as for Bergson, in order to study a phenomenon such as the evolution of human knowledge, it is essential to recognize the blind spots created by that very evolution and, where possible, to overcome the analytic bias towards 'facts' as quantifiable, equivalent, archivable units of information.[2] What Bergson identifies in the mechanizing habits of his own intellect is an expression of a proto-mechanizing tendency that is virtually endemic to life: the tendency for a cell, organism or group to extract the energy it needs in order to perpetuate itself from its environment – which, importantly, includes other organisms (CE: 253). Yet only in *Two Sources* does he directly link this tendency to mechanization in the social sense of industrialization and its concomitant ethico-political transformations. Here he associates the mechanizing tendencies that he had already identified as aspects of the biological development of life and the psychic functioning of the human, with the human tendency towards violent conflict. This tendency is so embedded in human social and biological existence that Bergson refers to it as a 'war-instinct', explaining it as follows: 'the origin of war is ownership, individual or collective, and since humanity is predestined to ownership by its structure, war is natural' (MR: 284).

It is this deep embedding of the tendency towards war within the biological origins of human society that renders the overriding concern of *Two Sources* – the overcoming or subverting of the destructive threat of warfare – so difficult. What renders the task so urgent is the ever-increasing scale of this threat under the conditions of modern mechanization – the social processes of industrialization intensifying and extending the reach of the human's older, endemic mechanizing tendencies. With the globalization of modern mechanized warfare, the destruction of life on an unseen scale emerges as a realistic possibility, and the destruction of the species or life as a whole becomes thinkable:

> At the pace at which science is moving, that day is not far off when one of the two adversaries, through some secret process which he was holding in reserve, will have the means of annihilating his opponent. The vanquished may vanish off the face of the earth. (MR: 287)

Understandably in the years following the First World War and his own subsequent diplomatic and political efforts to avert future conflicts, Bergson perceived the destructive technologies of mechanized warfare as the most obvious and most threatening modern expression of the war-instinct. Yet he also emphasized that even without direct military conflict, the rise of mechanization (in the sense of industrialization) still brings about the mass destruction of human life – for example through illness and starvation as a result of the ongoing appropriation of industry to serve the needs of the few. Mechanization may take place through a range of means other than war, such as enslavement, labour markets, ideological manipulation, population management, not to mention the wide-reaching instrumentalization of nonhuman life. We should also bear in mind that, although his remarks concerning a secret weapon with the capacity to make the vanquished 'vanish off the face of the earth' seem to anticipate nuclear warfare, the Nazi genocide during the Second World War may ultimately have come closest to realizing Bergson's fears; what made this possible was a combination of mechanization in the sense of a readiness to treat other humans as non-living, with another form of mechanization in the shape of a massive, bureaucratic infrastructure.

Thus although, at a socio-philosophical level, *Two Sources* can be understood as an enquiry into the nature and origins of morality and religion in human society, the motivation for this enquiry is urgently ethical and political, primarily directed towards the problem of overcoming the war-instinct. This task appears, in the inter-war period in which Bergson is writing, to be shifting its status, from that of a question of great moral significance to one whose accomplishment may well be a necessary condition for human future survival.

It can thus be argued that Bergson undertakes his enquiry into morality and religion because it is in these spheres that the suppression of the war-instinct has previously been achieved. Understanding first how this suppression or challenge was ever possible, and second, why it has only ever been partially successful – and then posing the question of how it might be renewed in an era which has seen mechanization cross a new threshold in terms of its destructive scale and power, are three necessary stages in this undertaking; and as we will see, fabulation plays a crucial role in each of them.

The biological origins of society

A fundamental premise of *Two Sources* is that social evolution is an extension or continuation of biological evolution: '[...] the evolution of life along its two main lines has been accomplished in the direction of social life. [...] since life is organization, [...] we pass by imperceptible transitions from the relation between cells in an organism to the relation between individuals in society' (MR: 94). The way Bergson links biology and society here differs subtly but crucially from the association implied in the analogy between organism and society used by many early social theorists, such as Comte, Spencer, Schaeffle and Durkheim.[3] For such thinkers, the analogy was a means by which the young field of the study of society could borrow legitimacy and methodological weight from the more established study of living organisms in the biological sciences. Bergson's emphasis, however, is on the *relations* among cells and individuals in a manner that presupposes neither the primacy of these units, nor the whole (organism/society) of which they are part, and that sees a formal identity, rather than analogy, between these relationships as considered in different spheres.[4] Thus he moves us away from both the organism and analogy, towards a general principle of life as an organizing tendency, of which both the organism *and* society are products: 'society therefore is not self-explanatory; so we must search below the social accretions, get down to Life, of which human societies, as indeed the human species altogether, are but manifestations' (MR: 100).

As I noted above, Bergson had argued in *Creative Evolution* that the essence of life is to procure energy from the material world (which it then expends in various ways) (CE: 253). Thus he can state that 'life is, more than anything else, a tendency to act on inert matter' (CE: 96). This apparently circular definition (life is what acts upon the non-living) can also be read as an indication of its inherent mechanizing tendency (whatever life acts upon is by this action constituted, in some sense, as non-living). What Bergson refers to as the 'two main lines' of animal evolution are differentiated by the means, in general, by which they carry out this task: along one line, epitomized by hymenopteran species such as bees and ants, instinct is emphasized; the other line, in which humanity emerges, has tended to emphasize intellect. Bergson is careful not to over-define or essentialize these dominant characteristics (among other issues, such an analytical approach would produce an account shaped in advance by the intellectual perspective). While instinct and intellect constitute 'radically different kinds of knowledge' (CE: 143), they nevertheless share a common biological origin, and even at the extremes represented by hymenopteran and human species, the dominance of one never completely eradicates the other: 'There is no intelligence in which some traces of instinct are not to be discovered, more especially no instinct that is not surrounded with a fringe of intelligence' (CE: 136).

In the same vein, it would be excessive to link intellect or intelligence exclusively to consciousness, regarding instinct as wholly unconscious – though they can be said generally to tend in these directions (CE: 145). Rehearsing an approach he had developed in the first chapter of *Matter and Memory*, Bergson here suggests that the degree of consciousness found in a living system is relative to the size of the gap between actual and potential action – which is effectively to identify it with the organism's capacity for hesitation or choice (CE: 144–5).[5] The fact that Bergson retains this definition across his work is particularly significant in light of its proximity with Dick's ethics of balking, a point to which we will return later. At this stage in *Creative Evolution*, Bergson reformulates the dualism of intellect and intuition discussed above, arguing that intellect is predisposed to that which is material, solid (CE: 153), to that which is or may be conceived as discontinuous, immobile (CE: 154–5). Intuition, in contrast, is attuned to the apprehension of 'true continuity, real mobility, reciprocal penetration – in a word, that creative evolution which is life', yet requires the mind to 'twist about on itself' in order to escape the fixities of habitual, intellectual thinking (CE: 162).

What Bergson does not do in *Creative Evolution* is link his account of the dominance of intellect to its social context. There are hints at a wider socio-ethical dimension, for example in his observation that the intellect's tendency to find causality everywhere 'expresses the very mechanism of our industry' in which the same parts are repeatedly combined in a repeated series of movements to build the same products (CE: 164). Yet on the whole his consideration of the intellect as situated within a society – among other intellects – extends only as far as a consideration of language as equally tailored towards analytic, immobile, materialist ways of knowing. Only in *Two Sources* does he address directly the social and moral consequences of being governed by an intellect whose dominant characteristic is '*a natural inability to comprehend life*' (CE: 165, original emphasis). A society of such beings would seem to be one doomed to fail: a society of asocial schizoids, unable to sympathize or respond emotionally to one another (although see Dick's *Clans of the Alphane Moon* (1975 [1964]) for a speculative exploration of how some kind of social order might emerge among a diverse group of largely anti-social organisms).

That Bergson was still able, in *Creative Evolution*, to pass over this fundamental contradiction or tension at the heart of the social is likely not only due to the particular focus of his study, but to the fact that, as he had already argued, intellect is never wholly without instinct – so that intellect's inability to grasp life does not place such an understanding beyond the human entirely. Indeed, it is only this co-existence of intellect and instinct that makes intuition possible. The simple fact of the endurance of societies of organisms dominated by intellect may be taken to reflect the success, however limited, of this balance between intellect, instinct and intuition. Yet the hugely transformed historical circumstances that followed the First World War would surely have made it difficult for any European to take it as a given that society was naturally able, or would continue, to overcome its asocial tendencies. The question of how the intellect's failure to understand life impacts on human societies, indeed, of how it leads humans in social groups and as a species to self-destruction, becomes crucial for Bergson at this moment, as for many of his contemporaries.

Countering the intellect

Though Bergson challenged the neo-Darwinist views of evolution that portrayed it as an entirely automatic, mechanistic process, natural selection remains crucial to his conception of creative evolution (CE: 23–4; cf. Pearson 2002: 79–81). According to this understanding, natural selection is 'not purely accidental, although accident has a large place in it; and it does not depend solely on the initiative of individuals, although individuals collaborate in it' (CE: 170–1). In *Two Sources*, this perspective manifests as a form of functionalism (to use a certain Darwin-influenced sociological vocabulary): any aspect of a phenomenon which endures, in particular a phenomenon which involves life, such as a species, an organism, a society, but also a religion, an idea, a dream, can be expected to perform (or to have performed in the past) some function relevant to that endurance. Hence Bergson reasons that since both the major lines of evolution, with their respective emphases on instinct and intellect, have led to social life, sociality must likewise have favoured life's fundamental activity of extracting energy from matter.

Yet where social life among species governed by instinct operates as though by necessary laws, such that the activity of every organism is subsumed under the activity of the collective, intelligence brings with it certain individualistic traits that threaten all possibility of social cohesion. Bergson suggests three particular ways in which this happens. The first is the possibility, indeed the likelihood, that the individual will place his or her own interests above those of the group: 'roused to thought, he will turn to himself and think only of leading a pleasant life' (MR: 121). The second arises from awareness of mortality: since intelligence provides the human individual with 'the faculty of observing with no view to immediate utility' (MR: 130), it is quite easy for her to acquire a sense of certainty regarding her own death. As Bergson puts it, '[s]eeing that every living thing about him ends by dying he is convinced that he will die too'

(MR: 130). The same ability to reason from observation leads to a third type of threat resulting from recognition of 'the depressing margin of the unexpected between the initiative taken and the effect desired' (MR: 140). This apparent primal ancestor of our modern Murphy's Law (roughly stated, when something can go wrong, it will go wrong) may be conceived as an attitude of rational pessimism – the observation that, when there are countless things that could easily go wrong, failure is virtually guaranteed. All three of these effects of intelligence seem to pose a huge threat to any form of social collaboration – whether through individualistic self-interest leading to antagonism, violence and abuse, or through the depression and resignation that could be expected to accompany a sense of mortality and the ultimate futility of all one's endeavours, including the primary struggle to survive.

These are problems that do not arise in the case of societies governed by instinct, such as the bee-hive and the ant-hill, in which 'the individual lives for the community alone' (MR: 121). Bergson therefore attempts to identify the trait that has brought about an equivalent effect in the other main branch of evolution, epitomized by vertebrate species and characterized by the emergence of intellect. The earliest widespread social phenomenon in which he discerns counter-measures against the anti-social side-effects of intelligence is religion, and he gives an account of the ways religion – in what he takes to be its most basic elements – counters the threats posed by intelligence. The likelihood of a person acting exclusively in their own interests, at the expense of others, is countered by the disciplining social pressure that operates through the development of proto-religious customs. Knowledge of one's mortality is countered by belief in the possibility of survival beyond the death of the body. (Bergson notes that the benefit to society of the belief in an after-life consists not only in ensuring that its individuals do not regress into debilitated states of depressed inactivity or self-destruction, but also in providing the condition of trans-generational endurance and stability required by social institutions – especially in societies that do not yet possess other signs of such continuity, in the form of laws, information systems, or long-lasting architectural structures.) Meanwhile, the possibility of being supported in one's endeavours by invisible forces, whether in the form of deities, magic, spirits, or other animist or animatist entities, can help overcome rational pessimism. In short, '[p]rimitive religion […] is a precaution against the danger man runs, as soon as he thinks at all, of thinking of himself alone. It is therefore […] a defensive reaction of nature against intelligence' (MR: 123–4). Bergson thus joins a number of early twentieth-century thinkers – some of the most influential being Freud, Durkheim and Malinowski – in attributing to the earliest or simplest forms of religion the function of holding together social groups against the disintegrating effects of individualism. The specificity of Bergson's approach, however, lies in the emphasis he places on the evolved capacity which makes religion possible in the first place. It is this capacity that he terms fabulation.

At the point at which intellect, having brought new benefits to the organism and the species in terms of the capacity for survival, also begins to manifest certain new threats, instinct returns to counter intelligence's potential danger to itself. However, since humans have evolved in a manner which renders instinct subservient to intellect, it cannot directly intervene; or at least, it may supersede intellect only briefly in order to induce it to counter its own seemingly accurate, but potentially self-destructive observations:

> If this counterpoise cannot be instinct itself, for the very reason that its place has been taken by intelligence, the same effect must be produced by a virtuality of instinct, or if you prefer it, the residue of instinct which survives on the fringe of intelligence: it cannot exercise direct action, but since intelligence works on representations, it will call up 'imaginary' ones, which will hold their own against the representation of reality and will succeed, through the agency of the intelligence itself, in counteracting the work of intelligence. This would be the explanation of the fabulation function. (MR: 119)

All the means by which religion, in what have been understood as its incipient or elementary forms, and in general, counters the individualistic tendencies of intellect, depend at some level on a human capacity to believe in that which, from a materialist perspective, would be considered non-actual. The idea of a soul that is not wholly coincident with the body, like the notion of animist forces that may punish or favour humans' activities by invisibly controlling aspects of the environment or the actions of others, requires a capacity for believing in the enduring reality of that which has no immediate or substantial material presence. Bergson suggests that fabulation, the capacity for inventing and believing in such entities, forces and ideas, must have co-evolved with intellect, possibly as a function of instinct.

Though we may consciously direct this capacity for fictionalizing in any direction, its primary function – the reason it has evolved, and, from a social point of view, its ongoing usefulness – lies in its ability to enable survival against (vastly) unfavourable odds. The archetypal situation in which the fabulation function operates is one of critical threat – that is, in which the life of an individual or a group seems to be in intense, imminent danger, and from which the habitual intellectual mode of thought offers no means of escape – either because it does not perceive the danger, or because it sees it as inescapable. In order to illustrate this process by which fabulation 'counteracts' intelligence, Bergson recounts the following modern example from 'psychical research':

> A lady was on the upper floor of an hotel. The gate provided for the lift happened to be open. As the gate was so contrived as to be open only if the lift were stopped at that floor, she naturally thought the lift was there and rushed forward to take it. All of a sudden she felt herself flung backwards; the man entrusted with the working of the lift had just appeared and was pushing her back on to the landing. At this point she emerged from her fit of abstraction. She was amazed to see that neither man nor lift were there. The mechanism being out of order, it was possible for the gate to be open at her floor, though the lift was still down below. She had been about to fling herself into the gaping void; a miraculous hallucination had saved her life. (MR: 120)

Despite its apparent cultural and historical remove from the context of the origins of religion, this example is informative in a number of ways (and would be a suitable scenario for illuminating the theory of fabulation even if it were itself 'only' a fiction). Bergson's primary purpose is to illustrate the way a person may react to something instinctively before the intellect has had time to reflect on it. The fabulation of a 'fictitious hallucinatory perception' may be employed as part of this instinctive reaction to 'evoke and explain the apparently unjustified movement' (MR: 120–1), and dissuade the intellect from resisting. In addition, it demonstrates that the relationship Bergson identifies between fabulation and salvation entails the issue of immediate, physical survival ('a miraculous hallucination had saved her life'), and furthermore, that he sees fabulation as a general psychological characteristic – neither restricted to the sphere of religion, nor belonging to what some nineteenth- and early twentieth-century thinkers viewed as the 'pre-modern' mind.

Furthermore, this example shows how, for Bergson, fabulation and the religious phenomena to which it gives rise are no more social than individual in essence. Any given instance of 'salvation' through fabulation may in itself seem to have little significance for society as a whole; yet aggregated, a number of such incidents, especially when we consider them in the context of the more widespread threats discussed above, such as interpersonal violence, defeatism, a fear of death, and so on, may make the difference between survival and extinction for a species or large group. By the same token, individuals are saved in such situations only by virtue of the shared biological characteristic of fabulation, and sometimes by the socialized fabulations for which it is responsible (i.e. shared religious beliefs and practices). The survival of the individual and the group are mutually enhancing:

> we have, indeed, seen that the fabulation function, innate in the individual, has as its first object the consolidation of society; but we know that it is also intended to support the individual himself, and that, moreover, such is the interest of society [...] The individual and society thus condition each other, circle-wise. (MR: 198–9)

Fabulation's function is thus to restore the balance, or circularity, originally a simple biological or ecological reality, that was threatened by the individualism of the intellect. As we will begin to see in the following chapter, the disjunction between personal and social realities is a driving force in Dick's science fiction plots – and indeed, it is generally through fabulation that his characters (attempt to) cope with this disjunction. This theme, which as we have already noted, Dick himself often conceives in the Heraclitean vocabulary of the distinction between the *idios kosmos* and the *koinos kosmos*, may be observed throughout his work, although particularly illustrative examples can be found in *Time Out of Joint* (2003c [1959]), in which the main character unknowingly (initially) lives in an entire fake town constructed entirely for his benefit, or *Flow My Tears, the Policeman Said* (2001 [1974]), in which the protagonist Jason Taverner is a world-famous celebrity whose identity is suddenly erased from the popular consciousness. As Umberto Rossi (2011) argues, one cumulative effect of Dick's fictions is to underscore the interminable instability of attempts to restore this balance between individual and social worlds (at least, for forms of life that have deviated from the pseudo-mechanistic evolutionary path in which instinct dominates).

Bergson's example of the malfunctioning lift shaft may also remind us (if slightly obliquely) that the dangers the woman evades arise not only from the lift's machinery, but from her own intellect's mechanistic tendencies. As Dick once said in an interview, 'the entire universe and all the parts therein continually malfunction. But the great merit of the human being is that the human being is isomorphic with his malfunctioning universe. I mean, he too is somewhat malfunctioning' (Dick, in Anton and Fuchs 1996: 43). In *Ubik* (2000c [1969]), another of Dick's novels in which the disjunction between private and shared worlds is central, the main characters struggle to understand why certain technological objects have begun to revert to their earlier equivalent forms. Yet it is irresolvably uncertain whether it is the actual machines or the characters' own psychological mechanisms that are changing. This is made especially clear when, in a strange parallel to the example cited by Bergson, two characters find themselves hesitating on the point of entering a lift. While Al Hammond perceives the lift as having reverted to a 1910 model with an open cage and a lift operator inside, his colleague Joe Chip sees the modern automated version to which he is accustomed. By concentrating on his memory of the lift's modern form, Hammond is able to restore it, causing yet another apparently fictional lift operator – whose function again is to instigate attempts to overcome the difference between two versions of reality – to vanish (2000c: 124–5).

Fabulation, then, is Bergson's tentative answer to the question of what it is that makes social life possible among individuals with intellect. It is the faculty which prevents what he terms the war-instinct from becoming dominant. However, the history of human culture, which, to paraphrase Walter Benjamin, is simultaneously a history of barbarism, testifies to the limited scope of this overcoming: thus we should view fabulation not as the conqueror of the war-instinct, but as the marker and enabler of the *possibility* of going against the war-instinct – a possibility whose actualization hangs constantly in the balance, both during the course of a person's daily existence, and through the course of human history.

The morality of violence

The limited success of fabulation in suppressing the war-instinct, according to Bergson's account, had provided humanity through most of its existence with a reasonable chance of overall survival, however violent and self-destructive its path may have been. Yet it seemed that with the advent of the modern era these chances were dropping dramatically. Thus, having posited the value of fabulation in opposing the mechanizing dimension of intellect, Bergson addresses the question of its limitations, both in general, and in the particular social-historical context of modernity.

A substantial part of *Two Sources* addresses the ways widespread, localized instances of fabulation may gradually give rise to forms of religion approaching its recognizable institutionalized versions. Through this account, one can trace the trajectory of mechanization as it is countered by fabulation within the group, only to return at the inter-social level. For mechanization is not banished by proto-religious fabulations such as the soul or gods, any more than the principles of entropy or gravity are banished by the growth of an embryo or a bird in flight. Nevertheless, its effects are clearly sufficiently resisted in certain circumstances to allow social groups to function and grow, as shared moral codes, rituals and religious beliefs take on organized shape, effectively aggregating the various localized instances in which fabulation dissuades individuals from anti-social behaviour, or improves their own survival prospects (and thus restoring the functional unity that bound these two effects at the level of biological survival).

One might ask what it is – barring the intervention of some supernatural intelligence – that causes this process to take place: that is, what causes the jump from scattered, localized fabulations in individual experience to the organized fabulations of religion? But for Bergson, fabulation does not so much *cause* social cohesion, as remove the obstacles which intellect places in the way of a biological tendency that long precedes the evolution of so-called *homo sapiens*. Even if, as Bergson argues in both *Creative Evolution* and *Two Sources*, vertebrate evolution gradually leads towards the dominance of intellect over instinct, both are means of fulfilling a tendency towards cohesion, coordination – in a sense, a proto-sociality – which precedes them as a fundamental characteristic of life. Lynn Margulis' serial endosymbiosis theory, which suggests that the formation of new organisms through the symbiotic merging of separate cellular entities has been fundamental to the evolution of multicellular life, could be seen as a sophisticated contemporary version of such a principle.[6]

Thus, before there is social obligation, there is obligation in general, which is 'among the most specific phenomena of life' (MR: 29). The crucial role fabulation plays in the emergence of human society is not in causing collaboration among individuals, but in sufficiently diminishing the extent to which intellect hinders such collaboration. Yet this essentially means allowing instinct to direct behaviour, which, as in the kind of society represented by the ant-hill, only suppresses individualistic behaviour for the benefit of that society. Whatever morality develops on this basis is, in Bergson's vocabulary, 'closed', in that none of its imperatives or responsibilities are extended to those beyond the particular social group in question: 'In a word, the social instinct which we have detected at the basis of social obligation always has in view – instinct being relatively unchangeable – a closed society, however large' (MR 32). The kind of morality that is made possible by fabulation is 'an attitude which is that of discipline in the face of the enemy' (MR 31). The members of the closed society are bound together by an equally closed morality, in that their love and respect for one another – or their partial obedience to prohibitions against mutual mistreatment – are based on mutual dependence and the pressure to defend themselves collectively against external threats. The corollary is that anyone considered outside the closed society is automatically assigned a status whereby, at a minimum, they lack the protection of any moral code operating within that society, and in many circumstances will be considered equivalent to material resources for consumption or use. Members of the closed society are likely to be permitted, if not encouraged, by their moral and religious frameworks to kill, enslave, steal from or otherwise abuse those who do not belong to their group. Thus fabulation, in offsetting the dangers of intellect within the social group, can be said to establish the conditions for, and even encourage the return of mechanization at an inter-social level.

One might counter this aspect of Bergson's theory by asking why, if it is correct, does closed morality not always lead to the total annihilation of one social group when two come into contact? But just as fabulation does not suppress individualism and the war-instinct entirely – indeed, it apparently does just enough to prevent human societies from collapsing – the closed morality to which it gives rise does not lead to a permanent state of violent aggression between closed societies. There are plenty of factors which would counter such a possibility. For one thing, even a closed society that regards members of an external group as entirely undeserving of any moral obligation will not necessarily see conflict with that group as in its own interests, depending on what it stands to lose and gain through such action. Another consideration must be that the longer contact continues, the less distinct the separation between two groups becomes, such that at some point a closed society must, at least partially, extend its morality to those who were not counted among its members when contact was first made. This happens regardless of whether the contact takes place primarily through war, trade, occupation, migration or other forms of cultural interaction. Presumably the only sets of circumstance in which this is not the case are those where annihilation takes place virtually immediately, and those in which a great effort is made to maintain isolation (i.e. those scenarios in which nothing significantly changes for the closed society in question as a result of contact).

Aside from these mitigating factors, however, there is a crucial further element which may, and has, prevented closed morality from becoming totalized. In addition to the obligation or pressure that produces closed morality, there is a set of human characteristics which forms the basis for an entirely different form of morality.

Open morality and the misdirection of mechanism

What Bergson refers to as 'open morality' is, in its origins, no less biological than closed morality. Both closed and open tendencies are aspects of the creative movement of life out of which both human organisms and human society have evolved. Whereas he views closed morality as the manifestation at a human psychological and social level of a self-preserving tendency towards closure, found throughout the living world, open morality manifests the governing generative principle or creative force of life. These two tendencies had been central to Bergson's account of life in *Creative Evolution*. Returning to this perspective in *Two Sources*, he writes that a 'great current of creative energy is precipitated into matter, to wrest from it what it can. At most points, remember, it came to a stop; these stops are equivalent, in our eyes, to the phenomena of so many living species' (MR: 209). Species dominated by instinct are those 'whose activity ran indefinitely in the same circle' – that is, which took up positions of effective self-enclosure along the flow of evolution. However, that same flow continues to produce new forms, new possibilities – and in the case of humans, makes possible a capacity for invention (MR: 209–10). Hence, 'all morality, be it pressure or aspiration, is in essence biological' (MR: 101). This means that open morality – associated here with aspiration, in contrast to the pressure or obligation by which closed morality achieves sociality – is likewise a possibility immanent in all humans (if not all life).

The potential for open morality may lie dormant most of the time, yet even as a potential – one that can be traced back to the small but crucial difference between the ant-hill organized through instinct and the human society governed by a *virtual* instinct – it makes it possible to conceive of an open society, in contrast to the closed. Where the closed society denotes a group with a finite number of members who are in principle countable, known to one another, identifying with one another (even if above a certain size this can take place only through 'imagined communities' [Anderson 1983] which are equally dependent on fabulation), the open society does not attempt to limit its membership. Importantly, this means the absence of predefined limits in both geographical and temporal/historical senses, in that the open society would count within its membership as a *minimum* the whole of humanity, without placing rigid restrictions on who or what may count, either geographically or with regard to possible future encounters. To invoke 'humanity' as a whole, of course, has both political and biological (or biopolitical) implications: where used to refer to people (rather than an ethical quality), it easily tends towards the kind of closure Bergson associates with defining, delimiting a species (a process that can be understood to take place at the natural and the epistemological level); yet within the perspective of open morality and the open society, the identification of members or groups of members as 'human' or otherwise can only ever be considered grounds for inclusion, never exclusion.

We should note that Bergson's distinction between the closed and open society is a distinction between static and dynamic forms *that is itself dynamic*. That is, these are not two simple categories, into which we can classify given empirical examples of specific societies. Such would be a means of distinguishing according to closed thinking – and indeed, such classification forms a real, reductive though pragmatic component of much political thought and activity, especially in contexts such as national and global governance. The open society is more a principle or idea(l) that may affect and begin to transform the closed society. While a concrete instantiation of an open society may ultimately be unrealizable (and while any declaration of confidence in such an instantiation having taken place would negate itself, in declaring complete that which by nature must never be completed), as a principle, it indicates an always-possible process of 'opening' the closed society and closed morality.

Though Bergson does not make it explicit, this means that any conception of the open society must also involve fabulation – and in a dynamic fashion. That is, no particular representation, as for example found in a utopian text, describing the specific political and social characteristics of an imaginary society, will suffice: any detailed, prescriptive or descriptive account of the open society immediately begins to revert towards closure.[7] Nevertheless, remaining 'open' to the as-yet-unknown or not-yet-encountered member of a non-exclusionary society requires an imaginative gesture that would be impossible without the capacity to fictionalize. The notion of a fabulation which would resist the pressure to revert to closure (that is, to the support of the closed society with its closed morality) is an essential component of both the Bergsonian and Dickian soteriologies, one which will become clearer in the following chapters as we superimpose them upon one another.

It seems then that fabulation's success in thwarting the war-instinct has at best been partial, producing a precarious balance between social and anti-social behaviour. Closed morality has remained largely dominant, though the immanent potential for open morality, along with certain pragmatic constraints, has prevented this dominance from becoming total, just as fabulation prevents the individual intellect from destroying social life.

What calls this into doubt for Bergson (as, implicitly, for many of his contemporaries) is the coupling of humanity's immanent mechanizing tendencies with the rise of modern industrial mechanization. As Bergson puts it, the intelligence,

> pouring into these machines reserves of energy which nature (so heedless of economy) had never even thought of, has endowed us with powers beside which those of our body barely count: they will be altogether limitless when science is able to liberate the force which is enclosed, or rather condensed, in the slightest particle of ponderable matter. The material barrier has then well nigh vanished. (MR: 312)

This statement anticipates aspects of later twentieth- and twenty-first-century discourses of posthumanism, both in theoretical writing and science fiction, highlighting how the materialistic, mechanistic worldview that underpins a certain (dominant) strand of modern scientific and technological thinking may ultimately lead towards rather than away from experiences and ideas that demand to be thought within a spiritual or quasi-religious framework. Katherine Hayles' *How We Became Posthuman* (1999) and Erik Davis' *TechGnosis* (1998) give incisive accounts of several dimensions of such trends – both drawing on Dick's science fiction. As I suggested in the Introduction, and as much science fiction postulates, the most seemingly mechanistic approach may constitute a condition for sublime and spiritual experiences, rather than their abolition.

However, it is precisely humanity's failure to develop a spiritual maturity adequate to this new physical power that is Bergson's concern. Though the accelerated industrial forms of mechanization had led to dramatic expansions in the speed and scale of human destruction, through global mechanized warfare and the imperialist-capitalist subjugation of much of the planetary population, this was not inevitable: mechanization in the industrial sense did not automatically have to serve and intensify the mechanizing war-instinct, though in so doing it may well have contributed to the pervasive illusion of its inevitability. Indeed, the course taken is, in ethical terms, but also from an evolutionary biological viewpoint, a 'mistake': 'machinery, through a mistake at the points, has been switched on to a track at the end of which lies exaggerated luxury and comfort for the few, rather than liberation for all' (MR: 309).

In using a railway metaphor that alludes to both the train and the ability to control which track it runs on, Bergson re-emphasizes the fact that by 'mechanism' he means both the actual machinery of industrialization, and the general tendency of human beings elaborated above. Mechanism, in the joint sense of industry and the intelligence that organizes it, could, in the service of life, have ensured, first, food for all and, second, the elimination of large-scale violence. Instead, the 'mistake at the points' has taken mechanism in a different direction such that it increasingly threatens the destruction of humanity, either through the literal ending of lives, or through the large-scale reduction of life to a status approaching that of the mechanical.

Bergson continues his account of mechanized humanity's inability to wield adequately its newly acquired power through the image of a body that has suddenly undergone a dramatic increase in size. The great danger lies in the fact that,

> in this body, distended out of all proportion, the soul remains what it was, too small to fill it, too weak to guide it. Hence the gap between the two. Hence the tremendous social, political and international problems which are just so many definitions of this gap, and which provoke so many chaotic and ineffectual efforts to fill it. (MR: 310)

This image of the distended cosmic body may further remind us that Bergson's theme here – the question of modern and future humanity's (in)ability to wield its newly acquired technological power – would soon be established as a major theme in science fiction. As we will see, many of Dick's plots, especially in his early novels, can be read as documents of 'chaotic and ineffectual efforts' to address this gap between physical power and spiritual or moral maturity which resonate with an array of twentieth-century governmental strategies.

Where then, for Bergson, are we to find the 'bigger soul' that is needed to match this enlarged body? Where are the 'new reserves of potential energy – moral energy this time' (MR: 310) that would be equivalent to the material reserves of fossil fuels and atomic power? Bergson associates the outlook that would meet these requirements with a certain mysticism – though he is careful to distinguish what he refers to as 'true mysticism' from the 'counterfeit' forms which were already by the early twentieth century being criticized for their association with imperialist political programmes, and which would soon after come to be associated with Nazism and fascism (MR: 310–11). True mysticism is for Bergson completely incompatible with those counterfeit forms which link a deity or divine power exclusively to a particular human group (MR: 311). It is, rather, characterized by an open as opposed to a closed morality, by a universalizing as opposed to a particularizing predisposition. Considering the figure Bergson refers to as the true mystic in more detail should give us a clearer understanding of what for him is at stake in the task of opposing modern mechanization – in particular, why it is not a task that can be addressed through any approach that invokes a simple opposition between the material and the spiritual, between immanence and transcendence. Further, it will allow us to see how fabulation may – and perhaps must – be expected to play a key role in this task.

True mysticism: Immanent salvation

Bergson's two forms of morality, each with its own biological origin, also have their own respective affective characters, equating to two kinds of love. Whereas the citizens of the closed society may feel a kind of love for their fellow-citizens that is the result of shared traits and interests and the biological pressure towards social coherence (expressed in demonstrations of familial or tribal bonds, nationalist pride, religious ritual and so on), the kind of love associated with open morality is characterized by universal acceptance and an unreserved, expansive love extending through and beyond all specific individuals, indeed, potentially beyond the limits of any conventional understanding of humanity or even life. The former is associated with contentment, the latter with joy.

Doubtless most people have the potential for both kinds of affect, and a mixture of the two are probably common. However, it seems reasonable to suggest that it would be quite difficult for most people to live their lives consistently according to an open rather than closed morality. This would entail, to a large extent, the abandonment of long-acquired ties to particular groups, and the relinquishing, to a degree, of the protection of the closed society; in a world largely dominated by closed morality, to be unreservedly open is, almost certainly, to open oneself to abuse and exploitation.

Thus while moments of 'opening' may be widely experienced, the figure who is able to maintain such a perspective indefinitely, with confidence and intensity, is quite rare. Bergson identifies possible historical examples of such 'true mystics' in, for example, Jesus of Nazareth, Joan of Arc and Teresa of Avila. The scarcity of such individuals should in itself be a testament to the extreme difficulties humanity faces if it is to have any hope of continuing to suppress the war-instinct sufficiently in order to survive. Nevertheless, their existence at all suggests that such an achievement is not impossible.

Bergson describes as 'static religion' those forms which emerge in, or with, the closed society. This phrase indicates an affiliation with the biological tendency towards closure (by this point it should be clear that Bergson's 'two sources' correspond to modes not only of morality and religion, but also of social formation, love, identity, and other dimensions of human life). Like the tendency within life to produce self-enclosed species, static religion supports the constitution of the closed society, strengthening the sense of closed morality and group unity through, for example, the development of ritual, doctrine and narratives (which form the basis for future laws and more complex codes of social behaviour). True mysticism, however, represents a reconnection with the vital creative force that caused new forms to emerge and proliferate – the second source, that of the open tendency. To the extent that this results in religion, it should be considered 'dynamic religion'. Many of the traits we associate with religion in general, according to this schema, are seen as specific to static religion, making the true mystic as anti-religious as she is religious. Whether imagined or real, the true mystic is the figure who helps us 'get back into the creative impetus, and impel human nature forward instead of letting it revolve on one spot' (MR: 199). Any transcendence associated with mysticism and dynamic religion comes not from a deity, but through the acquired capacity for overcoming one's previous limitations, for reintroducing change, evolution, movement into what had become static.

In broad terms, a philosophical position of immanence is concerned with arguing that there is only one plane of reality; that nothing exists in a separate dimension, exterior to this worldly plane. Though it is generally viewed in opposition to a perspective involving transcendence (in a manner paralleling but not identical with the opposition between materialist and idealist perspectives), we can conceive of a compatible form of transcendence that would really only mark the difference between two notions of possibility or ability – that is, for example, between the ability to speak a foreign language and the ability to learn to speak that language given enough time; the difference hinges on whether one takes a static view of an individual or state (at a particular instant) or a dynamic view allowing for its continual change over time.

This is not to suggest that there is no hint of something like transcendence in the more religious sense involved here. When a change is so drastic as to be considered impossible within a given time-frame, its occurrence is rightly treated as 'miraculous', whether this entails a belief in the working of supernatural forces or consists of a metaphorical expression connoting the extreme improbability of the event that has taken place. The thought or experience of transcendence, as the above account of fabulation suggests, should be understood as a constitutive part of immanent reality, and as a component with the capacity to bring about concrete and occasionally hugely unlikely effects. Yet this should not be viewed as confirming the validity of an influential line of criticism of Bergson which has seen philosophers from Russell to Badiou claim that Bergson's vitalism itself involves an irreducibly transcendent dimension. (In relation to this criticism, see the discussion of Bergson and Badiou in Chapter 3, where I argue that their respective conceptions of life are quite compatible, if not convergent, at least with regard to their potential ethico-political valency and efficacy.) Especially in light of this common (mis)perception, it is worth emphasizing the extent to which Bergson's true mystic is a worldly figure.

The reason Bergson hesitates to include the figure of Buddha among his examples of true mystics is his supposed retirement from (or renunciation of) the world.[8] Likewise, the mysticism of Plotinus for Bergson failed to reach full maturity due to a lack of faith in action (MR: 225–6), even if it attains an experience of ecstasy which may well constitute the reconnection of the open soul with 'the creative effort which life itself manifests' (MR: 220). Where the classical Greek intellectualism represented by Plotinus has a reverence for pure thought which views action as 'a weakening of contemplation' (MR: 221), Bergson sees fully realized mysticism as being

> expressed in the bent for action, the faculty of adapting and re-adapting oneself to circumstances, in firmness combined with suppleness, in the prophetic discernment of what is possible and what is not, in the spirit of simplicity which triumphs over complications, in a word, supreme good sense. (MR: 228)

This 'spirit of simplicity' is fundamental to the attitude which gives the mystic an (often surprising) aptitude for accomplishment through direct worldly action. It causes her to ignore 'false problems', implicitly answering questions that have 'force[d] themselves on the attention of philosophers' and regarding as non-existent problems which 'should never have perplexed philosophers' (MR: 251).

Testament to the bent for action of the true mystic is found in 'what was accomplished in the field of action by a St Paul, a St Teresa, a St Catherine of Siena, a St Francis, a Joan of Arc' (MR: 228). Again, the extraordinary achievements of such figures can indeed seem to give them a miraculous or divine power. Yet Bergson's argument is that this in fact reflects a deeply practical ability based on 'an exceptional, deep-rooted mental healthiness' (MR: 228), and which is ultimately rooted in a biological rather than a divine source. Such figures do not transcend the world, but surpass the limits of a particular type of human with a particular view of the world – one that is based on false problems and the dominant fabulations of the closed society. If this creates the impression of superhuman ability, it nevertheless entails no necessary action or event that would be beyond immanent reality.

In recent years, conceptions of the posthuman have offered a number of ways of exploring such a perspective. Particularly relevant here is Bruce Clarke's notion of the 'evolutionary sublime', in which 'the human species finds it consummation [...] by absorption into a transcendental posthuman consortium' (2008: 191). For Bergson, the true mystic, in 'breaking the circle' of closed morality and re-identifying with the larger, ongoing, dynamic evolution of life, effectively becomes 'a species composed of a single individual' (MR: 268), and indeed, the appearance of each true mystic is 'like the creation of a new species' (MR: 95). Clarke is referring to a kind of biocultural evolution brought about by cross-species bonding, which is central to Octavia Butler's *Xenogenesis* trilogy, and which, as mentioned above, has through Margulis' work on endosymbiosis been recognized as likely to have been a major factor in the evolution of life on earth. With Bergson's true mystic, we do not see the bonding of two species, but in that the open soul reconnects with a creative tendency running through all life, we can say there is effectively a virtual hybridization or coupling with any – and therefore (virtually) all – species, which although not 'consummated' as it is in Clarke's Butlerian scenario, is nevertheless maintained by 'a great surge of love' (MR: 95). This notion of an evolutionary sublime, and of the combining of separate species as an evolutionary engine, resonates with many aspects of Dick's work that are discussed in subsequent chapters of this book, in particular the notion that his communications with Valis or Zebra represent a form of 'cross-bonding' between biological and informational entities.

An incomplete soteriology

In that *Two Sources* concerns the question of preserving humanity from its (self-)destruction, in circumstances where this seems a near-impossible task, it can be understood as an attempt to pursue a path or logic of salvation. This is, as I have suggested, a notion of salvation that should be viable within an immanent understanding of the world – yet one which remains salvation nonetheless. Thus *Two Sources* can be said to develop, among other things, an immanent soteriology. The value of the true mystic lies in her ability to span this seemingly insuperable separation between immanence and transcendence, which corresponds to the gap between modern humanity's distended body and its small soul (MR: 311) in constituting 'an individual being, capable of transcending the limitations imposed on the species by its material nature' (MR: 210–11).

Yet even Bergson admits that 'it will be just as well not to count too much on the coming of a great privileged soul' (MR: 312). No immanent soteriology can rely on the arrival of an absolutely transcendent figure from another world, whether Christ or Superman. The historical appearance of true mystics is rare and unpredictable, and true mysticism as a concept or attitude, even if conceived without a dependence on divine or supernatural qualities, does not appear to be one that is easy to adopt or maintain. The 'bent for action' characterizing the true mystic entails a practicality of an unusual kind: it is not through a great focus on practical problems, but by ignoring them (and thus revealing the extent to which they may be considered false problems) that the mystic is able to step over obstacles that would seem insurmountable to most of us. Even if the creative impetus whose intuition gives this figure her unusual capability is immanent within every living organism, a life lived continually 'in touch' with this impetus would seem to be practically impossible for most humans. And yet, for the open society to have a chance of emerging, or even for the closed society to begin 'opening' in any effective way, this quality would, according to Bergson's argument, have to be possessed by a large proportion of the population. How is it possible to seek salvation – from a very material threat of destruction – through the emulation of a figure for whom practical obstacles do not exist? Is there not something missing, here, right at the heart of Bergson's soteriology?

The problem here does not lie in identifying the social changes that need to occur. The following all appear in the 'Final Remarks' of *Two Sources* as quite reasonable goals which, if they could be achieved, would bring us most of the way towards the larger aim of overcoming the critical threat of mechanization: the abolition of war (MR: 286–90); the abandonment of 'the concern for comfort and luxury which has apparently become the main preoccupation of humanity' (MR: 298); the reversal of the subservience of agriculture to industry in order to ensure the universal fulfilment of the basic needs for survival (MR: 306); establishing gender equality (MR: 302–3); and broadening the scope of scientific research to include the spiritual (MR: 312–17).

Most of these goals would be shared by a variety of critical political traditions, in Bergson's time as today. The great difficulty is not working out what needs to be done on an abstract level (stop killing, feed everyone, treat each other well) but figuring out how to get enough people to adopt such goals, and to agree on an effective means of achieving them. Since this would necessarily involve the negation of a mechanizing tendency that is, as we have seen, implicit in the fundamental activity of intelligence, this is an incredibly difficult task – more so, perhaps, than even the most ethically or critically disposed often recognize. It is this difficulty which causes the thought of overcoming mechanization to involve an ineradicable dimension of salvation, of transcendence, even as this process is ultimately centred on the material preservation of life.

How then is this transcendent dimension to be maintained without the true mystic? It is here, I would suggest, that we ought to return to fabulation in seeking an answer. Although Bergson does not indicate this directly, the argument of *Two Sources* seems to point towards it from a number of angles. His overt discussion of the role of fabulation is almost entirely restricted to the sphere of static religion and the closed society. As we have seen, its original function and effect was to diminish the threats posed by the mechanizing characteristics of the individualistic intellect from destroying social cohesion. The cultural formations which it facilitated and continues to support in order to fulfil this function then become central to a closed morality which, while preserving life within a social group, reproduces the destructive tendencies of mechanization at an inter-social level. Yet to reject fabulation on this basis is to forget its primary role. Indeed, Bergson highlights this error of excess in situations where mysticism is rejected as a tool of imperialism – just as associations with the mystical, transcendent or religious have frequently been denounced since as supporting capitalism, fascism and other ideological structures. Generalized reactions of this kind tend to equate mysticism with mystification, whereas one does not necessarily imply the other. Likewise, to abandon fabulation as the facilitator of mechanization is to give up the saving potential that it offers, and which, I will argue, may well ultimately be invaluable in the struggle against the destructive power of modern mechanization.

Near the end of *Two Sources*, Bergson reminds the reader that the relationship between mechanization and mysticism – and, implicitly therefore, between mechanization and fabulation – is not one of a simple opposition:

> The origins of the process of mechanization are indeed more mystical than we might imagine. Machinery will find its true vocation again, it will render services in proportion to its power, only if mankind, which it has bowed still lower to the earth, can succeed, through it, in standing erect and looking heavenwards. (MR: 310)

Ostensibly Bergson is referring here to the machinery of the factory, of industrialization. He is accounting for a certain spirit of inventiveness that historically leads to modern technological advancement, yet is not easily separable from a wide range of spiritual and moral ideals. The suggestion is that industry may still, if properly organized, become a liberating rather than mechanizing force with regard to life. Yet in light of the more general sense of mechanization that I have emphasized, this statement may simultaneously be read as indicating that there is something inherent to those same oppressive mechanizing processes which might, if properly re-appropriated, offer the possibility of liberation. Fabulation would fit this description perfectly, as that which enables the global mechanization of humanity, by virtue of its role in the growth of closed morality and closed societies, yet which does so only on the basis of a prior salvific potential which these developments should not be allowed to eclipse.

Just as we should not blame science or technology for the uses to which they have been put – just as industrial production needs to be set on a new footing in the service of life and the open society – we should not confuse fabulation with specific ways it has been used. Fabulation too is a form of mechanism, an evolved faculty for constructing and believing in fictions which have the potential to save. When Bergson says that 'man will rise above earthly things only if a powerful equipment supplies him with the requisite fulcrum' (MR: 309) he may be referring not only to the possibility of effecting a more ethical organization of industrial technology, but also to the spiritual or moral technologies that may be required to bring this about: fabulation itself may well be the 'powerful equipment' that is required to 'rise above earthly things' – which is, after all, its fundamental function.

It is in this light that I read the last line of *Two Sources*: it is the task of humans, once they have determined whether they wish 'to go on living or not', to decide 'if they want merely to live, or intend to make just the extra effort required for fulfilling, even on their refractory planet, the essential function of the universe, which is a machine for the making of gods' (MR: 317). The making of gods can be understood as humanity's becoming-mystic – the evolution into the new species which is encapsulated occasionally in human history by the figure of the true mystic, and to which all humanity would need to aspire in order to have a chance at overcoming mechanization. Yet this final sentence also concerns a *machine*, with a *function* that has specifically to do with humanity's self-transcendence – to do with a kind of living that would be beyond 'merely living' (*vivre seulement*), and which would constitute a kind of salvation. Intentionally or not, this conclusion thus points towards a convergence between the fabulation function, itself a machine which creates saving fictions, including gods, and what, in a poetic tone, Bergson calls the essential function of the universe. Could fabulation, the machine which constructs gods and saviours in a fictional but culturally and psychologically effective mode, be the key to making those who create and respond to such fictions into gods and saviours themselves? In other words, might not fabulation be the technique by which humanity's self-transcendence, its salvation from its own mechanization, becomes conceivable?

Fabulation for the open

To begin exploring this possibility, before we move on to developing it more fully as both an active principle and a submerged theme in Dick's work, we might consider what roles fabulation can already be expected to play within the activity of the true mystic as the embodiment of an open morality. No doubt, Bergson's true mystic sees through the fabulated constructs of the closed society, especially where these lead to the oppression or mechanization of life, to forms of imperialism and abuse. But might not the mystic also make use of the great potential of fabulation towards her own ends? Would she, with such deep-rooted mental healthiness as Bergson attributes to her, reject one of the most powerful tools for salvation, on the basis that it has also led to oppression and violence? We should remember that the fictions which come to support closed morality may be a long way from the act of fictionalizing or fabulation that is at work in an immediate experience of the divine, or in the hallucination which saved the woman from falling into an empty lift shaft. Indeed, the huge difference which Bergson emphasizes in a wide range of contexts between the dynamic and the static, the closed and the open, could and should be applied to fabulation. The process of fabulation produces specific fictions which are taken up and passed on, elaborated and reduplicated, with certain elements becoming increasingly fixed across different re-tellings, solidifying as the counterparts of the religious or proto-religious institutions and doctrines that develop alongside them. They are the static fabulations of static religion, whereas the dynamic process of fabulating that gave rise to them corresponds to the attitude and morality of dynamic religion, in which an open, unbounded creativity is key. Just as Bergson critiqued, in *Creative Evolution*, the tendency to treat the series of particular evolved species as evolution itself, to identify the fictions invented and built into the fabric of cultural life by fabulation with the process of fabulating itself is to conflate two basically opposed tendencies.

The more successfully the fabulations that become religious doctrine are integrated into everyday existence, the more they are treated as though belonging to concrete reality. In this sense, the situation in which closed morality threatens to bring about destruction on a scale that threatens the species (as, putatively, when many formerly isolated closed societies come into prolonged contact) is directly analogous to that of the threat posed by the intellect within a given social group. Like intellect with respect to the individual, closed morality encourages the collective within which it is shared to act purely in their own interests, at the expense of any outsiders. Conversely, the individualistic ego can be said to have constituted all along a closed morality operating within a closed society of one member. The organism–society analogy was almost fulfilled – were it not for the fact that fabulation was able to 'open up' this unicellular society for a brief period, or in a limited way, such that socially destructive tendencies were diverted and deferred. If this deferral led to the reproduction of analogous circumstances at a multicellular level, should fabulation not subsequently be able to reprise its role?

When a true mystic – or indeed anyone critical of their socio-cultural environment – sees through the cultural fictions which are responsible for the spread and intensification of the mechanization of humans (and of the living in general), they are revealing as fictional that which had become apparent reality (or perhaps more accurately, rendering static fictions dynamic). Just as the woman approaching the empty lift shaft was rationally certain that the lift was there, the closed society often believes it is acting morally when it enslaves, attacks or otherwise abuses those outside its walls. In both cases, averting the threat to life – which means *saving* life – involves a counteracting of apparent reality, in which its salient aspects are revealed as fictional. In some sense, fabulation must always in some sense constitute meta-fabulation; the dynamic process of fabulating always operates against static fictions that have been falsely perceived as concrete, immutable reality.

A mode of fabulation adequate to the task of working towards the open society would thus have to be one that recognizes and counters the static products of former fabulations. It would need to acknowledge the saving effects they once produced, while critiquing the mechanizing closed morality – and perceptions of reality in general – to which they have made essential contributions. It would need to engage with the problematics of this process, of the ease with which the dynamic becomes static and with which anti-mechanizing (e.g. mystic, vitalistic, open) efforts give rise to mechanization in other forms and other sites; and it would need to develop strategies to prevent its own effects from inadvertently (re)producing mechanization elsewhere. This is what I believe we find in the writing, or rather, the *fabulations* of Philip K. Dick: a dynamic fabulating activity that emerges across a lifetime, becoming the driving force in an immanent soteriology, which, regardless of whether they are named, constitutes a prolonged search for both the open soul and the open society.

Conclusion

The presentation of Bergson in this chapter, especially where connections are made between earlier and later aspects of his thought, may have given the false impression that his philosophy forms a systematic whole. He himself denied this. While there are many convergences and common, indeed mutually enhancing concepts, theories and lines of philosophical investigation across his works, these have more to do with something like organic cohesion – resonances and continuities arising from sustained efforts of thought – than an abstract, systematic framework. As Mullarkey emphasizes, Bergson insisted on an inherent vagueness to his key terms, a degree of 'conceptual indefinability' corresponding to the lack of systemacity in nature or reality; any term or concept that is too rigidly defined is likely to become useless, if not detrimental, to the intuitive method in its attempts 'to adjust dynamically to reality' (Mullarkey 1999: 166). Bergson's concepts are deployed dynamically as opposed to in static forms, in order to approach a better understanding, rather than awaiting their own verification. This applies to fabulation as much as to any other element of his work – including his attempt to make an ethical contribution to the future of human society, that which I have termed his immanent soteriology.

If Bergson's account of fabulation is inherently incomplete, the first reason, then, is that as a way of attempting to understand crucial aspects of society and culture, the theory or concept of fabulation should be subordinated to and malleable in the face of the reality it attempts to describe, rather than attempting to fit the facts to its own rigid and prescriptive model; that is, it should be a useful and adaptive tool in the dynamic process by which that reality gradually becomes clearer – rather than positing an immediately clear abstraction and reducing the real to it. But a second reason is that that reality is itself changing, not only from the perspective of a given psyche, but on a historical and global scale: if *Two Sources* is to participate usefully in an ongoing ethico-political project – the overcoming of war-instinct in the context of modern mechanization – its key concepts must be able to adapt as that context develops.

Despite its focus on the *origins* of society, religion and morality, *Two Sources* is ultimately a future-oriented project. Though what follows may be characterized as an attempt to address the incompleteness of Bergson's immanent soteriology by developing the understanding of fabulation through Dick's work, ultimately such a project must aim to respect and maintain that incompleteness – which must be understood as constitutive of the openness of any genuine ethics. In this sense, Bergson's incomplete soteriology is also a soteriology of incompleteness, in a sense that, ultimately, may also characterize that of Dick.

2

Fabulating Salvation in Four Early Novels

In 1977, Dick wrote: 'I never knew of, nor did I experience or write about, a salvific entity' (E: 231). Yet in characteristic fashion, he immediately negated the statement by citing four or five of his previous works which do feature characters with some apparently transcendent saving power and function. In fact, salvation and saviour-figures can be identified throughout his work, starting long before the religious visions of 1974 that underpinned his late novels. As we will see, salvation in Dick's work is consistently tied to (the threat of) mechanization, in both the industrial-technological sense, and in terms of the more general (in) human and physical tendencies which Bergson, as we saw in the last chapter, identifies as preceding it (e.g. the war-instinct, determinism, entropy, closed morality). Indeed, in the same paragraph from which the above quotation is taken, Dick highlights as his two 'grand themes', false reality and 'androids programmed to imagine they are human (i.e. self-determining)' (E: 231), both of which are strongly linked to mechanization in its diverse forms.

We have already touched on some of the ways mechanization and salvation can, broadly, be viewed as themes common to science fiction in general. The historical rise of mechanization, in the industrial sense, forms a major part of the backdrop for the cultural emergence of science fiction as a modern genre, as well as inspiring many of its staple props and conceits. The theme of salvation has likewise played a central role in several of the main strands of science fiction, where the threatened destruction of a people or world becomes a generic plot scenario across a variety of its forms: not only do space opera, apocalyptic science fiction, dystopian fiction, superhero narratives and many other sub-genres typically take such threats as core plot elements, but they also frequently feature an overtly or covertly messianic protagonist charged with the task of averting disaster. Yet what I find particular to Dick is an engagement with these themes which links them to fabulation: not only thematically or in terms of plot, but in that the fiction or narrative itself effectively begins to perform a soteriological function. That is, Dick's most powerful writing operates in what, towards the end of the previous chapter, I suggested may be considered a dynamic or open mode of fabulation, which both obliterates and re-energizes static closed fictions which have become fixed aspects of reality (whether in a cultural, psychological, historical, or some other register). The function of this operation is to seek out possible modes and forms of salvation, though crucially, ones that would be viable within an immanent worldview.

The dynamic dimension of Dick's fabulations is less overt in the earlier works considered in this chapter, which remain closer (though by no means bound) to the science fiction conventions of the time and climate within which Dick began his career. The aim here will be to establish an overview of the thematic triangle mechanization–salvation–fabulation in Dick's work, before using it as a basis for the explorations of dynamic fabulation in the extended readings of particular novels that are the focus of subsequent chapters. In those readings, we will see how Dick's work pursues the question and possibility of immanent salvation through the opening up of closed (static) fictions which make up dominant reality, in contexts such as the nature of the human in relation to its perceived others, the experience of history, and the relationship between the divine and the mundane. Yet we may still observe in the earlier novels discussed in this chapter elements of at least an incipient mode of dynamic fabulation with regard to the genre of science fiction itself.

Critics have often discussed what they take to be Dick's subversions of the modes of traditional science fiction, suggesting for example that he writes 'meta-SF', 'distorting and modifying' its narrative devices (Pagetti 1992: 25); that his writing 'acts as a critique of the ideological presuppositions of the SF genre' (Fitting 1992b: 42); that he is 'an enthusiastic rather than a conventional writer of SF, so that he exploits the conventions of the genre rather than obeying them' (Palmer 2003: vii). Whatever conventional aspects of science fiction Dick's writing subverts might, in the Bergsonian sense, be considered 'closed', that is, representing the ossified results of a creative process of invention which had, in certain places and instances, ceased to evolve. To this extent, any attempt to subvert them can be seen as an attempt to undo this closure. Thus even if mechanization and salvation are already, in various forms, themes associated with a number of staples of the science fiction genre, we find that Dick's own uses of these forms, even in his early fiction, begin to subvert or open them to possible functions and associations that had been closed off from them in their becoming-generic. In this way, he already begins to develop the techniques which, I will argue, evolve into a more fully soteriological mode of open or dynamic fabulation.

We can already see in the triangulation of mechanization, salvation and fabulation at work in the four novels from the 1950s discussed here, the emergence of certain recurrent implied questions that will become crucial for Dick's fabulative soteriology: what are the necessary conditions for producing an open society that will resist the tendency to revert to closure? How does one seek salvation within an immanent understanding of reality? What mistakes arise from confusing a particular example or form of mechanization with mechanization in general? What are the possibilities and dangers of using fabulation to overcome seemingly insurmountable dangers? These are formulations – articulated here in a Bergsonian vocabulary – of problems with which Dick engages, both implicitly and overtly, throughout his life and work.

Solar Lottery (1972 [1955])

Many of Dick's narratives, especially in his earlier novels, take place against the background of the rise of mechanization in its most overt forms – war (global or interplanetary) and hyper-industrialization, along with their catastrophic effects. They are often set in the years following a Third World War that has heavily reduced the population, as in *The World Jones Made* (1993b [1956]), *Vulcan's Hammer* (1976c [1960]), *The Game-Players of Titan* (1991b [1963]) and *Dr Bloodmoney* (2000a [1965]) – or in the middle of such a war that appears to be ongoing – as in *Time Out of Joint* (2003c [1959]) and *The Penultimate Truth* (1978 [1964]). To an extent, this reflects the dominant images of mechanization that inspired social anxiety in Dick's own Western culture in the years following the Second World War. As Warrick writes, the horrifying memories of the nuclear holocaust and the continuing of international crises made it impossible to ignore the destructive powers of modern technology. Not surprisingly, much of Dick's early fiction mirrors this world of military unrest and technological mistrust (1987: 5). Yet the theme of Cold War fears does not come close to exhausting the ways mechanization is at work in Dick's 1950s and early 1960s novels. Against the background of the threat of humanity's destruction through warfare, the novels' main characters, and indeed whole societies, are threatened by mechanization in a range of other forms: exaggerated levels of industrialization and bureaucracy, conventional science fiction dangers such as the replacement of humans by androids and robots, paranoid supercomputers trying to take over the world, and, crucially, more physical and metaphysical mechanizing forces, such as determinism and entropy. Perhaps the most recognizably Dickian of these forms is 'androidization', the term which, as I suggested in the Introduction, Dick uses to refer both to the 'becoming alive' of the increasingly machinic environment, and the becoming-mechanistic (predictable, lacking empathy) of the human (Dick 1995c: 183, 191) – provided we recognize this concern with the artificial human as a partial subset of Dick's virtually constant theme, the artificial (re)construction of the real.

In the imagined future world of *Solar Lottery* (1972 [1955]), one of Dick's most popular 1950s novels, industrialization has apparently brought about its own demise through over-production: 'in the early twentieth century the problem of production had been solved; after that it was the problem of consumption that plagued society' (19). This led first to panicked reactions such as the mass burning of luxury goods, and then, by a 'gradual and profound' process, to a more over-arching transformation of the dominant worldview (20). This somewhat vague set-up seems to have the main function of enabling the socio-cultural scenario which really frames the action of the novel, one in which the whole human species, we are to understand, has undergone something like a total crisis of self-confidence: 'Nothing seemed stable or fixed; the universe was a sliding flux' (20). This is not a Heraclitean acceptance of the dynamic nature of the world, but an experience of chaos resulting from the breakdown of former certainties, which in Bergsonian terms amounts to the collapse of the stabilizing influences of closed morality: 'Nobody could count on anything … People lost faith in the belief that they could control their environment' (20).

In setting up this scenario, Dick thus imagines a future recurrence of something like the conditions depicted in many imagined accounts of human prehistory, whereby the figure of the human finds itself dominated by natural forces, possessing only a negligible capacity to exercise any control. In Bergson's account of the emergence of religion, such a situation is what led humans to fabulate environmental forces that are amenable to influence, and from which evolved the larger religious systems that came to dominate much of human history. Though there is currently no reason to think Dick had read or even encountered Bergson's *Two Sources*, he was quite familiar with accounts of animism and the so-called 'primitive' mind in modern psychology (Dick 1995c: 183). If such accounts of 'primitive' humanity's helplessness seem to have proliferated in the late nineteenth and early twentieth centuries, this may have much to do with an equivalent widespread experience of existential uncertainty belonging to the era of modern secularization and industrialization – the condition which Durkheim termed anomie, the experience of the loss of formerly guiding social norms. This may thus also be considered an implied referent of the *Solar Lottery* scenario.

The collective response to the lack of control brought about by randomness has been to embrace it: 'Statistical prediction became popular [...] the very concept of cause and effect died out' (20). At the institutional level, the result of this is the adoption of the 'lottery' system as the means of electing the global leader: any (legally recognized) citizen may supposedly be elected to the supreme office of 'Quizmaster' by the 'twitching' of a randomized machine known as 'the bottle'. In depicting a society which has lost faith in one of its most basic tenets, that of the relationship between cause and effect, Dick can also be read as extending to the whole of humanity a particular aspect of his own young experience, which he would later describe in very similar terms: 'in my worldview (head) there is no appreciation or recognition of causality as normally understood – and I recall that dilemma when I was 19 and found I simply could literally not see causality – while all other people do' (E 241 [27:3]). We may well see here the source of, or at least an early catalyst for, a tendency which, by the time of the *Exegesis*, had been expanded to almost every area of Dick's life: in what he experiences as the absence of causality, that is, the lack of an ability to understand why things happen and to act upon the world so that predictable effects result, he requires external agents to make decisions for him. In earlier *Exegesis* entries he makes several claims not to have written most of his books ('Nobody wrote them. The goddam typewriter wrote them; it's a magic typewriter'; E 22 [4: 41]); or to have been the medium for another agent, usually the living informational entity or force whose nature he ostensibly undertakes the writing of the *Exegesis* in order to understand. In fact, as early as 1962 Dick was consulting the *I Ching* for help in developing the plot of one of his most critically acclaimed works, *The Man in the High Castle* (1965 [1962]) (Sutin 1991: 109–10).

The fact that an absence of mechanical causation can lead Dick and the society of *Solar Lottery* to believe simultaneously in both randomness and superstitious agency as responsible for the course of events points to a certain equivalence, at least from a phenomenological or psychological point of view, between attributing events to 'chance', and to an external, quasi-transcendent agency. Bergson makes precisely this point in *Two Sources*, arguing that even when we use the term 'chance' to recognize that 'everything is capable of mechanical explanation', there is underlying it a 'spontaneous, semi-conscious thought, which superimposes on the mechanical sequence of cause and effect something totally different'; thus mechanism is treated 'as though possessing an intention' (MR: 148). In this light, the adoption of a lottery to 'select' the leader of the government can be regarded as equivalent to relying on a sign from God, to the extent that they are both ways of relinquishing the activity of decision-making while allowing the outcome of a decision nonetheless to be produced (in both cases, the act of decision-making is replaced by a virtual or fictional version of itself). Thus, as one character in the novel declares, becoming dependent on random chance has turned everyone into 'superstitious fools', constantly on the look-out for harbingers and collecting all manner of magic charms (59).

More religious forms of fabulation have not disappeared entirely from the world of *Solar Lottery*, however, and there remains a very small portion of the population who have responded to their loss of meaning and control in a more traditional way, by developing a new, quasi-religious sense of destiny. John Preston is a crackpot/visionary who, some time prior to the main events of the novel, claimed to have mystical knowledge of the existence of a habitable plane just outside the known solar system, which he named Flame Disc. Though Preston himself has not been seen since he departed in search of his legendary new world, and is widely believed to have perished somewhere out in space, a small group calling themselves the Preston Society has formed around his teachings – in particular the belief that humanity's chances of survival lie in the right (i.e. sufficiently enlightened) people finding Flame Disc and founding a new society. With no empirical evidence either in Preston's writings or elsewhere to back up his assertions, the Prestonites' endeavour – to pool their resources and, in contravention of political and legal rulings prohibiting space exploration, set out to find and colonize Flame Disc – is based entirely on faith.

Each of these strategies, the lottery system and the utopian quest, can be understood as an attempt to use fabulation to find salvation – from a mechanistic existence. Furthermore, each has as its starting point the collapse of the dominant cultural fictions of the closed society, and attempts to create a new, open society, in which all members will be genuinely equal. Thus both can be seen to gesture towards a mode of open or dynamic fabulation, and even if neither attempt can be considered successful, the flaws in each strategy are informative for understanding the challenges that such a mode might have to overcome.

Much of the novel's action revolves around the flawed nature of the lottery system, as the main characters engage in a series of struggles to gain the kinds of social and political advantages that it is supposed to rule out. This is principally achieved by developing means of overcoming randomness – rendering unpredictable processes determinate once again – while attempting to decrease the predictive capacity of their opponents. The engineer Leon Cartwright, a member of the Preston Society, achieves this by rigging the mechanics of the lottery system, while the Quizmaster he replaces, Reese Verrick, uses more traditional forms of political corruption and violence, including attempting to assassinate Cartwright. The outcome of their power struggle becomes dependent on who is best able to thwart (or manipulate) the laws of determinism and probability. Though this is most prominent in their attempts to overcome the huge odds which the lottery system stacks against every individual, it is a struggle that permeates the whole narrative. For example, Verrick's assassination attempt on Cartwright relies heavily on catching the target by surprise. Cartwright has a team of telepathic guards to help protect him against attacks by detecting would-be assassins before they can get near. However, Verrick tops this counter-strategy by sending as his assassin a mechanical humanoid shell which may be 'inhabited' from a distance by any one of a number of human operators, who are switched in and out at random. At any given moment, the assassin's intentions and plans are thus subject to radical change, rendering 'him' deeply unpredictable, even for telepaths.

As these struggles play out, it becomes quite clear that the lottery system is a failure as a means of creating an equal society. The obvious problem – that a particularly incompetent or tyrannical ruler might randomly be given power over everyone – is at least partially countered by the limited term of office, which seems to be unpredictable. The lottery system attempts to mechanically engineer something like the open society, by taking both the capacity and the responsibility for selecting a leader out of human hands. Though this constitutes an ingenious strategy for preventing the power-hungry from acquiring power, a common destructive trait among political systems, it does little to address an equally ubiquitous obstacle – that people may not adhere to its rules. Indeed, the widespread belief that the system is fair – which the actions of both Verrick and Cartwright reveal to be a fiction – almost automatically gives an advantage to whoever is able and willing to alter the system. Thus the lottery strategy correctly conceives of the source of the problem – that which Bergson terms the war-instinct; its flaw is in the presumption that it is possible to take this entirely out of the picture.

Cartwright and the Preston Society have an alternative strategy for attempting to create something like an open society, which necessarily also begins with the recognition that the existing system's apparent fairness is an illusion, a fiction.

Cartwright explains to the protagonist Ted Benteley how he realized that 'the rules were set up so I couldn't win. Who wants to play that kind of game? We're betting against the house, and the house always wins' (177). Thus, like Verrick, Cartwright decided to alter the rules: 'I said to myself, what sort of rules would be better? I sat down and worked them out. From then on I played according to them, as if they were already in operation' (178). As we saw in the previous chapter, fabulation's primary function is to construct hitherto non-existent alternatives in seeming no-win situations. Cartwright imagined different rules, and through playing by them (which entailed re-engineering the lottery mechanism), brought them into effect. This (counter-)fabulation constitutes a technical and moral attempt to harness the fictionalizing power by which the closed society has maintained itself, in order to push it in the direction of a more open form.

Cartwright's recognition of the transformative power of fabulation was also the motivation behind his early decision to follow Preston. His intervention in the lottery system is geared not towards acquiring power for himself, but towards enabling the members of the Preston Society to escape the galaxy in search of their mythic Flame Disc. As Cartwright says, 'Preston saw through the rules too. He wanted what I wanted, a game in which everybody stood a chance of winning' (178). By the end of the novel, the Prestonites have reached their destination, though there is no reason to believe that they will therefore succeed in building an open society. The narrative ends with this question quite evenly balanced, as they encounter a holographic projection of the now long-dead John Preston. He urges them, in terms which seem to echo the language of Bergson's *Creative Evolution*, '[t]o spread out, reach areas, experiences, comprehend and live in an evolving fashion. To push aside routine and repetition, to break out of mindless monotony and thrust forward. To keep moving on ...' (188). On the one hand, this sounds very much like a description of the force embodied in Bergson's true mystic, who reconnects with the open, creative tendency at the heart of life, breaking out of the closed circles of repetition. However, the tone may also remind us of those expansionist discourses which have so often accompanied physical acts of colonization, enslavement and inter-societal violence during the course of humanity's Earth-bound history. Thus, even as their reaching out towards the stars may present itself as a movement of openness, it might equally be interpreted as an attempt to render the Preston Society a fully closed society, absolutely cut off from the rest of humanity (one whose ethical openness may only then last for as long as they remain physically isolated). At this level, the conclusion of Dick's narrative taps into a dichotomy already at work in the burgeoning space race, with its strange conflation of the struggle for technological and military supremacy, with the dream of reaching other worlds and new forms of life.

If there is an incipient form of dynamic fabulation at work here, I would suggest it is most discernible in the absence of any final authorial judgement on Preston's call to 'keep moving on …' The novel closes with these words, at the end of a passage consisting mostly of dialogue. One can read Preston's speech as a conventional science fiction paean to the human urge to expand and explore the universe, or equally as an implicit critique of that urge as an ongoing attempt to bring the world under human control, to mechanize and exploit it under the cover of noble ideals. The latter possibility is raised by the fact that these words emerge from a holographic representation of Preston as a paralysed old man (in reality already dead), unaware of his (its) listeners (188). Does his weakness, coupled with his ignorance of those he is attempting to inspire, undermine the strength of his message, or does he himself embody humanity's unquenchable drive to survive, to continue growing, however great the obstacles? The narrator or author gives us no interpretive clues or suggestions, leaving the final words to the inhuman hologram, and it seems that our only option is to accept the ambiguity. Yet in doing so, we may have cause to reflect on the relationship between these two seemingly opposing tendencies, and question whether their sources are really so disparate. The expansionist drive, which in human history has become such a mechanizing force, may yet have its roots in a creative openness that constitutes both a biological and ethical willingness to reach out towards the radically other, and to seek self-renewal and self-transformation through such contact. This raises the possibility of reactivating this dynamic tendency that has been heavily restricted and ossified within the static, mechanizing, forms to which it has given rise (imperialism, colonization, conquest, etc.). At the same time, it reminds us how easily an ethical outlook rooted in openness to alterity can be transformed into its opposite, a closed, mechanizing force.

Whether the Flame Disc settlers will inaugurate a new path for humanity leading towards its salvation, or a continuation of the mechanizing tendency they seek to escape, is an absolutely open question. The task they (and the readers) face is to accept their capacity to determine which way they will go – to decide, as Bergson puts it, whether or not they wish to go beyond 'mere living'. Ultimately it may be that this ambiguity is a fundamental requirement of any attempt to construct an open society, just as incompleteness may need to be built in to an adequately immanent soteriology.

The World Jones Made (1993b [1956])

Like many of Dick's novels, *Jones* is set in the aftermath of a third global war: in this world, the Cold War had become hot, with China and the USA as the main antagonists. Following the end of hostilities, the remainder of the human race, still suffering the effects of radioactive fallout, is in the process of rebuilding, mostly starting from the rural areas which have been seen the least destruction – a scenario which Dick would develop more fully and with complex utopian sensibilities in *Dr Bloodmoney*, as explored by Fredric Jameson (1992) among others. As in *Solar Lottery*, fear of destruction through warfare has led to a radical transformation of the social structure. At the centre of this transformation is the universal adoption of 'Relativism' as a core legal and moral doctrine, stringently enforced by a brutal police state. Relativism forbids any person from treating as true that which is uncertain: all expressions of opinion, personal belief, all religious or other unproven views are banned.

This may thus effectively be understood as a ban on fabulation, or at least on belief in the fictional, understood as that which is not (at least within the official perspective of the governing authorities) demonstrably, empirically real. The reasoning behind Relativism is that all disagreements, and therefore all wars, are based on differences between people(s). To an extent, this implies a recognition of the role played by fictionalizing in the closed morality that fuels inter-societal wars. Yet it also constitutes a failure to appreciate that fabulation plays such a fundamental role in human existence that it will remain a factor in determining the path taken by a society, regardless of any conscious or cultural prohibition.

Though it is practically impossible fully to obey the laws of Relativism, the authorities stamp out, often through violent means, any transgression they regard as even potentially dangerous. The result is a kind of monochrome mirror-image of multiculturalism, a forced, artificially neutral homogeneity. Thus, like *Solar Lottery*, the novel dramatizes a flawed strategy which, in attempting to eradicate one mechanizing threat (warfare), replaces it with another (state oppression). In a further parallel, a quasi-religious movement develops in opposition to the political situation, centred on the eponymous Jones.

Following exposure to the radiation brought about by nuclear war, Jones was born a mutant. He has the unique trait of experiencing his life a year in advance: the present experienced by others is for him a fading memory. Near the start of the novel, he is arrested for making predictions, an act that is seen as a contravention of the doctrine of Relativism. Yet when all of Jones' predictions turn out to be accurate, and the police are forced to accept that he is making statements of truth rather than opinion, they have no option but to release him (an event which he has naturally already foreseen). Jones' fame spreads and he soon acquires a large cult-like and increasingly militaristic following which is able to avoid defeat by the security forces thanks to the strategic advantages provided by their leader's foresight.

Jones' eventual goal, like that of John Preston, is for humanity to spread outwards towards the stars. His project does not share the moral ambiguity of the Prestonites' endeavour, however, as it is explicitly couched in a closed morality, beginning with a campaign to destroy a (presumed) enemy rather than an attempt to reach out towards other worlds. Jones predicts the arrival on Earth of an alien species popularly referred to as 'drifters', and uses his followers to form violent mobs to repel the supposed invasion – with the long-term aim of pursuing them to their home-world and initiating a new era of aggressive human expansion. However, Jones realizes too late (though still a year before everyone else) that the drifters are benign, and that his great Crusade will not get beyond a few local star systems: having perceived the human race as an irritating virus, the fully developed adults whose embryos are the drifters will seal off humanity indefinitely within their local area of space. The journey to the stars with which Jones has ignited the popular imagination will be halted virtually the moment it begins.

Thus the flaws in the social system of Relativism are mirrored in Jones' alternative strategy. He too, in trusting his knowledge of future events as certain and concrete, has failed to recognize the extent to which fictionalizing continues to infuse this very knowledge: what he actually foresees are his own experiences one year ahead (rather than some objective account of future history), and his fallacy is in believing that these experiences correspond directly to reality. If the state fails to appreciate that its attempt to escape mechanization is itself mechanizing, that its abolition of fabulation is based on a fabulation, Jones fails to recognize how easily the saviour may turn into its opposite: yet a senior agent, Kaminski, compares him within a few pages to both the Messiah – 'Him Who John foretold' (84) – and the devil – 'That's the worst thing about our world … it's permitted the beast to come' (81). The way Jones' messiah complex leads him towards the position of anti-messiah, the delusional would-be destroyer of a whole race, has clear parallels with Hitler's 'crusade' against Jews, which Dick would later confirm were intentional (Lord RC 2006: 66). Both history and science fiction testify here to the potential scale of destruction that may result from closed morality – the analogy between the two highlighting that genocidal destruction is not the result of some unprecedented evil force, but an immanent potential virtually intrinsic to social formation.

For all his foresight, Jones is unable to alter the future: everything he does, he has seen himself doing in advance. His visionary knowledge is more a wearying burden than a gift; in the final year of his life he must experience not only his own future death, but the subsequent post-mortem deterioration of his corporeal and spiritual being, its devolution to mineral form (163–4). Thus Jones is just as much a victim of his own self-fulfilling prophecies as others. His promotion of the attacks on the drifters is motivated by his anticipation of the fear and panic they will inspire – ignoring the fact that he will be fuelling this fear by what he thinks is simply a reaction to it. Again we see Dick putting into a dramatic setting his own mistrust of causality. But we may also read this cyclical destabilization of linear cause–effect relations as analogous to the typical moral reaction of the closed society to encountering outsiders: in treating them in advance as an enemy, they construct them as such, and their expectations appear to be confirmed.

By the end of the novel, Jones is aware of his mistake, recognizing the continuity between the determining influence of his foresight on the world and the mechanizing tendencies that had already come close to causing humanity to destroy itself through nuclear war. His struggle with determinism culminates in the realization that any future-oriented strategy intended to move humanity towards an open society must necessarily involve a degree of uncertainty with regard to the future in order to have a chance of succeeding. His final action is thus to take himself, as the determining force, out of the situation. He deliberately gets himself shot and killed, leaving behind a recorded prophecy that points to the future success of the movement that will be based on his martyrdom: 'The new religion. The crucified god, slain for the glory of man. Certain to reappear, someday; a death not in vain. Temples, myths, sacred texts. Relativism wasn't coming back in, not in this world. Not after this' (188).

Thus Jones continues his fabulation – reopening it where it had turned towards closure – making possible the continuation of his cult by removing himself as the factor most responsible for rendering it deterministic. The journey of interstellar conquest will not succeed, but the oppressive police state will be overthrown. Whether this will ultimately be better or worse for the species remains an open question – but such uncertainty is at least preferable to the determinate future which was steadily closing humanity in on itself. Jones is sure that his followers would eventually have turned against him had he not died, this being the first piece of foresight he draws on that does not come from his precognitive talent – that is, the first which comes from speculation about imagined future possibilities beyond his direct knowledge. His decision to get himself killed is the only action arising from such speculation. Until this point, Jones has acted as if according to the natural laws governing raw matter, as if he himself were governed by determinism: in his first and only gesture of free will, there is at least the chance, albeit minimal, of opening up the potential for something like salvation. At the same time, the novel has emphasized the affiliation between religious and anti-religious attempts to safeguard the future, as well as further illustrating the ease with which fabulation that is intended to promote openness can revert to closure.

Vulcan's Hammer (1976c [1960])

Solar Lottery and *The World Jones Made* depict strategies of countering the war-instinct in which the aim is to neutralize certain human traits that are identified as its source, such as self-interest, conflict over cultural differences, and group competition. In *Vulcan's Hammer* those in power have gone one step further and eliminated the human element altogether from the decision-making processes of world governance, placing a supercomputer called Vulcan 3 in control.

Managing Director Jason Dill (the highest human figure of authority in the new system) explains to a class of schoolchildren that 'something drastic had to be done, because another war would destroy mankind. Something, some ultimate principle of organization, was needed. International control' (19). This fear of mutual self-destruction and a sense of the need for some preventative mechanism could be seen as inflecting the politics not only of the Cold War period, but of occidental politics generally since the First World War (at least until the beginning of the twenty-first century, when terrorism, or perhaps the unpredictable catastrophe more generally, might be said to have taken over from international warfare as the greatest perceived threat to a Western nation's security). Dill's sentiments echo precisely those of Bergson at the end of *Two Sources* when he expresses concern that one antagonist will soon have the capacity to remove the other from the face of the planet. The international mechanism which Bergson hoped might have a chance at averting such an event was the League of Nations, forerunner of the United Nations. In the scenario of *Vulcan's Hammer* such organizations are already viewed as failures, and the only viable path is perceived to lie in making literally (automatically, mechanically) binding the commitments which in a human organization depend on the sustained or continually renewed goodwill and consent of its members. Thus, following the nuclear war, the 'combined nations of the world' have agreed to 'subordinate themselves in a realistic manner – not in the idealistic fashion of the UN days – to a common supranational authority, for the good of all mankind' (19).

The logic here is that humans will never be able to value the survival of humanity as a whole above the survival – or even above the well-being – of the particular group within humanity to which they belong. If a human-controlled organization will always revert or succumb to closed society thinking, the reasoning goes, humanity's survival can only be assured by removing humans altogether from the highest positions of power. In fact, this ultimately does little more than replay an already archetypal human displacement of power or governance on to divine or other supernatural entities.

As with the justifications for the lottery system and Relativism, the flaws in this logic become apparent by the end of *Vulcan's Hammer*: instead of working to counter closed morality per se, the strategy used here simply replaces one form of closed thinking and self-interest with another. Vulcan 3 swiftly develops an interest in its own survival, and is prepared to destroy human life on a massive scale to protect itself. Even prior to this, the removal of humans from the decision-making processes has rendered the human organization called Unity, which is responsible for carrying out Vulcan 3's policies, nothing more than a massive bureaucracy that already represents the mechanization of human society: 'The Unity Building rang and vibrated with the sounds of endless calculators, statistics machines, vidphones, teletypes, and the innumerable electric typewriters of the minor clerks' (8). It is also made clear that human competitiveness and antagonism continue to flourish under these mechanized conditions: virtually every character working for Unity displays both a ruthless desire to climb higher in the organization, and a deep suspicion of colleagues harbouring similar ambitions. One of the second-tier directors, William Barris, notes that '[i]t's this sort of reasoning that's made us into the thing we are. The paranoid suspicions of one another. [...] Some unity, with each of us eying the other, watching for any mistake, any sign' (11).

Once again, a cult movement opposes the government and the new socio-political order. This time the organization, whose members call themselves the Healers, operates out of a pseudo-Luddite hatred of the mechanisms that have taken power away from humans. They cultivate a religious appearance, wearing monks' robes and referring to their key figures by the title of 'Father'. Their aim

is to restore humanity's control over its own destiny by destroying both Vulcan 3 and Unity, seeing the latter as merely a machinic extension of the former, with humans as its moving parts. The leader of the Healers, Father Fields, eventually succeeds in convincing Barris that Vulcan 3 is a dire threat to humanity (rather than its guardian), and their combined efforts, after a desperate struggle, succeed in destroying the supercomputer. Yet even more so than in *Solar Lottery* or *Jones*, the triumph of the protagonists over an immediate mechanizing threat does not result in a particularly uplifting conclusion. This is primarily because the human resistance represented by the Healers turns out to be as mechanistic in origin as the supercomputer they have defeated: Vulcan 2, the predecessor to Vulcan 3, dreamed up the idea of the Healers, having anticipated that its replacement would develop self-awareness and turn against humanity. As Father Fields ultimately realizes, his organization was just as much a mechanical appendage as Unity: 'We humans [...] we were pawns of those two things. They played us off against one another, like inanimate pieces. The things became alive and the living organisms were reduced to things' (153).

Vulcan's Hammer could be considered quite a clichéd genre narrative, with a plot which pits humans against evil supercomputers and characters who lack any real depth engaging in desperate physical struggles to save the world. Yet at least in the way its ending undercuts the humans' victory over the computers, it manages to avoid any essentialist reaffirmation of the human/machine distinction. Indeed, in portraying the Unity organization as a great, inefficient machine, and its human characters as mechanizing in their instrumental treatment of one another, it can be said to undermine such a distinction, in a way that anticipates the posthumanist ethics of later works such as *Do Androids Dream of Electric Sheep?* (1993a [1968]) and *We Can Build You* (1977b [1972]). In fact, it would not be ridiculous to suggest that there may be connections that are more than superficial between the thematics of mechanization within the novel's plot and the mechanical use of certain genre tropes in their deployment – such that the human characters' lack of depth, the subsumption of any flickers of personality within the mechanical way in which they go through the motions of a conventional science fiction adventure, could be seen as contributing to the effect of inverting and destabilizing the human/machine distinction.

Father Fields' realization that he and his followers were pawns of the computers is representative of a broader point implicit in the narrative as a whole, as in the other two novels thus far in this chapter – that mechanization is not defeated by the formation of closed societies to oppose it; such groups will always risk becoming an extension or alternative form of mechanization, even if (or because) they destroy the particular mechanisms they are targeting. This mistake is repeatedly dramatized in Dick's early novels, both by political strategists and religious or mystical saviour-figures. The Quiz/lottery system, Relativism and Vulcan 3 are outright failures, reinforcing rather than countering the threat of mechanization. Meanwhile the strategies associated with forms of mysticism – Preston's utopianism, Jones' Crusade and the Healers' movement are at least partially successful within the diegetic worlds in which they appear, in that they overcome an immediate, critical threat, and at least offer the possibility of future survival. This points to the importance for Dick, as for Bergson, of mysticism as a necessary element in the human struggle to overcome mechanization. But the successes in these scenarios do not ring as true as the struggles themselves: an adequate saviour-figure or concept of salvation still appears to be a long way off for Dick.

Time Out of Joint (2003c [1959])

Thus far we have encountered mechanization in Dick's early novels in a range of forms: industrialization, war (in terms of both the human motivations behind it and the technological means by which it is waged on an increasingly global scale), determinism, entropy, cybernetic machines in the form of bureaucracy and supercomputers. Nevertheless, there is much similarity between the settings of the three novels discussed above, which deploy relatively conventional science fiction scenarios, even if there is some implicit critique or incipient subversion of genre conventions. In *Time Out of Joint* the setting is (for the first two-thirds of the narrative, at any rate) very different, having more in common with the mainstream novels that Dick had been writing alongside his science fiction in the 1950s, but which had failed to find sufficient favour with publishers.[1] Nevertheless, mechanization can again be regarded as central to *Joint*, in a different, though no less important form to those we have considered so far. Here it is the 'world' itself – or more specifically the habitational and perceptual environment of the protagonist – that has been mechanized, in the sense that it has been replaced by an artificial construction. Though intricate, the fake world, as is usually the case in a Dickian narrative, ultimately has certain characteristics that will allow its artificiality to be discerned. Indeed, this motif, already apparent elsewhere in other early novels such as *The Cosmic Puppets* (2006 [1957]) and *Eye in the Sky* (2003a [1957]) would be central to many of Dick's later novels, and has come to be regarded as one of the most recognizable, defining traits of his fiction.

When Ragle Gumm sees a soft-drink stand dissolve before his eyes, to be replaced by a slip of paper on which is printed 'SOFT-DRINK STAND', he believes he is going mad. In fact, as another character, Major Bill Black later observes, he is just starting to become sane – while those around him continue to accept a reality that is illusory. As in *Hamlet*, the source of the novel's title, the insane behaviour of those surrounding the protagonist (in this case a society striving to destroy itself), has driven him into a form of madness of his own – though a madness which only appears so due to the irrationality of everyone else. The illusion is fabulative in that it is the product of a fictionalizing activity undertaken for the purposes of preserving (saving) lives: like Hamlet's, it is a madness with a method.

Ragle Gumm's world at the beginning of the novel is a replica of a certain idyllic image of suburban 1950s California. He makes a daily living by entering a newspaper competition called 'Where Will the Little Green Man Be Next?' – which he has a particular talent for winning. Based on data provided and a large amount of intuition, the contestant has to pinpoint a specific set of spatial and temporal coordinates within a grid of thousands of possibilities. However, as he will discover in the final part of the novel, this seemingly trivial competition is actually a complex military exercise. Beyond the boundaries of his small town is a very different world, in which Earth is engaged in a civil war that appears to have its roots in the different factions' opposed attitudes to space exploration and expansion. The dominant ideology of the mainstream is that humans should not leave the planet, encapsulated in their slogan 'One Happy World' (182). The militant, pro-exploration dissidents have taken refuge on the moon, earning them the label 'Lunatics', and from there they maintain a limited but steady series of missile attacks against Earth.

Ragle Gumm formerly had the role of predicting these strikes for the military, a task for which he possessed a unique aptitude: yet the responsibility eventually became too much and drove him into a state of psychosis. Turning the task of making the predictions into a puzzle was his own psychological mechanism for shielding himself from the stress. Along with this, he retreated into a fantasy of the safer, idyllic suburbia of his childhood. As Major Bill Black explains, once the military understood what was happening to Ragle's mind, they realized that they could make use of the fantasy to keep him performing his life-saving work: 'So we found a system by which we could let him live in his stress-free world. Relatively stress-free, I mean. And still plot our missile intercepts for us. He could do it without the sense of load on his shoulders. The lives of all mankind' (200). Hence a physical version of Ragle's fantasy world was constructed and populated with complementary inhabitants – many of them having their own memories altered to fit in with his psychosis.

This is a somewhat different fabulative strategy to those we have encountered thus far, in that it arises, initially at least, by unconscious mechanism rather than socio-political design. Nevertheless, it shares the function of preserving lives from destruction through war, by virtue of an intuitive activity (guessing the bomb strike targets) which simultaneously generates or sustains illusions that will render them acceptable to the intellect. It also turns out to be fundamentally flawed, in that ultimately, as in the novels discussed above, it merely replaces one form of mechanization with another, such that further counter-strategies are needed.

The construction of the artificial town has a mechanizing effect not only on Ragle's own life, but with regard to wider society: by the time he has escaped to the outside world and recovered his repressed memories, he will realize that ultimately it is only his participation that is keeping the war against the Lunatics going. As we have seen, the fabulation which saves one group may be the engine of mechanization at an inter-social level. Ragle recalls that, prior to his descent into a fantasy world, he was on the verge of changing sides. He had come to appreciate the simplicity of the Lunatics' urge, and its essential harmlessness: 'It had nothing to do with minerals, resources, scientific measurement … exploration and profit. Those were excuses. The actual reason lay outside their conscious minds' (204). Thus at the novel's close he finally actualizes his decision to join the Lunatics, knowing that, rather than exposing the Earth to devastating attacks, he will be ending the war (210).

The artificial world which Ragle Gumm has collaborated with his society in building for himself reflects other ways in which we inhabit (and help maintain) artificial worlds. The construction of his nostalgic image of 1950s suburbia is a microcosm of what the 'One Happy World' government wants all its people to believe in – a world which regards itself as totally self-sufficient, and seeks to maintain its isolation from the rest of the universe (a perfect closed society). This resonates with the self-conceptions and governmental strategies of many 'real-world' societies, from isolationist policies on trade and integration, to the policing of international migration. Ragle Gumm's attempts to evade the authorities and escape the bounds of his artificial town could be considered in the context of numerous attempted border crossings in other political realities, highlighting the way every struggle to move beyond a physical, geographical boundary may simultaneously constitute an attempt to enter a literally, metaphysically and politically alternative world.

The fake town of *Joint* can also be taken to reflect the ways in which we inhabit false realities in psychological and epistemological senses. A central concern in Bergson's early work had been to account for the reasons and means by which the intellect's habitual way of perceiving and interacting with the world renders into separate objects material that at a more fundamental level can be considered continuous. Experiencing time and matter as composed of divisible units – days, hours, seconds, objects, entities, atoms – serves our practical needs, whether we are planning everyday activities, looking for food, constructing tools, or undertaking a scientific study. Seemingly separate memories come and go within our conscious experience – generally in ways that are filtered or organized by the most pressing concerns of the thinking, bodily entity – leading us to understand memory as made up of smaller units that are stored somewhere in our physiological structure, from Plato's wax tablet to the modern image of the brain as a processor of information.[2] However pragmatic, indeed necessary, it may be to make these separations in our perception of time and matter, for Bergson we are in error when we treat these (useful) artificial constructions as corresponding to the fundamental nature of temporality, memory, or objective reality:

> That which is commonly called a *fact* is not reality as it appears to immediate intuition, but an adaptation of the real to the interests of practice and to the exigencies of social life. Pure intuition [...] is that of an undivided continuity. We break this continuity into elements laid side by side [...] But [...] we feel ourselves obliged to establish between the severed terms a bond which can only then be external and superadded. For the living unity, which was born from internal continuity, we substitute the factitious unity of an empty diagram as lifeless as the parts which it holds together. (1988 [1896]): 183)

The adjective 'factitious', a translation of the French *factice*, meaning artificial, forced or simulated, underscores the connection Bergson makes here between the notion of a constructed version of reality, and 'facts': reality understood as a collection of facts – ideas or statements habitually taken as given – is already an artificial reality, a factitious unity. The conventional association of fact with truth, in opposition to fiction, is reversed; this provides us with a philosophical basis for understanding an effect repeatedly produced by Dick's narratives. Although Bergson would not develop the notion of fabulation until long after he wrote *Matter and Memory*, the notion of a factitious unity may usefully be applied to the understanding of closed morality as the product of past fabulations. Where intuition uses fabulation to save the intellect from itself, the urgency of such instantaneous, dynamic processes is subsequently transmuted into the mundane, though equally survival-oriented practicality of the intellect: the latter adapts the saving fabulation into a coherent worldview, a factitious unity, including a closed morality, which serves 'the interests of practice and the exigencies of social life'. In other words, closed morality is the ethical dimension of the fabulated worldview of a closed society or culture, with which its members' individual moral outlooks are pressured towards conformity in just the same way as perceptions of physical reality are constantly adapting to social norms.

The world Ragle Gumm attempts to escape can thus be considered a factitious unity, a world made of facts that are both as artificial *and* as substantial as the fake objects and buildings which also structure it (and, conversely, those artificial objects are just as *in*substantial as facts – which is one way of understanding the significance of the way the ice cream van and other objects in the novel are suddenly transformed into words on scraps of paper). The task which occupies Ragle for the main part of the novel consists in an effort to engage what Bergson might call his intuitive knowledge of the past, which has been obscured from his intellectual understanding. First he perceives the small incongruities in the factitious unities that constitute his physical surroundings and his false psychological construction of the past. Then he focuses his attention on the objects and events which bring these inconsistencies to the fore – such as pages from a telephone book containing numbers that should not exist, a picture of Marilyn Monroe portraying her as an international star (whereas she is unknown in Ragle's 1950s world), and a small-scale model of an underground Civil Defence factory, the full-sized version of which is supposed to be in its planning stages, but which he remembers having walked around inside (150). Reflecting on such objects brings back more and more related aspects of the forgotten past. Finally, having found a way through the illusion to what lies beyond, confirming its factitious nature in the process, he is presented with a copy of *Time* magazine with his picture on the cover and his biography inside, and uses the facts presented in the magazine as focal points for reconnecting with the rest of his suppressed memory: 'In his hands the pages of the magazine opened, spread out, presented him with the world of reality. Names, faces, experiences drifted up at him and resumed their existences' (192). This whole process can be read as a fabulative activity in which, in order to escape one false, mechanically engineered world, he must construct another out of bits and pieces he finds scattered around (the telephone book and the magazine are unearthed in a rubbish dump), which, while initially seeming far-fetched, eventually amounts to something which rings far truer than the substantial world that appears to his immediate perception. As we will see, much later when writing his *Exegesis*, Dick himself would undertake an equivalent activity in order to construct his own saviour as an ecological arrangement of textual, ideational and physical materials.

Conclusion: Super–everyman to solar shoe salesman

Dick's early novels are often viewed by critics as inferior to his mature work. Among the characteristically Dickian elements they are taken to lack is the figure of the flawed central protagonist. As Rickman writes, 'the protagonists of *Eye in the Sky*, *The Cosmic Puppets*, *Time Out of Joint* and *Dr. Futurity* all are at first baffled by the insane worlds they find themselves in, but once they figure out what's wrong they move forcefully to correct it' (1988b: 19). In this sense, Dick's early protagonists are not very far from the archetypal no-nonsense hero of pulp science fiction and space opera. Popular early twentieth-century examples such as John Carter of Mars, Buck Rogers and Flash Gordon had given rise to a plethora of protagonists in the same mould, dominating the comic strips and pulp science fiction magazines Dick read and collected as a teenager in the 1940s.

In most of Dick's later novels, however, and certainly his most celebrated, the pragmatic, confident qualities of the conventional science fiction hero are undermined or eschewed in favour of 'unheroic' characteristics such as pessimism, depression and paranoia. The most recognizable Dickian protagonist is a 'little man', a small businessman or employee with a certain set of practical skills, in which he may possess some talent, though which is nevertheless not widely recognized, partly due to the low social standing of the area in which he works, and partly due to his own lack of self-confidence. He is also often afflicted by an inability to sustain functional marital relationships or to handle his finances, and may be prone to depressive and possibly suicidal tendencies. Yet with all this, he also possesses some spark, some irreducible capacity for hope or resistance, which ultimately keeps open, however slightly, the possibility of redemption, for himself and others. The following assessment of Joe Chip, the protagonist of *Ubik* (2000c [1969]), by his boss Glen Runciter, epitomizes this combination of elements:

> He had a peculiar defeated quality hanging over him, and yet, underneath, he did not seem to have given up. A vague and ragged hint of vitality lurked behind the resignation; it seemed to Runciter that Joe most nearly could be accused of feigning spiritual downfall ... the real article, however, was not there. (47–8)

Other typical examples would be Chuck Rittersdorf in *Clans of the Alphane Moon* (1975 [1964]) and Joe Fernwright in *Galactic Pot-Healer* (2005a [1969]) (which I discuss in some detail in Chapter 5). John Sladek's excellent parody, 'Solar Shoe-Salesman' (1973), demonstrates just how recognizably Dickian this figure had become by the early 1970s.

Joanna Russ has suggested that the typical pulp science fiction protagonist, 'if not Everyman, is a glamorized version of Super-everyman' (1975). This genre staple offers, in a sense, a ready-made 'immanent saviour': exceptional in many ways, he is usually a biologically normal human being, who through a combination of unusual circumstances and his own special talents ends up saving others, usually on a massive scale. In transmuting this figure into the downtrodden, near-hopeless 'solar shoe-salesman', Dick manages to make the hero's saving achievements seem simultaneously more impressive *and* less removed from the capabilities of the ordinary reader. In other words, Dick immanentizes the fantastic pulp science fiction hero, bringing him down to our level (or pushing him down beneath it).

In some of the later novels, this immanentizing becomes central to the way the plot develops within the narrative. Jason Taverner in *Flow My Tears, the Policeman Said* (2001 [1974]) is a genetically superior, intelligent, handsome and talented celebrity who suddenly finds his identity erased, forcing him to struggle to survive as an undocumented criminal within a punitive police state. Rick Deckard in *Do Androids Dream of Electric Sheep?* (1993a [1968]), as discussed in Chapter 5, begins as a seemingly typical, no-nonsense, upbeat hero, but is gradually worn down to a state of absolute exhaustion and self-doubt by the end of the novel. In such cases, it is as though Dick has plucked a hero out of a different, more conventional science fiction narrative, in which they confidently exercise mastery over their environment however volatile it becomes, and has thrown them into an unfamiliar universe in which their classically heroic traits are of much less use: these scenarios in a sense thus metafictively reproduce, in a metaphysically and ontologically distorted mirrored version, the physical transportation to another world that, in a pulp narrative tends to mark the beginning of the hero's thrilling adventures (e.g. Buck Rogers going into suspended animation, Flash Gordon's abduction, John Carter being transported to Mars). Yet if the 'solar shoe-salesman' is not yet a standard in Dick's 1950s novels, there are plenty of signs that he is moving in that direction. Most of the protagonists in the four novels discussed in this chapter, as well as other early novels, demonstrate signs of unhappiness or depression at some point or other. Despite inhabiting an idyllic world constructed from his happy childhood memories, Ragle Gumm initially views himself as something of a loser, a single, middle-aged man who lives with his sister's family and is unable to do a real job. Floyd Jones, as we have seen, is a depressive figure throughout most of his narrative, which culminates in a kind of vicarious suicide. Moreover, each is barely able to cope with the saviour status that has been conferred upon him. If there is subversion at work in Dick's early novels, four examples of which have been discussed here, it is one that appears to be in the process of evolution. That is, Dick is primarily attempting to write publishable, rather than subversive science fiction, to earn a living and establish himself as a writer; yet during this process he displays a growing dissatisfaction with many conventions of the genre, which he begins to rework in various ways. What we may also see in these early novels are early signs that one of the resources science fiction offers Dick as a genre is an engagement with questions of salvation – even if the religious context of such questions is often submerged within plots of alien contact, futuristic technologies, space travel and so on. Nevertheless, we may already observe Dick in these early novels trying out various kinds of saviour-figure, testing their viability in a variety of different critical scenarios involving a range of forms of mechanization, and repeatedly discovering that fabulation plays key roles in his characters' attempts to save themselves and others. As we will see, versions of this immanentizing process can be observed in Dick's treatment of various types of saviour-figure, whether this means dressing a deity in a Paisley shawl, afflicting it with amnesia, or causing it to manifest in the commodified form of a spray-can of deodorant.

3

The Empire that Never Ended

When the victor grants the conquered populations a semblance of independence, the grouping lasts longer: witness the Roman Empire.
(Bergson, MR: 276)

Destruction of Rome ends, and Rome perpetuates itself into an infinitude of fake time. It is as if a spurious ontological matrix or receptacle for Rome is obligingly spun out, and Rome unrolls forever into it in a plethora of disguises.
(Dick, E: 414)

A recurrent aspect of Dick's 2-3-74 visions was the experience that the Roman Empire had somehow persisted, and that it continued to constitute the background of his contemporary reality. In at least one vision, he recalled witnessing 1970s California fading out and first-century Rome fading in to replace it. This vision gave rise to a variety of attempts to explain its significance, which became intertwined with the general speculating and theorizing about 2-3-74 which constitute the *Exegesis*. Other fabulations fed into these explanations – such as a dream in which he was searching in an old science fiction store for a serial novel called *The Empire Never Ended*, a phrase which became a favourite refrain in Dick's late years, appearing prominently in *VALIS* (1991d [1981]: 48; E: 421). A further dimension of Dick's understanding of the Roman Empire as contemporaneous with his world came through his experiences of hearing the thoughts of someone he understood to be living in that period. These ruminations ranged across a variety of theological and philosophical topics, and often seemed to take the form of phrases in classical languages. One of Dick's theories regarding this figure, who he often referred to as Thomas or Firebright, was that he was a secret early Christian engaged in a militant and spiritual struggle against the Empire, though he also came up with many others, such as the notion that he was actually being tricked by the medieval scholar Erasmus, who was citing his classical predecessors (E: 107–8), or that it was his deceased friend Bishop Jim Pike (E: 22–3).

These experiences have often been dismissed, along with Dick's writing relating to his visions in general, as aspects of insanity. Even an admirer such as Steve Erikson writes, in a footnote in the *Exegesis*, 'Dick was in many ways a genius and visionary, but this Rome business is just stone screwy' (E: 382). Yet the idea that ancient imperial Rome and modernity in some sense coincide has recently been explored seriously by a number of theologians and philosophers in the context of a 'rediscovery' of the contemporary political value of the writings of Saint Paul. Admittedly, for thinkers such as Taubes (2004 [1993]), Badiou (2003 [1997]), Agamben (2005 [2000]), Milbank (2008) and Žižek (2010) the coincidence is social and political, based partly on historical continuity (the Roman Empire and the birth of Christianity as conditioning subsequent Western history) and partly on analogy (the conditions of empire in the time of Saint Paul mirroring those of modern global capitalism). Yet Dick's attempts to understand his Rome experiences address many of the questions that arise in the context of these recent exercises in the philosophy of religion and political theology. Furthermore, the fact that Dick begins with a fabulation – a direct vision – rather than with an analogy or by following a line of socio-historical argument, may well be informative in terms of certain aspects that these approaches have in common, namely, in their attribution of a particular power and role to fiction and fictionalizing in their conceptions of the Roman Empire and Paul's struggles against it.

Of particular interest in the contemporary philosophical engagement with Paul's writing is the frequency with which modern readers touch upon the value (for immanent reality, political and otherwise) of the transcendent elements of certain supposedly ethical and religious fabulating activities. Yet although this dimension of Paul is present in various recent philosophical engagements, it is seldom emphasized. According to the perspective I will pursue here, Paul may be understood as one of the first immanent soteriologists (or, at least, one of the most influential), with figures such as Bergson and Dick among his spiritual heirs (some of the first being found among the early Christian Gnostics), not only due to the similarity of certain aspects of their respective undertakings, but in their use of a mode of dynamic fabulation of which Paul can be considered an early theorist and practitioner.

Saint Paul is one of the figures Bergson cites as an example of the 'true mystic'; he is also either the source, or the most frequent and easily recognizable theologico-philosophical referent, for Dick's ethics of *caritas*, even prior to Dick's own Dasmascene conversion experience in 1974 (McKee 2004: 33–7;

Rickman 1988b: 9–42). A consideration of Paul's own immanent soteriology, as partially rediscovered by Agamben, Badiou and others, will in this chapter allow us to develop a more technical and elaborate sense of how a dynamic mode of fabulation may work to undermine or open up the static fabulations it opposes, and to gain a more concrete understanding of its central role in an immanent soteriology. This will inform the examinations of specific works by Dick, and his fabulation of Valis, in the subsequent chapters of this book.

In examining Badiou's approach to Paul in the first part of this chapter, I will highlight what we might think of as the generalization of the Roman Empire which occurs in his reading, through which he establishes grounds for Paul's contemporary political relevance that are compatible with an atheist, immanence-based worldview. What Dick described in the citation above as Rome's interminable unfolding into 'a plethora of disguises' is found here in the form of a continuity which Badiou identifies between law, desire, death and empire. We will see how closely this account of a general imperialism parallels Bergson's account of mechanization in *Two Sources*. Both are effectively captured in Dick's image of the 'Black Iron Prison' – the phrase he used to refer to the oppressive form taken by imperial Rome when it emerged from beneath his Californian environment during the March 1974 visions, and which encapsulates what he perceived as its political and metaphysical power to confine and determine the living (i.e. to mechanize). We will also see how the universalism whose roots Badiou traces to Paul's opposition to the conditions of empire (and with this the birth of Christianity), mirrors Bergson's thinking of the open society.

In the second part of the chapter, we will turn to Agamben's account of Paul, and in particular the 'messianic tension' which he identifies in various forms as a technical feature of Paul's writing, and which can be understood as a means by which a particular power of fictionalizing can be used to 'open up' the closed fictions of empire and static religion. In dealing with both Agamben and Badiou, as with Paul himself, my overall concern is to bring out a crucial but apparently downplayed role of fictionalizing in these and related accounts of the struggle against empire, which may inform and expand our understanding of the role of (dynamic) fabulation in challenging the closed society – and in so doing, offer something approaching a coherent ethico-philosophical basis for understanding the role of Dick's visions in his struggle against the Black Iron Prison, the empire that never ended.

A matter of life or (life under the sign of) death

Both Badiou and Agamben note Nietzsche's apparent hatred for the figure widely considered the institutional founder of the Christian Church, each suggesting that Nietzsche's savage attacks on Paul mask an underlying affinity. For Badiou, the denunciations are so extreme precisely because, far from being in direct opposition, the two are rival 'antiphilosophers' (SP: 71); while Agamben explains the apparent disjunction by interpreting *The Antichrist* as 'a messianic parody in which Nietzsche, in cloaking himself in the garments of the Antimessiah, is actually only reciting a script written by Paul' (TR: 111). If 'neutrality is impossible' when discussing Saint Paul (Wright, 2005: 15), it seems that (for modern philosophers at least) the crucial determining factor is not to be found among the ambiguities of language and doctrine, but in the way one understands – or decides to treat – the centrality Paul gives to the Resurrection. Nietzsche is enraged by the audacity with which some theologians interpret Paul's statements (1968: 169), yet unrestrainedly interprets the Cross as a sign of death, and Resurrection as the central lie responsible for rendering Christianity 'the *one* great curse' (1968: 186). In contrast, Agamben and Badiou view the Resurrection as the institution of an affirmative principle of life, and on this basis see Paul as representing, perhaps more than Jesus, the radical political potential within Christianity which the Church has done much to suppress during its subsequent history. Yet surprisingly, perhaps, and crucially for the relationship between fabulation and salvation, these drastically varying opinions concerning Paul agree on a fundamental point – that the Resurrection must be understood as a *fictional* event.

Deleuze, for his part, seems to have followed the Nietzschean view of the Resurrection as fixated on death rather than life, with the corresponding image of 'the black Saint Paul, who keeps Christ on the cross, ceaselessly leading him back to it' (Deleuze 1998: 37). In 1997, the same year that he published his book on Saint Paul, Badiou wrote that Deleuze's 'philosophy of life is essentially [...] a philosophy of death' (2000: 13). What Badiou found most distasteful in Deleuze's vitalism was a supposedly transcendent dimension that, in Badiou's eyes, was inherited from Bergson. In contrast, the 'strange enterprise' he himself undertook in approaching Paul was premised on the view that there is 'no transcendence, nothing sacred' in the latter's thought (SP: 1). Yet the convergences and shared ground between Badiou's Pauline universalism and Bergson's philosophy of the open society, and the common roles of mechanization and fiction or fabulation in their respective approaches to the contemporary value of religious thought, suggest that in each case we are faced with a soteriology of immanence. An examination of these convergences will provide us with a more detailed formal understanding of what dynamic fabulation does to invert or explode the static fictions of empire, closed morality, and other forms of particularist thinking, such that we may appreciate the ways Dick's fabulations – both in his writing and his visions – can be considered in the same vein, if not tradition, as Paul's fabulative soteriological techniques.

The open and the universal

Badiou begins *Saint Paul: The Foundation of Universalism* (2003 [1997]) by making clear his antipathy towards religion, characterizing Paul as a militant and a 'poet-thinker of the event' (SP: 2). Despite his feeling that Bergson laid himself 'much too open to [...] a recuperation of the injunctions of the Open by Christian spiritualism' (Badiou 2000: 99) this text thus shares with Bergson's *Two Sources* a basic assumption: that ideas conventionally associated with religion can be used to address the most pressing aspects of the contemporary social and political global situation, irrespective of whether one subscribes to any given set of religious beliefs. If Paul's value is not to do with religion, nearly two millennia of hindsight suggests that few figures have left themselves more open to recuperation by Christian spiritualism than Paul himself; and if a non-spiritualist Paul can be recovered from his canonized status within organized religion, then it should be a comparatively simpler matter to conceive of a non-spiritualist Bergson.

For both Bergson and Badiou, the existence or not of a transcendent God is largely irrelevant, and salvation is only a useful concept with regard to the actual physical and social conditions of our worldly existence. Bergson's use of the term 'mysticism' and his focus on the figure of the true mystic have little to do with what Badiou denounces as the 'obscurantist' discourse of 'the miraculous, or mystical', which attempts to justify commitment to an event or truth on the basis of a 'private resource of a miraculous communication with truth' (SP: 52). On the contrary, Bergson's mystics, as we have seen, possess a 'supreme good sense' (MR: 228) and 'prove to be great men of action, to the surprise of those for whom mysticism is nothing but visions, and raptures and ecstasies' (MR: 99). Admittedly, Bergson's mystic possesses these qualities by virtue of having re-established contact with the vital impetus or creative force of life, and it is in Bergson's vitalism that Badiou perceives an untenable dimension of transcendence. Yet even if the Badiou of *Deleuze* considers Bergson to have been 'extricated' from Christian spiritualism, 'modernized' and 'secularized' by Deleuze's 'astonishing undertaking' (2000: 99), it can be argued that the Bergson of *Two Sources* and the Badiou of *Saint Paul* are not so far apart as one might expect (2000: 99).

Badiou makes a crucial opposition between the 'principle of life' (on the side of truth, event) and a corresponding principle of death (on the side of law, sin). If one compares this opposition to Bergson's couplings of open and closed tendencies, mysticism and mechanism, it becomes increasingly difficult to identify the significant divergences, either at the level of philosophical worldview or in terms of potential political effects.

For Badiou, Paul's contemporaneity – which effectively resides in the coincidence of his thought with Badiou's own project – is his commitment to a genuine universality: 'Paul's unprecedented gesture consists in subtracting truth from the communitarian grasp, be it that of a people, a city, an empire, a territory, or a social class' (SP: 5). These examples of the communitarian are all instances of Bergson's closed society – whose 'essential characteristic is [...] to include at any moment a certain number of individuals, and exclude others' (MR: 30). Badiou's Paul aims at the universal (as one of its 'first theoreticians') through 'the termination of communitarian particularisms' (SP: 108) – '[t]here is neither Jew nor Greek, there is neither slave nor free, there is neither male nor female' (Gal. 3.28; SP: 9) – just as Bergson's 'open society [...] which is deemed in principle to embrace all humanity' (MR: 267) depends on the principled rejection of communitarian forms (closed societies) rather than their expansion to include more of humanity: 'Never shall we pass from the closed society to the open society, from the city to humanity, by any mere broadening out' (MR: 267).

As we have seen, Bergson refers to the open society as unrealizable in practice (MR: 84). Its extension to all humanity must thus be considered as operative 'in principle' rather than in fact – an abstract definition which parallels Badiou's use of sets to distinguish universalism from particularism.[1] Translated into such terms, Bergson's open society designates the set of all humans, while closed societies are subsets of this set. However, the closed society does not present itself as a mere subset, but rather attempts to substitute itself for the set of humanity as a whole: that is, as we have seen, in terms of treatment, moral responsibility and so on, it counts only its own members as members of 'humanity'. The open society, meanwhile, must recognize itself as fundamentally incomplete: those committed to it extend moral consideration beyond every putative human, indeed, potentially to all life (and ultimately perhaps to any part of the material universe with the potential for openness). These formal qualities of the closed and open society parallel very closely what Badiou describes as 'particularizing' and 'universalist' multiplicities:

- The particularizing multiplicity, the one accompanied by its own limit, marked by the predicate of its limit. The law is its cipher or letter.
- The multiplicity that, exceeding itself, upholds universality. Its being in excess of itself precludes its being represented as a totality. Superabundance cannot be assigned to any Whole. (SP: 78)

Badiou's particularizing multiplicity is thus determined, just like the closed society, by its limits, its boundaries, while the multiplicity that upholds universality cannot become a totality, but remains 'in excess of itself', just as the open society must include all humanity only by going beyond it: 'We must, in a single bound, be carried far beyond [humanity], and, without having made it our goal, reach it by outstripping it' (MR: 33). Bergson and Badiou are both concerned with a genuine universalism as opposed to a particularity presenting (fabulating, disguising) itself as such; both recognize that the genuinely universal cannot present itself as a totality, but must be characterized by superabundance, uncountability, openness.

The life–death chiasmus

Even if Bergson relies on an intuition of the creative force of life, while for Badiou 'life' names a more abstract (though in his eyes political) principle requiring a declaration of fidelity to the event (in this case the event of Resurrection), there is a formal identity in the way both logics oppose a notion of life associated with truth and universality (or openness) to a notion of death associated with law and particularity (or closure). Furthermore, both thinkers attach great importance to the novel transformation of the human subject, which can be taken in both cases as a sign of a qualified posthumanist dimension. For Bergson, this involves life in its creative as opposed to homeostatic form, which through love is 'capable of transposing human life into another tone' (MR: 99); Badiou meanwhile is concerned with an 'affirmative life [...] restored and refounded' (SP: 61) whereby 'the subject participates in a new life' (SP: 86), in a reaction against the prior subsumption of life under death and the Law (SP: 62).

While the difference between a vitalist and an abstract conception of the (new) subject might be crucial to a comparison of the Bergsonian and

Badiouian (meta-)ontologies in themselves, with regard to the political and ethical question of the future of human existence, this significance diminishes. This can best be appreciated by considering that which each sets in opposition to 'life', by associating it with death. In Bergson's case, as we have seen, the primary target is mechanization, the process through which the living is rendered non-living, reduced to the status of raw material or technological instrument, either through biological death or the restriction of various forms of autonomy. For Badiou, the equivalent association is between the principle of death and the Law: 'First among the names of death […] is Law' (SP: 74).

Law is death because it is on the side of particularity, dealing with opinion and custom, which can never be inscribed in a truth (SP: 76). Referring to the law's 'unfailingly "statist" character', Badiou emphasizes that it 'enumerates, names, and controls the parts of a situation' (SP: 76). The clear convergence with Bergsonian mechanization here is further suggested by Badiou's description of its effect upon the subject as introducing an 'unconscious automatism with respect to which the involuntary subject is capable only of inventing death' (SP: 79). This automatism mirrors the obligation which for Bergson is instilled in each member of the closed society, and which renders obedience virtually automatic:

> It is impossible to live a family life, follow a profession, attend to the thousand and one cares of the day […] without obeying rules and submitting to obligations. Every instant we have to choose, and we naturally decide on what is in keeping with the rule. We are hardly conscious of this; there is no effort. (MR: 19)

This is not to say that Bergson considers us to be born this way: the processes of education and self-policing that enrol us in the social order (in Foucauldian terms, the disciplines that produce docility) still depend on a form of 'resistance to self' (MR: 20) – it is just that this resistance increasingly takes place in an 'instinctive or somnambulistic' way (MR: 26).

We have already considered how Dick's ethics of balking, in which resisting such automatic obedience, particularly in contexts where the well-being of others is at stake, virtually defines the human. We have also seen that, for Bergson, consciousness itself is closely tied to hesitation, to the potentially indefinite delaying of the automatic response. The same can effectively be said of Badiou and Paul: what is at stake is a principle or tendency whereby what should be uncountable is represented as countable, reducing free will to controlled, scheduled actions, substituting the particular (the closed) for what should be universal (open). Law is a principle of death by virtue of its dehumanizing effects on living humanity, as many readers of Paul have noted: 'In Paul's thought the *law*, which Christ gained mastery over after being born under its yoke (Gal. 4.4–5), comprises all the impersonal factors that condition man' (Segundo 1974: 39).

Furthermore, this automatism perpetuates itself, because such obedience generally entails the mechanizing of others (e.g. as when closed morality legitimates the killing or enslavement of non-members of the closed society). In viewing laws as 'stabilized customs', and suggesting that 'originally the whole of morality is custom' (MR: 123), Bergson effectively treats closed morality and law as co-extensive. This gives law an intrinsic imperialistic leaning, as it plays a crucial role in articulating the fabulations which present the closed or particular community as universal, and so attribute to all those outside the city walls the nonhuman status of resource or threat. Paul addresses this relationship between law and empire specifically in relation to his own context of the Roman Empire, but in such a way that his approach resonates with Bergson's account of the formation of societies in general, and becomes a source of Christian and Badiouian universalism. For all three thinkers, the law claims to operate in the service of life, while actually supporting a particular subset of the living or the human and in this sense operating against life in general. Thus Bergson refers to the 'mysticism of imperialism', whereby the local morality or law (symbolized by the gods of the city) is disguised as the prescription of a universal God (MR: 311), while Badiou, drawing on Paul, describes the law as the 'empire of death' (SP: 86).

Yet if the law helps support the growth of empire, then the greater and more encompassing empire becomes, the more the falseness of its claim to universality should become visible. To illustrate this, we may conceive of closed societies – small groups or tribes – living in total isolation. Until the moment two such groups come into direct contact there has, for their members, been a *de facto* coincidence between the particular and the universal, the community and the species, that has prevented the question of their incommensurability *de jure* from being raised. Suddenly, with contact, the difference acquires a fundamental significance, and an immanent visibility. While power relations between different groups remain hierarchical and simple, this visibility may remain at a minimum – or at least, its acknowledgement may be seldom voiced; but as societies become more complex, as individuals and groups intermingle, whether through conquest, trade or migration, as different closed societies are superimposed on one another, as new communitarian particularisms emerge and others dissolve – then it is likely to become increasingly common for the particularism of the law, of governing customs and dominant religions, to be observed. Such conditions are created as large empires form, and intensified when they come into contact with one another: and one might argue that these conditions characterize Paul's time and ours in particular – the eras of the Roman Empire and of late capitalism or global modernity.

Badiou sees Paul as our contemporary precisely because he 'wanted to destroy a model of society based on social inequality, imperialism, and slavery' – which is why Pasolini could conceive of a film about Paul set in modern times but 'without modifying any of his statements' (SP: 37).[2] Likewise, Bergson, as we have seen, finds exemplary figures of the open(ing) soul in the early Christian mystics, including Jesus and Saint Paul, while at the same time situating the contemporary importance of such mysticism within the context of the modern mechanization of life, twentieth-century warfare and the threat of humanity's self-annihilation.

Badiou and Bergson each deploy a logic of salvation against the subjection of life to a principle of death – against its automatization, mechanization, destruction; both accounts of this subjection attend to the concurrent animation of life's opposite – the process whereby that which is inanimate, dead, mechanical – is given life, as it were, artificially. The automatized activity of the closed society or particularity presents itself as open, universal (MR: 38–9). The mistaking of closed morality for open, of mechanical activity for life, is as we have seen a central element in many of Dick's early novels, which depict one flawed attempt at social engineering after another failing (usually spectacularly) to eradicate large-scale violence. Bergson suggests that, in the modern era especially, desire for commodities and comfort, for 'easier material conditions', has become a frenzy; the mechanisms or tools, the 'artificial organs' we have invented – increasingly take on a life of their own, inventing false needs and fulfilling them for the benefit of a few at the expense of the many (MR: 309). Bergson's allusion to the artificial life of the object echoes Marx's account of the commodity – famously exemplified in his image of the table that 'evolves out of its wooden brain grotesque ideas' (Marx 1976: 163), and both Marx and Bergson here anticipate the dream-controlling beds, stubborn doors and spray-can deities that populate Dick's worlds.

It is desire that gives life to the inanimate – whether in the form of the 'frenzy' for luxuries and morals or in Paul's use of the term *epithumia* to describe the sinful longing to possess ('coveting') (Rom. 7.7). Badiou writes that, 'the law is what gives life to desire. But in so doing, it constrains the subject so that he wants to follow only the path of death' (SP: 79). The desire to possess is inseparable from 'the profound desire to conform' (SP: 111) and both lead to progressive automatization or mechanization, whose terminus is death. Badiou represents this redistribution, whereby life is subordinated to a principle of death, and death is given artificial life, using the 'figure of the chiasmus death/life, coordinated by the law' (SP: 85). The rhetorical device of the chiasmus has the particular characteristic of inverting two parallel elements or terms, as in the famous saying attributed to Jesus that 'the first will be last, and the last will be first' (Matt. 20.16). In Badiou's life–death chiasmus, 'the law distributes life on the side of the path of death, and death on the side of the path of life' (SP: 82). A chiasmus implies two (opposed) meanings for each term, and the process of their reversal, a transformation of opposites. This rhetorical-conceptual doubled inversion is a central device in Paul's writing, as we will see in Agamben's reading below, where what Badiou terms a chiasmus is understood as the dividing of a division, the splitting of each of two opposed terms (here life and death) into two opposed meanings.

Identifying the proximity between Bergson's dynamic fabulation and Badiou's life–death chiasmus (which is explicitly presented as belonging to a non-transcendent, political register) re-emphasizes that Bergson's is an *immanent* soteriology, while expanding the vocabulary and collection of conceptual resources available for exploring its technical operation and effects. Together these resources are valuable for understanding not only Dick's use of fabulation, but his strange, immanence-inflected relationship to religion and mysticism – which likewise draws powerfully on Paul's struggle against the Roman Empire. As in the life–death chiasmus, dynamic fabulation simultaneously draws on and counters the effect of earlier fabulative activities that have congealed into the cultural fictions of the closed society. The (purportedly) open is revealed as closed, while the closed becomes open. In turn, this association brings out the importance of fiction or fabulation in Badiou and Paul: perceiving the fakeness of death masquerading as life, while reactivating the potential of that life which has been subsumed under the sign of death, requires an act of counter-fabulation, a conceiving of the non-actual as possible, for the purposes of *rendering* non-actual those fabulations which have taken on real, lived status. This fabulative dimension is most visible in the emphasis Badiou places – despite the high value he assigns to truth – on the importance of the fictionality of the Resurrection.

The fictitious event

For Badiou, it is at best irrelevant to Paul's logic of salvation whether or not Christ actually died and returned to life, whether or not he performed miracles, in short, whether he was the literal 'Son of God'. Paul makes Christ's death the 'evental site' that creates the conditions for the event of the Resurrection precisely *because* it makes Christ mortal, subtracting his subjectivity from all the transcendent qualities attributed to him by the writers of the other Gospels: 'Through Christ's death, God renounces his transcendent separation; he unseparates himself through filiation and shares in a constitutive dimension of the divided human subject' (SP: 70). Badiou also stresses that the Resurrection is not even a historical event, but rather, with regard to its miraculous nature, 'fictitious'. Again, fidelity to this event should in no way be based on the notion of a transcendent God or saviour-figure able to overcome the laws of nature by miraculous acts. Rather, the truth to which we are asked to be faithful – the truth of the Resurrection-event – is that 'a man [...] capable of inventing death, is also capable of inventing life' (SP: 69). The central role of the Resurrection-event in Badiou's Paul is thus to immanentize salvation, to make clear that it is an operation humans are capable of carrying out.[3] Fidelity to such an event is primarily a commitment to what in Badiou's philosophical vocabulary constitutes its 'truth'. Where is the universality to this particular truth, that humans are capable of their own salvation? At first glance, on this point Bergson might appear more Badiouian than Badiou. Whereas the current of life that Bergson's true mystic recovers is, at least in the terms of *Two Sources*, one that runs through all of us – our re-attachment to it waiting to be reawakened by the words and actions of an exemplary mystic figure (MR: 100) – Badiou's soteriology asks for fidelity to an event which many are certain did not take place. Yet this only points to the particular nature of the kind of truth and the kind of operation that (immanent) salvation represents. For the possibility of the salvation of humanity by humanity – and in immanent terms, this must mean escape from actual, physical, socio-political and environmental destruction, from the enslaving of love and free will under the laws of desire and determinism – depends in the first instance upon human belief in that possibility. The universality of the truth of this event is that any person is capable of believing in it as the signifier of a principle – of declaring themselves faithful to this principle. Indeed, it is the 'eventual declaration' that is a truth's 'principle of life' (SP: 27). This is, as we have seen, the point with which Bergson ends the *Two Sources*: humanity has the *capacity* for its own salvation, but – even before this becomes a question of will or resolve – lacks awareness of or *belief* in that capacity; likewise, much of humanity does not recognize the *necessity* of salvation – does not appreciate how critical its situation has become. He makes clear that 'a decision is imperative', that the possibility of escaping this great danger depends upon humanity choosing, seeking out, rather than stumbling upon or being directed towards a new path. In attaching such importance to the declaration of faith, Badiou, like Bergson, is addressing the problem (of the lack) of belief in the human need and capacity for self-salvation.

If taking on the responsibility for determining their own future entails humans or subjects making a commitment, in Badiou's terms, to a fictitious event, then this would seem to involve the direct and deliberate employment of what Bergson calls fabulation – the faith or belief in the non-actual in such a way that actual salvation may result. As Badiou puts it, 'faith is the declared thought of a possible power of thought' (SP: 88–9). This would correspond to a use of fabulation that openly acknowledges its fictionalizing character, and thus knowingly engages the soteriological potential of fiction.

The messianic tension

In examining aspects of the modern philosophical turn to Paul as political theologian, we are able to get a better sense of what an immanent soteriology might look like, of the role and shape of dynamic fabulation within it, and in the process acquire an understanding of some of the less obvious aspects of the affinity between Dick and Paul. Agamben, in focusing on particular technical devices of Paul's writing, emphasizes a performative-transformative power which not only resonates with what I have already identified as the key elements of the Bergsonian and Badiouian immanent soteriologies, but presages a number of effects which Dick's writing produces through similar devices.

Agamben attempts to establish Paul's contemporary relevance primarily through revealing a series of hidden influences of his messianism on modern thinkers – such as a connection between the Pauline *klesis* (vocation) and class in Marx (TR: 30); the origins of the Hegelian *Aufhebung* (via Martin Luther) in Paul's *katargesis* (literally meaning 'rendering-inactive') (TR: 99); the effect of Paul's use of the term *hos me* ('as (if) not') on Heidegger's development of the dialectic between the proper (*Eigentlichkeit*) and the improper (*Uneigentlichkeit*) (TR: 34); and the paradigm of messianic time (*ho nyn kairos*) as the undeclared source of Benjamin's 'Theses on the Philosophy of History'

(TR: 138–45). This more genealogical approach, attempting to (re-)establish a sense of a Pauline heritage within modern Continental philosophy, by no means indicates that Agamben's Paul lacks the potential Badiou attributes to him for directly addressing our contemporary global political situation.

For Agamben, the central operation of Pauline messianism is the putting to work, in various forms, of what he calls 'the messianic tension', which is constitutive of both his gestures towards universalism and the concept of 'messianic time'. One of the most prominent operations of this messianic tension is achieved through Paul's use of the *hos me*. This term, translated in the form 'as not' (*quasi non*), is for Agamben 'a special type of tensor' that sets a concept's semantic field not against that of another concept, but against itself (TR: 24). As Paul writes, in the messianic time of the now (*ho nyn kairos*), 'those who have wives may be as though they had none; and those who weep, as though they didn't weep; and those who rejoice, as though they didn't rejoice; and those who buy, as though they didn't possess' (1 Cor. 7.29–30).[4] In nearly every case, Agamben notes, the *hos me* contrasts neither one verb or state with another – nor two different verb tenses or different times – but negates the same verb, and in the same time-frame. It does 'not compare two distinct terms but puts each being and each term in a tension with itself' (TR: 43). We might say that each use of the *hos me* equates to the inversion of a term's meaning effected through a chiasmus. Agamben effectively reads Paul's rhetorical technique grammatically where Badiou reads it diagrammatically (the literal meaning of 'chiasmus' being 'X-shaped').

As with the chiasmus, we can thus already discern in Agamben's *hos me* indications that some kind of counter-fabulation is at work – the setting of some aspect of perceived reality against itself, for the purposes of salvation. Agamben identifies the same messianic tension in Paul's use of the term *klesis* (meaning 'calling', 'vocation'). By virtue of the fact that he is 'called' (*kletos*) by God to be an apostle, Paul is able to oppose every worldly *klesis*, every calling, profession, social position as designated by law and the state: '*The messianic vocation is the revocation of every vocation*' (TR: 23, original italics). Just as the *hos me* places a term and state of being in tension with itself rather than with another, the messianic vocation does not confer on Paul a social role that is superior to other roles, but revokes 'every factical vocation' (TR: 25). The divisions the state (or the closed society) makes, in the identification and organization of its people, in terms of the varying rights and freedoms it accords to or withholds from different groups, are thus nullified, at least so far as Paul is concerned, by this messianic *klesis*, which is bound inextricably to the operations of the *hos me*:

> The messianic vocation is not a right, nor does it furnish an identity; rather, it is a generic potentiality [*potenza*] that can be used without ever being owned. To be messianic, to live in the Messiah, signifies the expropriation of each and every juridical-factical property (circumcised/uncircumcised; free/slave; man/woman) under the form of the *as not*. (TR: 26)

Agamben concurs with Badiou in suggesting that Paul proceeds to universalism only through the rejection of particularisms, while the concepts or states opposed – fixed identity versus potentiality, ownership versus 'using without owning' – resonate with the Bergsonian opposition between closed and open. Furthermore, just as the soteriologies of both Bergson and Badiou are oriented around an immanent conception of salvation, so the messianic tension is used to make immanent (or, to use Agamben's phrase, to place in a 'zone of indistinction' between immanence and transcendence) those aspects of the discussion of salvation that in the other Gospels, and in the words of the biblical prophets, appear definitively transcendent. The *hos me*, as the linguistic tensor signifying and constituting the effect of messianic *klesis*, contracts what in a transcendent soteriology would be two times or epochs (the present dominated by oppressive worldly conditions and a mythical heavenly future) and two states of being (factical existence and an imagined, prophesied or fantastical other state) into the here and now: 'the messianic vocation is a movement of immanence, or, if one prefers, a zone of absolute indiscernability between immanence and transcendence, between this world and the future world' (TR: 25). For Agamben as for Badiou – perhaps for modern thought in general – Paul is deemed politically and philosophically valuable only to the extent that his writing or thought can be 'immanentized'. Yet I want to emphasize that such a process need not involve the total eradication of any thought or idea of transcendence: Paul's concern remains the rendering-thinkable of what has become unthinkable, for the purposes of a worldly transformation that would irreducibly constitute salvation.

The remnant and messianic time

The closest Agamben comes to the Bergsonian terminology of open and closed in this text is in his discussion of the relationship between the part (*meros*), the all (*pas, panta*) and the remnant (*leimma*). Analysing the relations between these key Pauline terms, Agamben argues that Paul views the present, factical state of human existence as being under the principle of *ek merous* – 'in part', or divided. Just as the closed society is characterized by discontinuity, countability – the segregation of groups, classes, races, the homogenization of people as slaves, workers, capital – so '[e]verything here is divided, everything is *ek merous*, "in part"' (TR: 55). Living 'in part' is a state which Paul describes as being 'under the Law', as opposed to living in the time of salvation, when 'all of Israel will be saved' (Rom. 11.26). For Agamben, the purpose of Paul's introduction of messianic tension is to overcome the seemingly insurmountable separation of these two states – the immanence of Law and the transcendence of salvation. Whether in the form of the *hos me* or some other (the 'cut of Apelles', the messianic *klesis*, the *euaggelion*), Agamben argues that Paul's messianic tensor works by introducing a remnant that cannot be restricted to either state – thus 'dividing' the division between them.

A key example is the division of the flesh/breath (*sarx/pneuma*) division. The (religious and political) division made by the law equates those who are Jewish according to the flesh (circumcised) with those who are spiritually saved – just as we saw above that the isolated closed society equates its own members with the whole of humanity (i.e. views only its corporally countable subjects as deserving of salvation, worthy of life). Paul introduces the *sarx/pneuma* division in order to upset this identification, making it possible to recognize that there are those who are Jewish according to the flesh (*sarx*), circumcised, yet who are not necessarily saved in terms of spirit (*pneuma*), while there will be those who are not circumcised but who are nevertheless saved in spirit. In other words, beyond the subset of Jews (according to the flesh) there will now be a remnant of non-Jews (according to the flesh) who are still Jews (according to the spirit); while among the non-Jews (according to the flesh) there will be a remnant of Jews (according to the flesh) who are not Jews (according to the spirit): the remnant is 'what prevents divisions from being exhaustive and excludes the parts and the all from the possibility of coinciding with themselves' (TR: 56). In this sense, it is 'not so much the object of salvation as its instrument' (TR: 56), performing the same operation as Badiou's life–death chiasmus. The primary soteriological activity thus moves from adherence to a particular closed morality, to the rejection of the latter, the detachment of salvation from any predetermination according to bodily signs or other forms of identification. It is dynamic in that it must open up any closed notion of salvation.

As we have seen, the immanent disjunction within the closed society is the difference which it fails to recognize between the totality of its members and the totality of humanity, between the particular and the universal. The discursive production of the remnant, whether this entails the recognition that there are humans beyond the walls of the city, or that those accounted for by a given morality do not yet (and never will) include all that should count, reveals this disjunction within the closed society, and inaugurates or promotes its opening. The remnant is the figure that reveals the false presentation of the part (*meros*) as all (*pas*), opening it to challenge and transformation: 'The remnant is therefore both an excess of the all with regard to the part, and of the part with regard to the all. It functions as a very peculiar kind of soteriological machine' (TR: 56). A figure for that which tends to go unnoticed or unrecognized is thus also an intensifier; it enhances tensions that had previously been ignored even as it puts their sustainability into question.

Dick's work can be described in these terms, as driven in part by the repeated discovery or production of the remnant. The basic pattern involves the depiction of a particular 'reality' with some unusual element(s); the production of a worldview or theory which accounts for this reality; and the discovery of a remnant, defined as something which does not fit within that worldview, something that remains unaccounted for when everything else seems to have been explained. That which is left over – whether object, subject, fact, event – drives the action, as its incommensurability with perceived reality leads to the realization that something is wrong with either the worldview or the world, and their partial or total collapse. Viewing this general Dickian structure in terms of the Pauline remnant sheds light on its soteriological function and potential.

Yet salvation for Dick and his characters can seldom, if ever, be considered something achieved with finality. Even when a new world, perspective or theory replaces that which has fallen apart, there will always be another remnant. We will see this in each of the following chapters, as Dick's discovery/production of remnants allows numerous fictions inherent to closed morality to be opened up. Wherever there is a clear, accepted division – such as real history from alternative history, the human from the android, the saved from the damned – something emerges which defies the efficacy of such categories, and which, despite attempts to modify category boundaries, refuses to go away. This leads, in the sense of Agamben/Paul, to a dividing of the division, such that every previously accepted category must be reconceived. Of the novels discussed in the previous chapter, *Time Out of Joint* constitutes the most typical example of this process, with the remnant taking the forms of inconsistent memories (e.g. of a missing light cord), slips of paper replacing absent objects, telephone numbers representing non-existent places and magazine articles about unheard-of celebrities – all functioning as part of the soteriological machine. In *The Man in the High Castle*, as we will see in the following chapter, small, solid objects play the role of remnant in transcending the split between 'mainstream' and alternative history. The remnant may also be a person – as in the case of Jason Taverner, the protagonist of *Flow My Tears, the Policeman Said* (2001 [1974]), who is contained by none of the socio-political categories set up to organize the world in which he finds himself – not only is his identity erased, but even classifications such as 'criminal' or 'without papers' fail to apply. Whereas aspects of Dick's novels often draw comparisons with Kafka, in the case of *Flow My Tears* it is as though the typical Kafkaesque relationship between a protagonist and an impenetrable bureaucratic apparatus, for instance in *The Castle* (1997 [1926]), where everything functions to close off, block, clamp, lock down, were reversed, so that Taverner, unlike K., slips through every checkpoint, entrapment, arrest or other attempt to hold him, right through to the home of the Police General and away again to his eventual freedom.

What Agamben calls 'messianic time', then, is as much a remnant or remainder as any object or category of personhood; it is the 'time that remains' once we subtract the notion of a transcendent future time of salvation, and a present time of suffering without redemption – each of which must be deemed unacceptable within a perspective which places high value on ending this suffering. In other words, in contradistinction to *both* the time under the law, when those who are weeping must continue to suffer, *and* the future/other time of salvation, when those who are (now) weeping under the law will (then) be rejoicing in eternal life, the *hos me* introduces the notion of those who are weeping now *as not* weeping *now*. Such a possibility, I suggest, involves an irreducible fabulative element, a capacity to believe in that which intellectual reason suggests must be impossible. Through such a belief, as we saw in our engagement with Bergson's *Two Sources*, fabulation makes the hitherto impossible become possible.

The magic of language

A final point to draw here from Agamben's reading of Paul concerns the way in which open or dynamic fabulation achieves its effects, not just in the register of abstract ideas, but in terms of lived experience: its potential (and its potency) lies in its ability to effect a recognition of both the necessity and the possibility of salvation – bridging the gap between immanence and transcendence not only theoretically, but in terms of the gap between perceived reality and the figures of salvation that are conventionally, at least from a modern secular perspective, treated as pure fiction. It is in this dimension of his fabulating, beyond his more overtly Pauline ethics, that Dick, consciously or not, can be seen to be operating a soteriological machine very similar to that of Paul.

Bringing the remnant to consciousness, providing perspectives which divide divisions otherwise taken for granted as circumscribing self-sufficient unities, constructing in language forms of the life–death chiasmus, are all ways of working and intensifying the messianic tension. Yet there is more to the soteriological role of fabulation than this: the importance of faith, raised by Badiou, is also recognized by Agamben, who poses an crucial question regarding the *euaggelion*, the promise of salvation in which faith (*pistis*) is placed in a direct relationship with presence (*parousia*): 'What is a logos that can enact a presence for whomever hears it and believes?' (TR: 89). Our Bergsonian answer to this question is, of course, 'fabulation' – though I would want to add that fabulation is by no means restricted to language or *logos*. Both Badiou and Agamben attend to the importance Paul effectively assigns to performativity when he writes: 'For man believes with his heart and is so justified, and he confesses with his lips and so is saved' (Rom. 10.10; cited in Badiou, SP: 88).[5] For Badiou, Paul is calling for a 'declaration of fidelity' to the Resurrection-event that would not only state a belief in humanity's capacity to create new life, but enable that capacity: 'The announcement is power for the salvation of he who believes' (Rom. 1.16). Meanwhile Agamben suggests that, in order to think the *euaggelion*, in which the worded promise of salvation coincides with the object promised, we require 'an experience of language in which the text of the letter is at every point indistinguishable from the announcement and from the good announced' (TR: 90). The announcement entails a certain potentiality (*dynamis*), which must be complemented by faith (*pistis*) in order to be activated, to actualize that potential in action or *energeia*.

The importance of this performative declaration of faith lies in the fact that the possibility of salvation is a particular kind of future occurrence. That is, not only is it more likely to occur if one believes in it, but such fidelity is its necessary condition, and indeed, quite possibly a sufficient condition. It is worth noting here that if one were to attempt to produce such an effect through a novel, it would be useful to have some means by which elements described in the world of the novel could become literally 'true' or 'real' in the world of the reader – entailing a crossing or disrupting of the diegetic boundary. This type of effect is a hallmark of much late twentieth-century fiction that is often collectively referred to by literary critics as 'metafiction' (see Waugh 1984; Hutcheon 1985; Currie 1995). However, I would suggest that the metafictive elements of Dick's writing operate in a way that is more intensely affective – more immediate and organic, arising as a by-product of other elements – than in many of the more frequently cited examples of metafiction, such as works by Jorge Luis Borges, John Barth or William H. Gass. Dick's *The Man in the High Castle* has within its fictional world a novel which apparently describes the readers' own world (though with crucial differences that also call this into question). We will see in the following chapter how it is Juliana Frink's declaration of fidelity to the truth of Hawthorne Abendsen's alternative reality that constitutes her potential salvation, reflecting the possibility of the reader's own acquisition of faith in the performative truth of Dick's alternative reality. Yet it is in the more mundane details of the characters' experience, the ease with which we feel that they, despite belonging to a nightmarish alternative reality, might easily fit into our own, that the diegesis is rendered permeable. The affective immediacy with which Dick puts supposedly real and fictional worlds into contact resonates with the coincidence of word and object in Agamben's understanding of the *euaggelion*, in a way that contrasts starkly with the 'literary self-consciousness' (Waugh 1984: 21–61) and foregrounding of linguistic construction characterizing many critically attended examples of metafiction.

Agamben implies that the coincidence between word and thing is fundamentally related to the notion of faith, *pistis*, noting the latter's proximity to the ancient Greek *pistos*, which he identifies as meaning 'trustworthy' – worthy of another's faith. Such trustworthiness is often embodied in the *horkos*, an object that one holds while making an oath, and metonymically representing the oath itself (TR: 114). This object acts as a guarantee, supposedly being imbued with the power to kill the oath-maker should they fail to fulfil their pledge. In Dick's *Martian Time-Slip* (1999a [1964]), a 'water witch' given to the main character Jack Bohlen by the Bleekmen, the indigenous people of a newly colonized Mars, functions as a *horkos*, compressing the promise it symbolizes and the fulfilment of that pledge in a particular messianic temporality. The water witch is supposed to bring water to the bearer whenever they are in dire need – though in referring to water as 'the source of life', the donor indicates that it may be understood as a symbol for whatever it is that is required for salvation at a particular time of crisis (1999a: 25). Through the non-linear temporal twists of the story, the scene is later repeated, with differences: the second time around, another character, Arnie Kott, attempts to kill Jack before he receives the gift, yet one of the Bleekmen, perceiving his intention, shoots Arnie with a poisoned arrow. Thus the symbol of salvation, the water witch, is exchanged for the actual act of salvation – and in a peculiar temporality which simultaneously divides the present from itself, conflating two alternative time-frames.

Agamben takes the *horkos*, like the *euaggelion*, to be a signifier of 'a prejuridical sphere in which magic, religion, and law are absolutely indiscernible from one another' (TR: 114). It is this sphere to which the 'word of faith' – the *energeia* of the announcement – hearkens back – and from which it acquires its 'performative efficacy' (TR: 131). Agamben goes so far as to suggest that speech acts are themselves a hangover from this primordial cultural state: 'To do things with words could even be considered as a residue in language of a magical-juridical state of human existence, in which words and deeds, linguistic expression and real efficacy, coincide' (TR: 132). Paul's messianic announcement, and indeed the messianic tension that operates throughout the Pauline vocabulary, in such forms as the *hos me* and the messianic (re)vocation, *is* this performativity, going 'beyond the denotative relation between language and the world toward a different and more originary status of the word' (TR: 134). Agamben places the performative efficacy of the word of faith at the heart and origin of religious belief, exactly where Bergson locates fabulation.

When dealing with Paul, as with Bergson's true mystic, we are clearly concerned not only with an attempt to activate this performative efficacy, but to do so as a challenge to existing religious beliefs, as well as various other mechanizing cultural fictions which have been established on its basis (e.g. those which function through and as law, the state, imperialism). The performative power Agamben finds in Paul constitutes a *residue* of this magical-juridical state in language, meaning that it is not coterminous with, and quite likely precedes language. Hence language would be one cultural development among many which emerged from that less determinate state: such developments established the cohesion of the closed society, but are, in the hands of Paul, turned against themselves, through the messianic tension. This is how dynamic fabulation becomes (or reprises its originary status as) a counter-fabulation, targeting the fictions of the closed society to which fabulation first gave power, such as the divine authority of the Church, the superiority of an elite 'chosen' few, or the notion that salvation is dependent on corporal signs.

Sci-fi: The genre of 'as not'

Among the huge variety of definitions of modern science fiction that have been proposed and debated, one which seems to have particular currency, is the suggestion that it extrapolates novel scenarios from initial questions posed in the form 'what if …?' This bears an obvious proximity to the *hos me*, which as we have seen Agamben translates with the phrase *quasi non*, 'as (if) not'. Here is a clear formulation of the standard 'what if?' definition, taken from a guide to writing science fiction:

> Perhaps the crispest definition is that science fiction is a literature of 'what if?' What if we could travel in time? What if we were living on other planets? What if we made contact with alien races? And so on. The starting point is that the writer supposes things are different from how we know them to be.[6] (Evans 1988: 2)

The last sentence highlights something which is generally implicit in the phrase 'what if?' when used this way: the notion that in conceiving, writing, reading science fiction, we consider fantastic elements in direct contrast to known reality. This implication is echoed in Darko Suvin's more complex definition of science fiction as a 'literature of cognitive estrangement', which has been hugely influential, though much debated, in academic discussions of science fiction. Estrangement, as in the tradition of Schlovsky and Brecht, here entails 'confronting a set normative system – a Ptolemaic-type closed world picture – with a point of view or glance implying a new set of norms' (Suvin 1979: 374). The qualification that this must be 'cognitive' indicates that the basis of this new point of view is extrapolated from the empirical environment (Suvin 1979: 375).

What underpins these popular and academic definitions of science fiction is the recognition of its capacity for putting into close contact that which is *known* (commonly accepted) and that which is *known not to be* (commonly not believed). Such a capacity is arguably more literally captured by the 'as not' or *hos me*, with its explicit negating component, than the 'what if?' A science fiction plot conceived based on the question 'what if people could fly?' would probably not be set in a world where everyone has always been able to fly (the latter would be a more likely setting for what many would think of as 'fantasy'). Science fiction convention would have someone developing the ability to fly, whether through some advanced technology or the development of superheroic powers, within an otherwise realistic setting, that is, one which in other respects could be a world we recognize as our own, or one of its possible futures.

Without drawing any strong conclusions, we might find a further hint in this applicability of the *hos me* to science fiction that we are dealing with a genre particularly well suited to the activation of the messianic tension, offering valuable resources not only in its stock elements, but in its dominant conceptual mode, for a fabulative soteriology. Beyond 'fictionalizing the known', science fiction entails the (fabulative) construction of what is given *as not* given, the placing of certain factical states of being in tension with themselves. It sustains an inherent injunction to introduce the new into the world in *contrast* with that world, and may be one of the forms of modern fiction most connected to the original fabulation function. If the Bergsonian account of the originary binding of fiction to salvation is correct, science fiction retains great soteriological potential in the modern era, whether its themes are religious or not; and this may have much to do with its emergence in the context of mechanization, the set of conditions from which salvation is most critically required. Moreover, in its general orientation towards the future, science fiction has an in-built mechanism for the use of the messianic tension to produce messianic time.

Even if such a hypothesis carries any force, it certainly does not amount to a suggestion that all science fiction displays these salvational qualities, or operates in the dynamic or open mode of fabulation I am exploring here: on the contrary, much science fiction probably feeds into the very closed fabulations – dominant, carefully limited notions of the human, its society, technology and ethics – which make up the mechanizing forms of closed morality today. Yet it might still be suggested that there is an inherent, structural potential, a messianic *dynamis* in science fiction as a genre or method, which the *energeia* of Philip Dick's works among others – driven, like Paul's soteriological writing by love or *caritas* (as both Agamben and Badiou are careful to emphasize) – brings into effect.

Conclusion: Gnostic politics

In some of its central aspects, the recent engagement with Paul's political theology could be said to echo a very old gnostic tradition of Pauline exegesis, one that has largely been absent from mainstream Christian theology due to the historical portrayal of Paul as anti-gnostic. Elaine Pagels' work on the relation of gnosticism to Paul and the New Testament, however, presents this tradition as one in which Paul has already long been used as a challenge to hierarchy, not only in the form of Empire, but of the Church itself.

Both Agamben and Badiou challenge a literal reading of Paul's writing on the separation of Jews and non-Jews – Agamben, as we have seen, arguing that Paul further divides and thus destabilizes this separation, Badiou identifying in it the universalist principle that '"ethnic" or cultural difference, of which the opposition between Greek and Jew is in [Paul's] time [...] the prototype, is no longer significant with regard to the real' (SP: 57). Yet as Pagels has shown, the notion of a literal interpretation of Paul's discussion of the separation of Jews and Gentiles was already 'a dated issue' for the Valentinian gnostic readers of the second century (1992: 6). For them, the universalist Paul, who recognizes an obligation to both Jews and non-Jews, Greeks and barbarians, is already legible, and indeed constitutes an important gnostic source. In this sense, the dominant interpretation of Paul that became the basis of institutionalized Christianity can be considered a rendering static or closed of the dynamic, open fabulations of Paul's writing: from the Valentinian perspective, as from the perspectives of Agamben and Badiou, the real Paul – or the Paul worth maintaining as real – is the one who attempts to resist this closure, to prevent the particular from dominating the universal, the closed from replacing the open.

The question of the ontological status of the Resurrection has a central place in this struggle. By tying the inheritance of Jesus's leadership to those who had actually witnessed his literal, physical return, those concerned with establishing the early Christian Church could restrict authority to a select few, requiring all contemporary and subsequent community leaders to derive their authority from the apostles and their successors. In contrast, according to Pagels, gnostic Christians saw the Resurrection as a spiritual truth rather than an actual event, a symbolic expression of the possibility that anyone might be 'resurrected from the dead' at any time, to become spiritually alive (2006: 41–2) – precisely the process Badiou describes using the figure of the life–death chiasmus. Dick's novel *Counter-Clock World* (1977a [1967]) could be read as illustrating a similar position, in rendering Resurrection commonplace due to a cosmic event that reverses certain biological and temporal processes, and yet having it result neither in salvation nor in everlasting life: that it is spiritual rather than physical renewal that is essential is underscored by the swiftly aborted return of a widely anticipated saviour-figure (the Anarch Peak), and the general fate of those who live out their lives in anticipation of a precisely dated end, following a decline into the dementia of childhood.

The importance they laid on the spiritual/symbolic dimension of Resurrection does not mean that the gnostics disdained visions of Christ's return. It is the literal interpretation of such visions that they refused. In the gnostic 'Treatise on the Resurrection', for example, the author makes the very Badiouian point that resurrection stands for 'the transformation of things, and a transition into newness', a symbol representing the fact that everyone is capable of considering themselves 'risen' – and that despite its primarily symbolic value, it should be viewed as a truth against which it is the rest of the world that is an illusion (Robinson 1990: 56). The conflict between early orthodox and gnostic

Christianity can thus be construed not as a struggle over different versions of the truth, between competing historical accounts, but as the competition between a simple and a sophisticated understanding of the relationship between truth and fiction, reality and unreality. This is bound up with the shift from Hellenic to Hellenistic (e.g. Alexandrian) thought, whereby, as Whitehead put it in *Adventures of Ideas* (1942 [1933]: 125-6), an emphasis on 'delight, speculation, discursive literature' was gradually replaced by an emphasis on thoroughness, specialist exactitude and scholarly authority; the pregnant ambiguities and perplexities expressed by Plato, were replaced by a requirement that ideas be judged simply 'right or wrong' (Whitehead 1942: 126). The authority of the Church, at least in the period of its emergence, likewise relies on maintaining a simple opposition between true and false, real and fake, in which every declared event and fact must be situated on one side or the other: Jesus really, literally appeared to this person, and not to this one; this is a miracle, a sign of divine action, while this is not; these people have divine authority, these are false claimants. Gnostic Christianity, in contrast, can be read as finding reality in the visionary experience itself. Thus when Bishop Irenaeus attacks Valentinian gnostics for creating 'imaginary fiction', 'new forms of mythological poetry' and for relying on feeling and intuition rather than divine authority (Pagels 2006: 48), he is criticizing precisely what those same gnostics see as a great resource, the soteriological use of fiction (or in other words, fabulation).[7]

The Paul of Badiou, Agamben and other modern thinkers, rediscovered as a political theologian and thinker of universalism, can thus be identified with a gnostic Paul. Pagels' argument is only possible in light of the discovery of the Nag Hammadi texts, a large collection of gnostic writings discovered in Egypt in 1945 (but which did not appear in a modern translation until the 1970s). This discovery was also of great interest to Dick, whose identification with gnosticism recurs throughout the pages of the *Exgesis*, as well as having a great influence on his late novels (see the discussion of *VALIS* in Chapter 6 of this book, and Erik Davis' account of gnosticism and the contemporary information society, *TechGnosis* (1998), in which he draws on Dick's mystical experiences). The argument for a gnostic Paul allows us to see the compatibility between these two strands of religious/theological thought, and their complementarity as Dickian influences, where otherwise the appeal of one might have seemed to contradict the other. Whether consciously or not, what Dick finds in each, as in science fiction as a genre of 'as not', is a saving power of fiction.

For the Valentian gnostics, to understand Paul was to recognize that in order to write for both a specialized and a general audience, he wrote his letters 'in two ways at once' (Clement of Alexandria, quoted in Pagels 1992: 7). We may identify these two ways as static and dynamic respectively. The reader or listener still strongly bound to a particular closed fabulation as part of a closed morality, regarding, for example, the Resurrection as literal historical occurrence, will hear a confirmation of her beliefs in Paul's writing and preaching. A group formed on the basis of such views regards itself as God's chosen people, the initiated elite, in a closed form modelled on the select group of the apostles; its boundaries are maintained, however great the number within them becomes. This notion of the 'initiated' is inverted, however, if one takes Paul's texts as highlighting and embodying the constitutive role of the fictional – of symbolic and spiritual truth – in religious experience. Whereas the special *gnosis* (knowledge) by which the gnostic Christians defined themselves may give them the outward appearance of cultish mystics, what it really amounts to is the knowledge that anyone may have a relationship with the divine, through creative activity, through fictionalizing, and that all claims to privileged, exclusive access to God are themselves pure, static fictions. As Pagels puts it, 'on this theory, the structure of authority can never be fixed into an institutional framework: it must remain spontaneous, charismatic, and open' (2006: 53).

This is not therefore a straightforward case of two layers of meaning. As we saw in the context of Bergson's *Two Sources*, the distinction between static and dynamic must *itself* be considered dynamic, as opposed to simply descriptive. Paul's sense of dual responsibility, which leads him to write simultaneously 'in two ways', is itself a dynamic gesture of opening, attempting to affect the static meaning over which it is superimposed. In addressing those who are believers according to the spirit, he identifies a dynamic and boundless 'elite' composed of those who will allow any individual to count themselves as a member – effectively an anti-elite – in place of those who would restrict religious authority to their own limited group, defined according to specific ritualistic, bodily and doctrinal criteria. Political theology is a useful term – intended to indicate, I think, the relevance of Paul's writings for an era and a worldview characterized by an immanent, materialist perspective, in which 'salvation' must entail earthly emancipation, through political struggle. Yet we should not neglect that the very severity of the material conditions which necessitate this emancipation render the adequate thinking of it, let alone its achievement, at the very limits of human possibility. The transcendent dimension of the soteriological is of great value to Paul in his urgent quest to transform the world, politically and culturally. In this sense he is a political soteriologist; and it this, rather than theology or even religious belief, that Dick shares with Paul. Dick's vision of ancient Rome as a present condition, experienced in the form of an instantaneous fabulation, allows him to address and explore intellectually what he already grasps intuitively – that salvation must come from himself, from his own creative capacity. The difficulty, and the continual task faced by his or any other immanent soteriology, is to allow the intellect to go on treating the saviour as someone who comes from outside.

In the remaining three chapters, focused on extended readings of particular novels, we will see how Dick approaches this task, which requires him not simply to write, but perhaps to think simultaneously 'in two ways' that on the surface may seem contradictory. In doing so, his dynamic fabulation opens up the closed fabulations which have come to make up the more powerful and established aspects of the dominant 'reality' of the human, its history, and its spiritual and technological environments.

4

Objects of Salvation: *The Man in the High Castle*

[The science fiction writer's] story or novel is in a sense a protest, but not a political one; it is a protest against concrete reality in an unusual way.

(Dick 1995b [1974]: 74)

The fabulation of history

Dick's *The Man in the High Castle* (1965 [1962]) is an example of what is sometimes regarded as a sub-genre of science fiction, the alternative history novel. A typical alternative history narrative realistically presents a world which has diverged from the recognizable, historical 'real-world' course of events, imagining how things would have turned out differently if a certain event had (or had not) taken place. Whether such narratives should be considered science fiction at all is open to question: going by genre convention, one might classify as science fiction only those examples in which the divergence between timelines is produced by a future technology such as time travel. Yet whether we engage in such classificatory exercises or not, the defining traits of the alternative history narrative resonate strongly with the idea of narrating reality 'as not', which I suggested in the previous chapter might be a useful way to think the potentiality of science fiction as a genre. Whether such narratives, and *The Man in the High Castle* in particular, also share the Pauline connotations of the 'as not', entering into a certain soteriological mode, is a question to be addressed in the course of this chapter.

For the purposes of this account of *High Castle*, I will use the term 'mainstream history' to refer to the historical timeline from which the history of the novel ostensibly diverges. This is in recognition of the fact that what the alternative timeline is set against need not be understood as an absolutely 'real' or 'true' history, but that it at least corresponds broadly to the dominant Western cultural and political understanding and accounts of modern history. Even if its truth-status is radically open to question from a range of critical, constructionist and subaltern perspectives, mainstream history can nevertheless be expected to be recognizable to the majority of Dick's readers to date, as that which they have likely encountered in school textbooks, mainstream media and everyday discourse.

In the alternative timeline of *High Castle*, the primary difference from mainstream history is that the Axis powers were victorious rather than having been defeated in the Second World War, leading to the occupation of the United States (along with most of the world) by Nazi and Japanese forces. Publishers of the novel have naturally exploited the potential shock-value of this premise: the covers of many editions, especially those published in English, are dominated by a swastika, one of the most hated symbols of the post-war Western world, usually shown imposing itself upon a conventionally definitive symbol of the USA – a Coke bottle, a hamburger, the American flag, or simply a map of the United States. (The publishers of Philip Roth's more recent alternative history novel *The Plot Against America* [2004] used a similar strategy by showing on its cover a US postage stamp bearing a swastika.) This exploitation simultaneously operates on the verbal level, for example through re-titling translations, as in the Italian *La svastica sul sole* (*The Swastika on the Sun*), or more generally through tag-lines making claims about the novel's power and content: the first edition announced itself on the front cover as 'an electrifying novel of our world as it might have been', with similar phrases appearing in the marketing text on the backs of many editions.

Indeed, as one reads *High Castle* and the implications of a post-war world subjugated to Nazi ideology unfold, there is plenty to fulfil the publishers' promises of horror: in the world of the novel, the holocaust is an ongoing process that, in addition to pursuing Jews across the globe, has seen most of the population of Africa exterminated by systematic continental genocide. In Europe, the populations of most non-Axis countries are being reduced to the effective status of slaves, with the Mediterranean drained to provide farmland. Even in the less oppressive, Japanese-occupied areas such as the Western United States, where most of the novel takes place, racism and anti-semitism are institutionalized, and the most cherished freedoms of (mainstream) modern Western democracy, such as the rights to trial and free speech, are non-existent. Yet the novel's real power lies not in its ability to shock with its convincing, realistic depiction of an alternative nightmare world. On the contrary, the juxtaposition of the familiar world against a Nazi alternative could just as easily reassure readers as disturb them, by underlining the diametric opposition between the two. That is, if the novel simply enhanced the reader's sense of the ethical 'wrongness' of the world it depicts by drawing on its apparent ontological and historical inauthenticity, then simultaneously, the world of mainstream history would be confirmed as 'right', both morally and ontologically. But having invoked this binary opposition by its key premise, the more sophisticated trajectory followed by *High Castle* consists in gradually calling it into question.

Fredric Jameson has praised Dick's capacity for rendering the present historical in an era – 'consumer society, media society, the "society of the spectacle", late capitalism' – which is 'striking in its loss of a sense of the historical past and of historical futures' (2005: 355). Though Jameson has in mind Dickian scenarios in which it is a fantasized future that renders the present historical, *High Castle* achieves a similar effect by its depiction of an alternative present whose historicity we cannot avoid: purely in recognizing its basic premise, the reader is made conscious of the historical (mainstream) timeline from which the narrative diverges (the 'what if?' is immediately an 'as not'). Furthermore, the most horrifying aspects of the novel's world are tied to a past moment of catastrophe in just the same way that our own present can be said to derive its ahistorical imaginary from a moment perceived as one of salvation. One early edition was advertised as depicting a 'nightmare from which it might just be possible to awake': although Dick would likely have appreciated the reference to Joyce, a writer he particularly admired (and whose use of interior monologue in the early chapters of *Ulysses* appears to have influenced the style of *High Castle*), this phrase is representative of an ahistorical tendency of mainstream history that can be seen in various forms throughout the modern culture industry. The indirect suggestion is that the nightmare into which the novel's characters have fallen – and from which the real world was saved with the defeat of Nazism in 1945 – is history itself; whereas it is in fact the mainstream (ahistorical) history, haunted and reassured by this nightmare (a bad dream, but just a bad dream) that the novel opens up to critical consideration. Meanwhile, the visual symbols of a Nazi-ruled USA which adorn the covers of many editions may unwittingly hint at an already-emergent association whose very inconceivability their publishers intended to invoke.

In Agamben's Pauline vocabulary, as explored in the previous chapter, *High Castle* can be said to introduce a division within the division, destabilizing the binary of the two timelines set up by its premise. The first step is to reveal that the initial division is already operative in the Western world's perception of its own history as 'saved' by the defeat of Nazism – a self-perception which already implicitly defines itself in opposition to an alternative 'damned' history of the kind seemingly given form by the novel. The second step is to establish a dichotomy within this distinction, suggesting that we the readers are still partially inhabiting the nightmare alternative that the novel initially allows us to understand as imaginary, while simultaneously allowing us to see that its characters, even within this hell, are neither universally nor hopelessly condemned. In this sense the novel effects the Pauline operation of making their condition of being saved or damned according to the flesh (according to their ontological, material or socio-historical conditions) cease to coincide with being saved or damned according to the spirit (according to their ethical potential).

Thus while *High Castle* might represent the ultimate vision of a mechanized world, all humanity, and indeed the natural environment, being reduced to the status of mere resource for the benefit of a self-aggrandizing (yet still internecine and self-destructive) elite – nevertheless it remains possible for its characters to exhibit moral freedom, resistance to mechanization, and thus maintain the potential for the open society. Hence where several commentators see the notion that 'Nazism really triumphed in World War II' (Rieder 1992: 224) as the novel's central message, I am primarily interested in what the novel *does* with this notion as already playing a (possibly suppressed or virtual) role in the post-war Western psyche, as a counterpart to the more overtly and often ritualistically affirmed notion that Nazism, and in some ways mechanization in general, were decisively defeated at the end of the Second World War.

The dynamic fabulation at work here therefore renders both the 'damned' timeline and the 'saved' timeline 'as not', rendering visible or re-animating the evidence suppressed within each of them that worlds and their histories are continually in the process of being *made*, and as such always open to transformation. This involves shaking off what Dick, as we will see below, refers to as 'the tyranny of the concrete', that is, the false impression that the world is inevitably, fixedly the way it is (a deterministic, thus mechanistic outlook). Importantly, this process which operates at the level of reading is mirrored in the experience of some of the characters: a work of fiction within the novel, Hawthorne Abendsen's alternative reality novel, depicts a world in which the Allies won the Second World War, and is responsible, with the help of another text, the *I Ching*, for making certain inhabitants of the world of *High Castle* aware of the possible existence of other timelines such as the mainstream history familiar to the reader. By this device, the extra-diegetic world is brought within the novel, just as we come to recognize the supposedly fictional nightmare timeline as already a part of our own conception of history.

The world described in Abendsen's book, *The Grasshopper Lies Heavy*, is not quite identical with mainstream history, however. For example, rather than staying in power throughout the war, Roosevelt stands down in 1940 and is replaced by a man named Tugwell who, at the time of Pearl Harbor, is 'so smart that he has all the ships out to sea' (69). As a result of victory the British Empire, rather than collapsing, becomes larger than it was before the war (85). Many critics have understandably focused, as Adam Roberts (2002) has noted, on the relativist conception of history opened up by this further alternative, to the neglect of the elements which constitute the novel's 'sophisticated, and consciously artistic' achievements, in particular the small, collectible objects which are central to the everyday concerns of many characters as well as to key developments in the plot. In fact, as I will argue here, both these dimensions are essential and mutually dependent. Such objects are not only central to the techniques Dick uses to establish the alternative history as tangible and believable, but also integral to the means by which the simple opposition between two closed fabulations (mainstream history and its nightmare alternative) is destabilized or 'opened up' in the course of the novel's dynamic fabulating.

The capacity of such objects to perform these roles can be read as an index of the peculiar relationship between immanence and transcendence which seems to be concentrated in them. Furthermore, these small, solid objects function as both the symbols and the potential way out of an absolute state of mechanization, represented in their seemingly irreducible objecthood: however wide the range of what we perceive as objects, within which we might include, for example, planets, images, numbers, memories and systems; and however rigorously we might maintain the perspective of a process ontology, in which no entity is ever wholly isolated from the rest of the world – nevertheless the small, solid item we can hold in our hands for most of us is the quintessential object. Such objects as they circulate throughout *High Castle* can be taken to represent an absolute state of de-subjectivization, loss of living agency, coupled with the process of (re)vitalization of the lifeless. The fact that, in their very objecthood, they paradoxically take on a kind of agency, taking over precisely at the points in the plot when the human characters seem to have given up on their own free will altogether, offers a glimmer of hope for even the most lifeless, the most mechanized life.

Mechanization and paralysis

A condition which besets several of the main characters of *High Castle*, notably Frank Frink, his ex-wife Juliana Frink and the Japanese diplomat Tagomi, is one in which they repeatedly find themselves desperately unable to make decisions – to perceive, let alone select, an acceptable course of action. The general context for this condition is the seeming impossibility of an adequate response to the Nazi violence which has apparently surpassed all conceivable boundaries of scale and intensity; yet it is frequently a specific, personal act of violence, perhaps concentrating the general threat, that triggers the near-paralysed state. The absolute mechanization of human and natural resources represented by the extermination and subjugation of human life in Africa and Europe is something with which these characters, who still possess a limited degree of freedom as occupiers and occupied, must live every day, and yet which, when they pay direct attention to it – for example, when it is concentrated into a direct and personal danger – seems virtually impossible to endure. Both Juliana Frink and Tagomi, for example, when threatened with assassination, are forced to kill in order to preserve their own lives and the lives of others. Yet in order to do so, it seems they must enter a state of absolute depersonalization, in which all conscious agency seems to have been abandoned, at least during and immediately following their own acts of violence. Furthermore, as we will see, the return of reflective consciousness in both cases does not bring with it a recovery of agency, but rather a prolonged helplessness in which they feel unable to move in any direction.

Perhaps the most powerful expression of this state in the novel – and the one which results most directly from interacting with the core of the Nazi regime – comes when Mr Tagomi attends a meeting with other Japanese diplomats to discuss candidates for the Nazi leadership, following the death of Hitler's first successor Martin Bormann. Tagomi hears personality descriptions of the candidates: the ruthless Goering, characterized by 'self-glorification in ancient emperor fashion'; Goebbels, driven by the desire for power for its own sake; the pathologically schizophrenic Heydrich, who 'holds human struggle to be series of games'; von Schirach, the mastermind behind the post-war racial extermination programmes; and Seyss-Inquart, the man responsible for 'the decision to make holocaust of African continent' (93–6). Listening to these accounts, Tagomi is gradually overcome with nausea and has to leave the meeting (96). In addition to being reminded of the horrendous atrocities carried out by these figures and listening to accounts of their power-driven, inhuman characters, what seems to overwhelm him is the inescapability, the totalizing reach of these palpable, inhuman destructive forces, which infuse every single one of the contenders for the next world leader. Tagomi is perceiving the future of his world as 'a sort of Darwinian struggle between competing psychopathologies', as J. G. Ballard once pessimistically described his view of humanity's twenty-first-century future (2005: 20).

If evil can be considered the signifier of a quality that would make a world absolutely unliveable, this situation causes it to coincide with concrete reality, inescapable, absolute and ubiquitous: 'There is evil! It's actual, like cement … It's an ingredient in us. In the world. Poured over us, filtering into our bodies, minds, hearts, into the pavement itself' (97). The global Nazi machine appears to have succeeded in rendering almost the whole planet as what Heidegger termed 'standing reserve' (*Bestand*) (1993 [1954]: 322); or, to use a different vocabulary, it has reduced human and all other forms of life to the status of Agamben's 'bare life', a life beyond all political and moral existence, which he regards as the ultimate effect of the Nazi concentration camps (1998: 166–80). On the one hand, the objectification, or depersonalization of every individual, to the extent that they are deprived of agency, acting mechanically or not at all; on the other, the perceived irreversibility or finality of this condition, the sense that the Nazi programme will complete itself without deviation in a mechanical, ineluctable progression.

Where is anything like salvation to be found under such conditions? Whatever form it might take, we would have to anticipate that it could only be considered salvation in the most minimal sense: lives once lost cannot be literally restored – though life, in certain places and in certain senses, can. However, as I have suggested, if there is any non-transcendent possibility of salvation, it must constitutively entail the revealing of the impossibility of a saving event as a fiction; moreover, this revealing may itself take place through the fictionalizing of a possible escape route (which will subsequently turn out to have had or taken purchase in reality): a fabulation is always a counter-fabulation. In a sense, the conditions that make salvation necessary are those that make it possible (if still extremely unlikely). This is not just the logical consequence of a circularity of definitions (whereby escape from danger is considered 'salvation' only when it is perceived as impossible). Ultimately, there must also be a perceived nonhuman element to any conception or experience of salvation – the appeal to the transcendent is an appeal to something beyond the self, beyond the present self-world system in which the one seeking salvation recognizes the limits of his or her possible actions and effects: and it may just be that in the alienating, depersonalizing effects of mechanization, the conditions for conceiving of an aspect of oneself as other, as nonhuman, begin to emerge (providing there is some living remnant of subjectivity to experience its own mechanization).

Thus resistance to, or salvation from, the oppressive forces of mechanization, at least in the Nazi-dominated world of *High Castle*, will necessarily be limited, and will not take place through any large-scale military assault – there is no secret weapon or hidden elite/messianic force ready to launch a surprise attack and bring down the evil regime against all odds, in the manner of much mainstream science fiction, especially film, from *Star Wars* to *The Matrix*. Rather, whatever hope there is for salvation comes in the form of small, solid, objects that seem to epitomize triviality in contrast to the large historical and political forces transforming human life; yet it is precisely in this triviality that their transformative potential lies. As Rossi writes, in Dick, 'small events are actually cosmic; God is in the gutter; trash (be it science fiction, or any other mass product of cultural industry, or actual rubbish) is actually the most precious thing in the world' (2011: 90). Or, to cite Dick himself: 'Size is inversely proportional to hierarchical reality. We assume cosmic = most important = largest. (Cosmos = cosmic.) Wrong. Look for the seed' (E: 508).

Worldly remains

One category of these small, solid objects consists of antique Americana and ephemera. The collection and trading of these mementos of a culture now dwindling under colonialist rule are activities important to the professional and social lives of several key characters, forming the focus for their everyday concerns and anxieties. At the outset of the novel, Robert Childan, an American antiques dealer, is depressed to find on opening up his shop one morning that the Civil War recruiting poster he had ordered for Mr Tagomi, an important client, has not yet arrived. Having explained the situation to Tagomi, Childan experiences existential dread.

> 'A substitute, then. Your recommendation, Mr Chil*dan*?' Tagomi deliberately mispronounced the name; insult within the code that made Childan's ears burn. Place pulled, the dreadful mortification of their situation. Robert Childan's aspirations and fears and torments rose up and exposed themselves, swamping him, stopping his tongue. He stammered, his hand sticky on the phone. The air

of his store smelled of the marigolds; the music played on, but he felt as if he were falling into some distant sea.

'Well ...' he managed to mutter. 'Butter churn. Ice cream maker circa 1900.' His mind refused to think. Just when you forget about it; just when you fool yourself. He was thirty-eight years old, and he could remember the pre-war days, the other times. Franklin D. Roosevelt and the World's Fair; the former better world. (10)

Tagomi's mispronounciation of Childan's name – the simple shifting of emphasis from one syllable to another – encodes a whole set of power relations between occupier and occupied, cutting through the deceptively sweet normality of the marigold-scented air of Childan's shop to remind him of the true 'dreadful mortification' of his world. There is a similarly slight and equally suggestive difference between the two men's perspectives on the objects being traded – the Civil War poster, the butter churn, the Mickey Mouse watch Tagomi will eventually select as a substitute. In their apparently singular physicality, any of these objects can function as a synecdoche for either of two vastly different worlds (which later in the novel will be transposed on to the metaphysical relationships between alternative timelines). Even with his passionate collector's interest, for Tagomi the items in Childan's shop will never be much more than curiosities, exotic artefacts belonging to a dead culture, having no intrinsic significance in terms of the context of their original production and use (hence a Mickey Mouse watch is interchangeable with a Civil War recruitment poster). For Childan, regardless of the pride he takes in his business – 'his displays [...] really were the best of their kind on the Coast' (10) – these objects remain integral to his own past, nostalgically associated with Roosevelt and the World's Fair, remnants and reminders of a 'former, better world'.

Throughout the novel, objects such as these play the joint role of allowing the reader to identify with elements of the diegetic world, in particular the quotidian concerns of the main characters, without losing the sense of the extreme difference between the mainstream and alternative realities. They suture the novel's modernist-realist style to the irreality of its counter-factual setting. This capacity derives partially from their existence in both timelines (thus on both sides of the diegetic boundary), having been produced before the supposed point of divergence – apparently the 1934 assassination attempt on Roosevelt, successful in the world of *High Castle* but a failure in mainstream history. Antiques and ephemera, in *any* history, have already acquired new social, artistic and/or cultural significance. In this case, they have transcended two historical breaks – one effected by war and conquest, the other by the meta-ontological structure of which we as readers (along with some readers of *The Grasshopper Lies Heavy*) have a privileged awareness. In other words, the division is divided: although we may think of Dick's readers as real, and his characters as fake, such a distinction only applies in terms of what for us (or those readers) is raw physicality, that which Saint Paul identifies as flesh (*sarx*). According to the spirit (*pneuma*), the reality or fakeness of the histories and narratives of people depend on criteria other than their fleshly existence.

One of the most prominent and determining small objects in terms of the novel's plot is the Colt .44 pistol. One or several identical iterations of this antique firearm play(s) key roles throughout the novel. There are still enough Colt .44s in existence to allow Robert Childan to trade them, yet few enough to prevent the market being swamped. What he does not know is that the pieces he sells are actually fakes. Frank Frink, one of the few remaining Jews to have escaped Nazi detection, thus himself existing under a fake identity, works for a company that manufactures a wide range of 'antiques', the Colt .44 being one of his specialities. When he and a colleague wish to leave the company in order to set up their own business making authentic, contemporary jewellery, they allow Childan to discover that a Colt he has purchased is a fake, in order to blackmail their boss into putting up the money for their new venture. The plan succeeds, allowing Frink to begin creating what we are led to understand is some of the first genuine, original American art produced since the war, and which it is suggested may be a sign of and contributor to the gradual re-emergence of a living cultural identity.

It is also a Colt .44 – probably not the same one, but quite possibly also originating in Frink's workshop – that is pivotal in saving the lives of Tagomi and others at a critical moment, and enabling them to play a key role in averting another genocide. The Nazis have developed a secret plan to make 'an enormous nuclear attack' (182) on Japan, their supposed ally, and take possession of its territories. As a diplomat, Tagomi has been able to orchestrate a meeting between a Nazi counter-intelligence officer and a retired Japanese general, both posing as businessmen, with the purpose of passing on the details of the plot to the Japanese. During the meeting, Nazi thugs break into the embassy in an attempt to kill the three men and prevent the information from changing hands. Mr Tagomi, forced into an act of violence completely against his peaceful nature, uses his 'perfectly preserved U.S. 1860 Civil War Colt .44' – 'mature use heretofore delayed' (186) to kill the assassins. Not only does the gun, which Tagomi has never intended to use as a weapon, save the lives of the three men, but it is likely responsible for preventing an act of genocide and possibly a new global war. As if to underline the fact that small, antique artefacts are shaping world history, the evidence itself is transmitted in a silver cigarette case.

We have already been provided with the object's likely biography, its journey from Frink's workshop to Childan's shop to Tagomi's office; in the scene itself, its pivotal role is in direct contrast to the automatism displayed by its human counterpart. Tagomi is surprisingly composed and unemotional for one who is, in addition to being unaccustomed to such situations, of an extremely non-violent temperament. He is described carefully removing the revolver from its teakwood box, and carrying out the lengthy process of loading it with powder, ball and cap ammunition. There is almost a sense that he has allowed the pistol to take over his actions, as he performs the mechanical routines of loading and shooting that he has carried out countless times in 'vainglorious swift-draw practising and firing' (186). Only after the event will 'the most convincingly virtuous person in Dick's novels' (Palmer 2003: 109) show any uncertainty about having had to kill other humans – though when this time comes, his sense of guilt is immense.

The status of the antique is such that it is markedly mundane, yet at the same time lifted out of its ordinary world, in effect transcending itself as functional object by acquiring new roles; in this case, an object that has become culturally equivalent to a Mickey Mouse watch is transformed into a weapon that not only saves lives, but under highly improbable circumstances achieves the unlikely task of avoiding a genocidal nuclear attack – effectively carrying out an 'act' of salvation, its agency underlined by the mechanical movements of its human operator.

But if the gun is crucial in enacting salvation within the novel's diegesis, it (along with several similar handheld objects) also has a central role across this boundary – first in rendering the nightmare world believable (and thus its characters sympathetic), and second in establishing the possibility of salvation even under such conditions. The latter effect is in large part due to their apparent insignificance – their smallness in both physical and social terms. If people have the time and emotional capacity to be concerned about such trivialities, this signifies that the nightmare they inhabit cannot be total: even under such conditions, there is room for the everyday, for trivial, useless objects and pursuits. However, in *High Castle*, matters of literary technique cannot be easily restricted to the extra-diegetic sphere: the notion of a bridge between reader and character is already a theme of the novel – not in that its characters are also concerned with questions of literary aesthetics, as in some metafictional writing, but in that they seek a literal, ontological bridge between their world and ours. This is the purpose and significance of Abendsen's *Grasshopper* for the characters of *High Castle*. An empathetic reader of *High Castle* is not only empathizing with a person in dire circumstances, but with the experience of finding oneself to be a character trapped in an artificial world – an ontological dilemma which Dick's novels have come to epitomize. The centrality of this theme in Dick's writing and thought is another basis on which we might suggest that his novels are accidentally or organically, rather than self-consciously, metafictional: his key concerns could not avoid disrupting the boundary between the diegesis, the world in which the action takes place, and the extra-diegetic dimension in which form, technique, and the social context of reader and writer determine the work.

Openings between worlds

In light of the above, it should not be wholly surprising to find that one small, solid object transforms itself from a metaphorical to a literal bridge between worlds at another key moment in the story, allowing Tagomi briefly to cross over into what seems to be the world of mainstream history. In a state of shock following the assassination attempt and the violence he was forced to perpetrate, Tagomi wanders the city seemingly at random.[1] Eventually he finds himself at Childan's shop, where he intends to get rid of the Colt .44; now that it has reverted from antique to weapon, he views it with disgust. Childan will not take the gun (which he now suspects of being fake), but instead sells Tagomi a small silver pin in the shape of a triangle, one of the new pieces of jewellery that Frank Frink has recently made. Whether it is sales patter or a genuine belief, Childan suggests that the piece possesses some extraordinary redemptive power. Tagomi is sceptical but desperate. Finding a quiet spot in a park, he uses an array of strategies to get the triangle to yield its supposed power to him – pleading, threatening, meditating, approaching the object systematically with each of his five senses; finally, just as he feels enlightenment approaching, he is interrupted by a cop, and abandons the exercise, along with the triangle, in disgust (222). Only gradually, as he attempts to find his way back through the city, does he realize that the silver triangle has done something to him – or his world – after all.

Somehow, he has crossed over into another reality, one which seems, due to the attitudes of the people there, and the presence of certain landmarks such as the Embarcadero Freeway, to be the 'real', mainstream world of 1960s San Francisco. Tagomi is deeply disoriented to find that the streets are no longer filled with pedecabs – a rickshaw-like import of the occupying culture – and that other familiar objects such as the cable cars he earlier described as 'oddly yet extant' (213) have now disappeared. Such differences, along with the heavily increased motor traffic and pollution in the air, and, most chillingly as far as he is concerned, the refusal of the white people in a diner to give up their seats for him, cause him to imagine he has passed into the spirit-world of the dead:

> The silver triangle disoriented me. I broke from my moorings and hence stand on nothing. So much for my endeavour. Lesson to me for ever. One seeks to contravene one's perceptions – why? So that one can wander utterly lost, without signposts or guide? (224)

Dick has Tagomi express here the sense of despair that, at various times, accompanied his own attempts to move beyond the appearance of ordinary reality – to 'contravene his perceptions'. The tone anticipates in particular some of his lowest moments during the writing of the *Exegesis*, more than a decade later. There, and to a degree throughout his life, he had found himself moving beyond the perception of obvious reality in search of a deeper, underlying truth. Frequently ecstatic and full of wonder in his attempts to develop this understanding, the *Exegesis* is also punctuated with moments of extreme self-doubt, in which Dick expresses the loneliness and despair of having penetrated the artificiality of the world, without being granted full access to the transcendental reality he believes to lie beneath it (see, for example, E: 285).

Just as pain and salvation seem to be inseparable in Dick's 2–3–74 experiences, Tagomi's immediate appraisal of his crossing between worlds as a hellish torture, a punishment for his recent acts of violence, seems to be integral to its simultaneously containing the potential for redemption. On recovering the silver pin and using it again as a bridge to return to his own familiar universe, Tagomi finds his state of paralysis has passed, and feels the urge to re-engage with the routine of his quotidian existence: 'Duty calls. Customary day once again' (226). However, once back at the embassy, he refuses to follow customary procedure, and, in the epitome of Dickian 'balking', instead of signing paperwork which would authorize the handing over of a Jewish citizen to the Nazi government, he uses his authority to have him released – not knowing that this man – Frank Frink – is the creator of both the Colt .44 that saved his life and the silver triangle responsible for his seemingly revelatory, albeit painful experience.

The silver pin, in bridging immanence and transcendence, or rather, in rendering transcendent that which presented itself as not only immanent but intransigent, enables acts of salvation in circumstances where death and destruction seemed unavoidable. As emphasized in the scene depicting the contenders for the Nazi leadership, Tagomi and many others experience the world of *High Castle* as unbearable, an experience that is intensified by the sense of its seemingly unchangeable nature. Like the Roman Empire or the Black Iron Prison, its very power depends on collective global acceptance of the fact that it will not yield to either internal or external pressure to change. Opening up the possibility, the conceivability, of an alternative world – even if the immediate experience of it is, as in Tagomi's case, equally unbearable – challenges the source of Roman or Nazi or any mechanizing power, i.e. the belief which maintains it. In enabling this challenge, the silver triangle plays the role Agamben ascribes to the *horkos*: it has acted as guarantor of the promise made by Childan that it would open a 'new view in your heart' (217), doing so only on the basis of Tagomi's willingness to place faith in this promise. Tagomi's excursion into a nightmare alternative universe, like that of the reader of *High Castle*, offers an opportunity to grapple with the notion that while any world may be unbearable, no world is beyond transformation.

The jewellery created by Frank Frink does not share with antiques the property of transcending the gap, sometimes made by history, sometimes by social hierarchy, between function and artefact, between a culture of use and a culture of collection. Indeed, it is in a sense extracted from cultural context in general, not only in that it has no pre-existing model, but in that it is created by an individual whose cultural identity, both as a Jew and as a former citizen of the United States, has been nullified by the dominant Nazi regime. Thus the existence of both the silver triangle and its creator *despite* their official non-existence, already constitutes a challenge to the dominant reality: they are remnants in the sense of Agamben's Paul – upsetting the correspondence between world and worldview (*Weltanschauung*). The fiction which Nazism increasingly seeks to make into a reality, in part by treating it as largely already accomplished, is that of its own totality: having divided the world into Nazis and non-Nazis, it has sought to eradicate members of the latter category until its own particularism achieves a quasi-universal status. This is a kind of demonic inversion of open morality: everyone will be equal when everyone regarded as inferior has been removed. Such a world would not contain Frank Frink or his creations; their presence indicates the continued non-existence of such a world.

Thus the silver triangle seems to have a kind of moral power by virtue of existing outside the dominant conception of history or reality (the one which, within the world of the novel, is treated as its own 'mainstream'). Metaphorically, it is genetic proof of the limits of Nazism and of the fakeness of a particular world. In a metaphysical twist, Dick inserts this ahistorical quality directly into the object, almost as though it were a tangible magical ingredient that had the power to transport Tagomi into another world. A young Japanese collector describes this quality as *wu*:

> I recall a shrine in Hiroshima where a shinbone of some medieval saint could be examined. However, this is an artifact and that was a relic. This is alive in the now, whereas that merely remained [...]
>
> To have no historicity, and also no artistic, aesthetic worth, and yet to partake of some ethereal value – that is a marvel [...] One experiences awareness of wu in such trash as an old stick, or a rusty beer can by the side of the road. However, in those cases, the wu is in the viewer. It is a religious experience. Here, an artificer has put wu into the object, rather than merely witnessed the wu inherent in it. (171)

A piece of Edfrank jewellery, then, has more in common with Childan's antiques than may at first be apparent. While the antiques highlight the impermanence of particular cultural worlds by existing in more than one (traversing not only pre- and post-war cultures, but mainstream and alternative timelines), the silver triangle remains outside of all worlds, thus stubbornly revealing their insubstantiality. Though the antiques may be said to retain the material traces of their prior functions, the silver triangle *is* a material trace, its bare physical existence likewise constituting slight but crucial evidence of the possibility of other worlds, of the non-totality of any given (e.g. Nazi) world.

Thus at a range of levels, these objects form a pivot of shared reality around which whole worlds are juxtaposed against and potentially transformed into or exchanged for one another. They play precisely the role of Agamben's Pauline messianic tensors, setting a world (or aspects of it) against itself, making it conceivable 'as not' itself. It is worth noting that *wu*, like most Chinese characters, can perform many roles, and among other senses is found in Taoist thought in the principle of *wu wei*, sometimes translated as 'nonaction' (Watts 1975: 74–98). Though it may be advisable not to make too much of what is after all Dick's own selective use of elements of certain Eastern traditions, *wu* as performing a negating operation rather than designating nothingness or emptiness per se certainly resonates with the Pauline *hos me*, as well as with acts of balking such as Tagomi's refusal to sign the papers authorizing Frank Frink's execution. It is in setting a term or aspect of reality against itself, as though it were not so, that the silver pin, as well as the novels *High Castle* and *Grasshopper*, destabilize the supposed solidity and unchangeability of the world(s) in and beyond which they exist. This is one of the ways the novel opens up a minimal possibility of salvation through fabulation, for both its characters and its readers – whose very identification and even interchangeability contributes to and is reinforced by the breaking down of all straightforward boundaries between the fictional and the real.

The tyranny of the concrete

In opening up the closed fabulation of post-war Western history, one of *High Castle*'s strongest political-ethical effects, as many critics have noted, is to cause the reader to reflect on the extent to which the Nazi universe it presents is not simply a terrifying vision of 'our world as it might have been', but is actually integral to our world in a far more direct sense. Given the levels of violence and the wars that have pervaded global affairs since 1945, the number of deaths due to poverty and disease, and the very destruction of life that took place during the war itself, it is difficult to maintain any uncomplicated view of the Allied victory as a moment of global salvation – at least in any enduring sense. The defeat of Nazism brought neither redemption for those who had perpetrated and suffered violence, nor any effective restraint on subsequent violence occurring on a comparative scale.[2]

Yet the notion of the defeat of Nazism as a moment of salvation has been so well established in post-war Western culture that it is not unreasonable to suggest that it really does represent a bifurcation in history, in the cultural imagination if nowhere else (and where else is history?), leading to the creation of (at least) two post-war worlds. To what extent has the confidence of victory, the institutionalization of the idea that global catastrophe was averted, made it easier to allow further war, genocide and neglect of suffering to take place? Whether the novel's central message is that Nazism really did in some sense triumph at the end of the Second World War, or whether it simply constitutes a challenge to the self-certainty of mainstream history, has been debated by critics. The ending can be used to support either view. Juliana Frink, having made a journey to visit Hawthorne Abendsen, the author of the alternative history novel *The Grasshopper Lies Heavy*, questions him about his book. He confirms her suspicion that the *I Ching* played a major role in the composition of the novel, just as Dick averred of *High Castle* itself (DePrez 1976). Juliana then consults the *I Ching*, in the presence of Abendsen and his wife, asking why it 'wrote' *Grasshopper* – what message it intended to convey to them. The answer comes in the form of the hexagram *Chung Fu*, meaning 'Inner Truth', which they interpret as meaning that Abendsen's book is 'true' in its depiction of a world in which Germany and Japan lost the Second World War. Unlike Absendsen, Juliana is 'pleased and excited' to have learned this truth, even though it seemingly does nothing materially to change her situation. Where previously she has found choosing courses of action very difficult, a source of great anxiety, and relied like other characters on the *I Ching* for guidance, now when she is asked about her future plans she seems to have come to embrace her uncertainty: '"I don't know." The problem did not bother her' (248).

As John Rieder has noted, many readers and critics have been dissatisfied with the ambiguity of the novel's ending (1992: 223). Even Dick declared the *I Ching* a 'malicious spirit' for not providing a clear resolution (DePrez 1976: 8). Those who praise the ending often see in it a confirmation of the triumph of Nazism even within mainstream history (Rieder 1992: 224) – the *I Ching* both pointing to this condition, and suggesting that it is not absolute. Rieder's own reading refuses any conclusive interpretation, seeing in the ending a foregrounding of the radical instability of meaning, arguing that 'the novel promises only to create among its readers a form of community like that of the random coherence among the "moments" of hermeneutic activity codified in the *I Ching*: an apolitical collectivity, without a centre or a goal' (1992: 231). I would agree that there is no impetus on the reader to decide whether the novel's conclusion has *either* a clear meaning *or* constitutes a failure to find such a meaning. However, for me this uncertainty is tied to the impossibility of any absolute clarification of the strange relations between fiction and reality, immanence and transcendence, which run throughout the novel. Moreover, there *is* a de-centred collectivity discernible in the novel, yet it is one that must at least, in its coherence with an immanent soteriology in which ontology and ethics cannot easily be separated, be considered pre- or proto-political. Rieder's description would be viable only if we were to take 'apolitical' to mean 'against particularism', rejecting worldly divisions – the very stance that renders Paul a political theologian for Agamben, Badiou and others.

In a 1974 essay, Dick cited Santayana's definition of waking life as 'dreaming under the control of the object' (1995b: 75), arguing that the role of the science fiction writer is to free us from 'that immediate object [...] to speculate us out of its total grip'. If successful, he continues, the writer will have

> cut us loose enough to put us in a third space, neither the concrete nor the abstract, but something unique, something connected to both [...] the daily tyranny of our immediate world, which we generally succumb to, becoming passive in the hands of and accepting as immutable, this is broken, this tyranny of concrete reality. (1995b: 75–6)

This cutting-loose, the breaking of the tyranny of concrete reality, is precisely what occurs for Tagomi when he crosses over into another universe, as it has for the reader of *High Castle* in experiencing something similar. In both cases, the alternative world is initially perceived as a kind of hell, yet turns out to offer something potentially redemptive or salvational, even if minimally so. Though Tagomi's saving of a single life may still seem negligible against the backdrop of the destruction of millions, it is the saving of a life nonetheless, and signifies the continued possibility of resistance, the non-omnipotence of the Nazi machine. Juliana Frink, similarly, appears to experience a new form of freedom at the end of the novel, finally embracing her lack of grounding in reality as the counterpart to the ending of the tyranny of the concrete. Both she and Tagomi, following their journeys, no longer feel completely powerless in the face of the Nazi machine. Where the future seemed unchangeable, predetermined in advance as if following a mechanistic programme, it now contains an element of indeterminacy once again. Where the Black Iron Prison seemed impenetrable, it now reveals small but unmistakable weaknesses. The last we know of Tagomi is that he is taken to hospital after suffering a heart attack; the question of whether he will survive or not is uncertain, reflecting his general state, and that of his world – critical, in the sense of being dire, but also in the sense of having an indeterminate future: being at the point of judgement, but not yet beyond it.

For dynamic fabulation to achieve its effects, the future must be rendered open, as it has been for Juliana at the novel's end. The sole effect of the 'truth' that has been revealed to her has been to alter her own relation to the apparently concrete: its tyranny has been destabilized by the recognition that even the most seemingly fixed, immutable aspects of reality are contingent, and therefore open to reconstruction. The indeterminacy of the future has been freed from its subsumption within Nazi psychopathology, becoming genuinely open once again. A key Dickian (though also Pauline) lesson is that the tyranny of any political or ideological regime is co-extensive with the tyranny of concrete reality, and that to a certain extent they are mutually enhancing. In the *Exegesis*, Dick suggests that his 2-3-74 visions came about through his withdrawing of his assent from reality (E: 319). When we treat what is around us as real we are not only perceiving, but *assenting* – we are, albeit in a largely unconscious or intuitive mode, confirming our belief in the reality of what we perceive.

This assent may be the fabulative element already at work in perception, the inventive aspect of even the most apparently simple reasoning or observation, implicit in Bergson's account of fabulation, and subsequently explored in depth in a variety of intellectual contexts, such as the constructionism of Nelson Goodman (1978), or Maturana and Varela's autopoietic account of cognition (1980; 1987). We can speculate that any organism with any form of cognition in a sense constructs the world that it perceives or lives, through those very processes of perception and habitation; that is, with Maturana and Varela, in a quite Heideggerian tone, we can say that '*every act of knowing brings forth a world*' (1987: 26; original italics). Conversely, any interruption of an act of knowing can interrupt this bringing-forth, not only making other worlds conceivable, but drawing attention to this actively productive or fabulative element in knowledge. The closed fabulation that the world is 'out there', independent of any of us, is opened up, such that our capacity to bring forth other worlds – to fabulate openly, endlessly – comes into focus. The tyranny of concrete reality, along with the tyranny of any particular 'world', including those produced by the 'knowledge' that Nazism was defeated or victorious in 1945, is broken.

Objects of salvation

What unites several of the main characters of *High Castle* is that they save one another without knowing or directly intending it. Frank Frink's manufacture of the Colt .44 and the silver pin save Tagomi, who in turn saves Frink, although they have no knowledge of one another's existence. Abendsen's novel, perhaps unintentionally, seems to have had some kind of salvation-like effect for Juliana, and presumably for his other readers, while Juliana in turn saves him by destroying his would-be assassin. In this sense, *High Castle* points towards an understanding of the necessarily impersonal dimension in any viable, that is, immanent, means of bringing about salvation. It also suggests that immanent salvation must in some sense consist of self-salvation: Frink (unknowingly) saves himself by (unknowingly) saving Tagomi; Abendsen does the same through Juliana. Though they are unaware of the consequences of their actions, all of these characters are in some way balking against the world they are part of, through an act of negation, a refusal to recognize it as all-powerful or themselves as absolutely helpless.

The small, solid objects which play a variety of active roles in *High Castle* thus represent both the 'tyranny of the concrete', and the possibility of its escape. We have seen how several characters experience something like a state of paralysis at critical moments, when they are seemingly unable to maintain agency faced with a lack of viable (e.g. ethically acceptable, or practically effective) courses of action. During these periods, their inability to act is revealed by the extent to which they seemingly give over control to the impersonal elements of the world around them, such as the Colt. 44, the small, silver triangle, and the *I Ching*. Having used his antique pistol to kill, Tagomi comes to hate it, but finds himself inexplicably tied to it, summing up their mutual bonding (and equality of agency) with the phrase, 'It in my grip, I in its' (215). Yet the same object has been crucial in saving him and others from destruction, and even in his attachment to it, leads him to the small, silver triangle which will allow him (if only momentarily) to escape the grip of concrete reality altogether.

Hence, on the one hand, this abandonment of will and subjecthood to the object is an index of the extent to which mechanizing forces have deprived the human subjects of *High Castle* of their individual agency at the levels of social and ontological existence. Being directed by seemingly purposeless objects, antique weapons, trinkets and random lines from a book, represents, with an ironic flourish, an absolute mechanization of the human: its subordination to its own mechanistic creations – though without the sublime qualities of a Frankensteinian narrative or the apocalyptic tone found in much modern (mainstream) science fiction film and television. On the contrary, here, it is those creations that are seemingly of least importance that take charge (though this does suggest a certain resonance with the marginalized status of rebellious nonhumans in other narratives, such as the machines of the *Terminator* films, the cylons of *Battlestar Galactica*, or indeed the original robot workers of Karel Čapek's 1920 play *R.U.R.* – a topic discussed in the following chapter).

Yet on the other hand, such objects also seem to constitute the source of whatever salvation the characters experience. Paradoxically, it is in giving in to their own objectification, and allowing impersonal signs and objects to determine their course, that the characters of *High Castle* recover some small degree of freedom. Thus the novel suggests that the route to (even a minimal chance of) salvation must pass through the form of oppression which makes it necessary – echoing Bergson's statement that humanity must make use of mechanism to get away from mechanism. This is why nonhuman objects play a crucial role in the seemingly contradictory process whereby one must experience both alienation from, and continuity with reality, in order to find a viable path. When Frank or Juliana Frink or Tagomi (or indeed anyone, anywhere) feels unable to act, and consults the *I Ching* (by manipulating other small, solid objects such as coins or yarrow stalks), or asks a small piece of metal to transport them to another world, they are not abandoning agency altogether but attempting to defer, or confer it, on to the object(s). To the extent that both constitute impulses to fabulate, there is little difference between what the characters experience at these moments and any other attempt to reach out to a transcendent power, to anything beyond oneself, for salvation. By an act of fabulation, the individual in need of salvation behaves *as though* an exterior force or intelligence were present, influencing events. The very situation of desperation that necessitates salvation involves the perception that all visible or known courses of action are insufficient: every capacity or quality at ones' disposal has been exhausted, and salvation, if it comes at all, must come from something beyond oneself. Yet the fact that supernatural help is not available, or unlikely in the extreme, means that something else must take place if it is to be achieved: fabulation enables the invention of or belief in saving forces, involving the attribution of powers to aspects of the world perceived to be beyond the self. Thus even though being deprived of agency, mechanized, is what leaves the human in dire need of salvation, nevertheless the giving up of human agency – in what may simultaneously be the human's most creative act – can also be seen as the essence of fabulation, the site of its soteriological potential.

If the object is able to perform the role of saviour – ambiguously, never guaranteeing or making salvation absolute – this may point to the essential role of a nonhuman or impersonal element in any logic of salvation. In more conventional (i.e. mystical or religious) discourses of salvation, this nonhuman element tends to take the forms of gods and spirits, or other supernatural powers. In science fiction it often comes in the form of a new technology, or an alien species, which is able to achieve the apparently impossible. Yet it is not as gods or artificial intelligences that such figures bring about salvation, but as representatives of the entry into the human world of nonhuman, yet non-mechanistic elements, which simultaneously reveals the human as always-already in part nonhuman, technological, objectified. We will see this in the following chapter as we look at examples of these more conventionally science-fictional forms of the nonhuman (androids, gods, aliens) rendered unconventional in typical Dickian manner. Then, when we come to our final sustained reading of a Dick work, in the chapter on *VALIS*, we will be in a position to consider the way all of these different strategies which dynamic fabulation offers for rendering dominant aspects of the world, the human, the self, 'as not', can be orchestrated together.

Conclusion: Reality fields

The object may stand in certain contexts, including that of the characters of *High Castle*, for our uncritical belief in the reality and fixity of the tangible. Yet the novel also suggests how the object may make possible the transformation of this view, allowing a dynamic, changeable world to come increasingly into being, simply through an enhanced critical perception of the ineradicably insubstantial dimension of any world – which persists down to its seemingly most solid, unchanging components, such as a lump of metal.

It may well be that we ought to replace the everyday usage of the opposition reality/fiction with the distinction static/dynamic. That which we perceive in our environment as unchanging, we generally come to regard as reality; whereas that which is constantly changing is much more difficult to pin down and thus count as 'real'. Dick once offered a definition of reality – which he returned to many times subsequently – as that which, when you stop believing in it, does not go away (1995d [1978]: 261). It was this definition that he modified in the above citation from the *Exegesis* where he suggested that one does not just believe in the real, but assents to it. In other entries from around the same time, May 1978, he discusses the notion of reality *fields*, in a line of thinking apparently arising from his reflections on a sentence which had come to him from what he referred to as the 'AI voice'. This voice, which he reported hearing especially shortly before falling asleep, seems to have functioned (like many of the forms of Valis-style 'communication') as a kind of filter enabling him to feed his own semi-conscious thoughts back to himself, as though coming from elsewhere. The phrase was: 'Perturbations in the reality field' (E: 333).

In considering this phrase, Dick moves away from a more conventional ontological view in which something is either real or not (where it either is or is not part of what he refers to as the 'all-in-all'), towards a view that what we experience as 'reality' may actually be considered one of a plurality of possible fields, changeable, able to become more or less intensely real, and, crucially, capable of being altered by something other than itself: 'When we talk about reality this is what we're talking about: *a* field – and *now* the significance of "perturbations" can be appreciated: something *more*, in the field or (more likely *beyond*) the field, disturbing it' (E: 335). This notion functions well as an understanding of what takes place in *High Castle* and other novels in which Dick attempts to challenge the tyranny of concrete reality. It also suggests a way of thinking about immanence and transcendence in relation to this challenge that moves beyond simplifying oppositions between materialism and mysticism. Something that is not a part of a given reality field will appear as transcendent from within that field, and may therefore have seemingly transcendent effects in introducing perturbations within it, perhaps collapsing it altogether. Yet it is immanent to its own reality field, and others it may construct. In this sense, Valis in relation to Dick's attempts to break down his own reality fields, or *Grasshopper*, the *I Ching* and the small solid objects of *High Castle* in relation to the Nazi-dominated reality field of the novel's characters, can be said to occupy (or consist in) what Deleuze and Guattari call the 'plane of immanence' or 'plane of consistency'. Replacing the notion of a transcendent plane which would underpin life, art, writing, as its hidden, organizing principle, the plane of immanence 'has no other regions than the tribes populating and moving around on it' (Deleuze and Guattari 1994: 36–37). Considering these 'tribes' as reality fields, we may see how the plane of immanence, immanent only to itself (Deleuze 2001: 27), may appear as transcendent within a given such field, yet has no existence other than through them; it partakes only of *wu*, nothingness. Elsewhere in the *Exegesis*, Dick's discussion of 'a sort of field theory about the human being' in which Valis or Zebra would constitute 'a supra-ego existence (phylogenic being-reality) [...] of which each human is merely an epiphenomenon' (E: 456) resonates with Simondon's notion of the 'preindividual field' of which the individual subject is an effect – also a key influence on Deleuze.

Dick's dynamic fabulation attempts to resist the most fixed, immovable facets of reality – of the world which stubbornly continues to exist when you turn away from it – in this case the Nazi state, or the Black Iron Prison – by positing something more 'real', more stubborn, in an act of balking that refuses to accept the mechanical necessity of what it opposes. The fabulation and perception of other reality fields, which are set against any given such field, constitutes the latter's absolute disruption and opens it to an infinite potential for transformation.

5

How We Became Post-Android

'Astral determinism' and 'Fate' designate the inexorable outcome of a closed system.
This is why I become not-I.

(Dick, E: 487)

What is it in the end that goes in the same direction as this 'I think' that insures the humanity and animal rationality that I am? Well, paradoxically it is nothing other than a mechanism, a machine, but this time a providential machination.

(Derrida 2008: 97)

In the previous chapter we began to see, through *The Man in the High Castle*, how both a notion of self-salvation, *and* a notion of self as nonhuman, may be jointly integral to an immanent soteriology. Here I want to pursue this further, through two particular categories of the nonhuman – the alien and the android, each of which can be said to have been integral to the human self-conception for a long time prior to the appearance of modern science fiction. These two representatives of radical otherness and uncanny similitude are figures through which certain elements of a dominant human self-conception establish and reinforce themselves. They are closed fabulations participating in the constitution of the human's (humanist) reality field, allowing it to differentiate itself from superior and inferior beings, corresponding to gods on the one hand, and animals on the other – though gods and animals that are always-already technologized, rendered instruments or resources for the pursuit of human goals. Through looking in some detail at two novels dealing with these themes, *Galactic Pot-Healer* (2005a [1969]) and *Do Androids Dream of Electric Sheep?* (1993a [1968]) we may appreciate the ways Dick's dynamic fabulation operates upon such closed fabulations, as part of his ongoing search for an adequate form and logic of salvation. In the final chapter, we will see how the theme of the *salvator salvandus*, the self-saving saviour, reaches its fullest development in *VALIS* (1991d [1981]), which I argue constitutes, alongside and in dialogue with the *Exegesis*, Dick's most immanently soteriological use of dynamic fabulation.

The mechanization of pot-healing

In contrast to the tangible sense of evil which infuses the mechanizing forces of *High Castle* or *Palmer Eldritch*, *Galactic Pot-Healer* addresses such threats in a lighter, semi-parodic tone. Mechanization, in many of the forms already discussed, still afflicts the inhabitants of the human society it presents from all sides. The protagonist, Joe Fernwright, is fixed rigidly in place, both physically and socially, within a hyper-bureaucratized social machine. His workspace is restricted to a single small cubicle in a building composed of thousands of identical units (7). This familiar figure of modern alienation, the featureless, grid-like office block, has here, in a manner not without parallels in the contemporary industrialization and capitalization of creativity, extended its reach to all areas of the workforce, erasing the distinctions between artisanal, imaginative, administrative and business careers. Joe is a 'pot-healer', a restorer of broken ceramics, but his vocation is no different from any other in terms of the way the workforce is organized. The social machine's first priority is to maintain its own equilibrium, as emphasized by its prioritizing the maintenance of the daily routine over its useful output; it is more important that Joe and all the others in his class turn up for work, sit in their cubicles all day and go home to their underground apartments at night, than whether they actually have any work to carry out. This is especially evident in Joe's case, since very few ceramics exist for him to 'heal'. Dick's parodic exposition of the contradictions of bureaucracy is carried down to the most mundane level, as a police officer hovers over the street and threatens to arrest Joe for walking too slowly on his way to work (4–5).

Joe's social mobility is just as rigidly managed as his pedestrian. The sole means by which he might be able to change career is a coin-operated automated service called Mr Job – yet the devaluation of the currency and the hyper-inflated economy, in which coins appear to have become the most valuable money-form, mean that no one can realistically make sufficient use of the service. That this automated device, the 'ultimate visage of black iron' (13), is simultaneously treated as a potential route to salvation and, in its machinic unresponsiveness, the antithesis of salvation, is highlighted when a colleague says, '[n]o prayers ... no nothing, will get that godbedamned machine to spit out one additional word' (12).

These mechanizing processes extend right into the private realm, in which an array of automated services have the primary function of perpetuating their involvement in Joe's life rather than actually improving it. His bed, for example, forces upon the sleeper a mandatory dream prescribed by the government – 'one dream for everyone. But, thank god, a different dream each night' (20). In an attempt to avoid being forced to dream, Joe throws the 'sex lever' to try to trick the bed into thinking he is not sleeping. However, it deduces from his weight that there is only one person present, and induces sleep. That night's unrefusable offering is a money-centred fantasy in which the dreamer has won a competition to have their design used on new bank-notes issued by the state (21–2). This closed fabulation displays the contradictory logic underlying the hyper-mechanization of modern society (a logic which possibly also highlights one of the underlying affinities between certain common capitalist and communist images of the ideal society): everyone dreams the same dream in which they are uniquely raised above the rest of society – everyone is the most important person in the world.

Other mechanisms in Joe's apartment display this same motif, offering 'services' which turn out to have the primary effect of mechanizing those they are apparently intended to serve. A free government information service offers information to all on virtually any subject, but access is restricted to a couple of minutes' usage per day; the private enterprise equivalent, Mr Encyclopedia, would cost Joe two years' saving for the same amount of information. A 3D projection on his apartment wall of 'a view of the sea and of towering redwoods' (14) is supposed to compensate for his having to live underground, yet it has been replaced by a black pane of glass because he is unable to keep up the monthly payments; and even if he could renew the lease he would have to pay more to re-activate the accompanying encephalic device that is supposed to convince him of the view's authenticity (yet another of the artificial aids to fabulation that proliferate in Dick's stories).

These are all caricatured examples of the outcome of what Bergson referred to as the 'mistake at the points' which has placed humans under the control of mechanism, rather than the reverse. In many of the above examples, we see uses of fabulation intended to help maintain the coherence of society, actually resulting in the mechanization of its citizens. Such effects can also be identified with aspects of Foucault's and Agamben's discussions of biopower, the management of life and lives that Agamben suggests marks the hidden affinity between democracy and totalitarianism (1998: 121–3). Mechanization characterizes modern society before such ideological distinctions as communist/capitalist or democratic/totalitarian, and closed fabulation operates in and threatens all such social forms, by virtue of its inadequacy to fulfil its primary function (of preventing the destruction of life) on increasingly global scales.

Joe occupies himself at work with what he calls 'the Game', a forerunner of the kinds of interactive online activities that by the early twenty-first century would become ubiquitous means of passing/wasting the time in which one is required to be sitting at a desk. His description of it sounds like a depressive reflection on social networking: 'Contact with others, he thought; through the Game our isolation is lanced and its body broken. We peep out, but what do we see, really? Mirror reflections of our own selves, our bloodless, feeble countenances, devoted to nothing in particular, insofar as I can fathom it. Death is very close, he thought' (10). Other than the Game, Joe's only hope of respite is his pot-healing talent, which at least offers the possibility of giving his life a purpose. He does not simply 'fix' a pot, reassembling the broken pieces, which would produce what Bergson terms a 'factitious unity'. Rather, in 'healing' a ceramic object, Joe considers himself to be re-establishing it in its pre-broken state as 'a single homogeneous unit' (15) in which '[e]verything fuses; everything flows' (65). As opposed to his job, which is not socially distinguished from those of the occupants of the thousands of other cubicles in his building, pot-healing is his singular calling, his vocation – within his own understanding, his reason for being: 'A ceramic pot was a wonderful thing, and each that he healed became an object that he loved, which he never forgot; the shape of it, the texture of it and its glaze, remained with him on and on' (3). Significantly, Joe's calling displays qualities of the Bergsonian mystic, re-establishing the continuity between the pot in its present state with its past, in a gesture extending love even to the level of the inanimate. It is perhaps appropriate in terms of the construction of the novel that this talent, the restoration of living existence where there is none, has been rendered virtually obsolete by the mechanized society in which he lives – and that a lack of pots for him to heal has placed him in a desperately depressive state: 'He had thought of suicide. Once he had thought of a major crime, of killing someone high up in the hierarchy of Peaceful International World Senate. But what good would that do?' (4). Joe is simultaneously able to consider himself 'the best pot-healer on earth' (3) and at the same time feel, since he is not called on to fulfil his vocation, that *my work isn't good enough*' (4, original italics).

Joe's chances of escaping the increasingly intolerable mechanizing conditions of his existence are thus extremely limited. In an all-or-nothing attempt to find a way out, he takes his savings – sixty-five quarters – to Mr Job. His hopes are obliterated when, on his way there, he is confronted by a large group of people even worse off than himself, 'the mass of Cleveland's unemployed – and unemployable' (33), who, on perceiving his sack of coins, surround him with 'a ring of outstretched, open hands' (34). By 'a strange impulse' he finds himself giving away his coins. This act of charity, alien to the mechanizing society, immediately brings two cops to confront him; when he reflexively offers one of them a quarter, they shoot him between the eyes with a laser beam (37).

The alien god

Joe's charitable act of giving away the coins – if ultimately rather futile – displays, literally, *caritas*, selfless love, however impermanently. In addition to attracting the attention of the police, it calls another unlooked-for entity to him, one who may well offer an unexpected possibility of salvation. The Glimmung is an alien being with powers that from an ordinary human perspective appear transcendent. It has already contacted Joe through both conventional and unconventional means (for example through the 'mail-tube' system at his office, and by causing a note to materialize in the water closet of his toilet). The Glimmung extracts Joe from his arrest by transmuting the police station into a giant aquarium and transporting him to a packing crate in a downtown basement, where he talks to him via a phone-in radio show before opening the crate. This convoluted, somewhat surreal procedure is typical of the way the Glimmung's apparently divine or miraculous qualities are repeatedly blended with comically mundane elements: at this first meeting, it appears as two great hoops, one of water and one of fire – 'the basis for the universe' – rotating about a central nucleus (41); yet draped over this impressive elemental form is a paisley shawl. This technique of undercutting, which Dick uses several times with the Glimmung, but also with the robot Willis and, crucially, with Joe at the very end of the novel – and always in the context of salvation – is a trope which repeatedly immanentizes a transcendent quality or figure, as part of the larger strategy of dynamic fabulation.

The Glimmung displays qualities of Bergson's true mystic and Pauline messianism. Both Joe and another character, Mali Yojez, attest to his/its ability to understand them intuitively, as if from the inside out, in contrast to the telepathy used, for example, by the police for surveillance. As Yojez puts it, 'Glimmung looked into the *basis* of my life; it was as if he saw all the way back through my life, saw it all pass along and lead here, to this point. And he saw that at this point it isn't worth living. Except for this' (57). The Glimmung reconnects a mechanized present in which life has been placed under the sign of death, with the continuity of that life's past, its continual growth, re-establishing at least the potential for a re-insertion in duration, a creatively evolving way of living.

Yet he has practical reasons for effecting this supposed spiritual renewal: the Glimmung is enlisting the talents of Joe, Mali Yojez and many others, in a great undertaking, the raising of the once-magnificent cathedral Heldscalla from the depths of the ocean on his home-world, Plowman's Planet. Importantly, he has selected them vocationally: 'The Raising will take great skill, many skills, many knowings and crafts, vast numbers of arts' (50). The Glimmung's contact with Joe and the others is thus emphatically a *calling* – his first note to Joe addresses him by vocation rather than by name: 'POT-HEALER, I NEED YOU' (13). In seeking their practical skills, the Glimmung assigns Joe and the others the status of 'being called' in the Pauline sense, whereby, according to Agamben, *klesis* ('calling') indicates a '*messianic vocation that is the revocation of every vocation*' (TR: 23, original italics). Joe's involvement in the Raising of Heldscalla, despite appearances, as Agamben says of the messianic vocation, 'does not entail substituting a less authentic vocation with a truer vocation' (2005: 23). (Such a substitution is what Joe had hoped to make by taking his coins to Mr Job – which for both the Glimmung and Agamben would have been to miss any chance of salvation, of the messianic.) Rather, the messianic quality of the Glimmung's Undertaking consists in its revocation of the former worldly situations – not only professions, but every determination based on social status, class and other divisions between people: '*Klesis* indicates the particular transformation that every juridical status and worldly condition undergoes because of, and only because of, its relation to the messianic event' (TR: 22).

The Glimmung's call to become part of his Undertaking is this messianic event for Joe and the others. Bringing the great cathedral up from its state of decay at the bottom of the ocean is a form of resurrection – as signified at the end of the novel, when the Undertaking is finally begun, and the cathedral is transformed into a foetal child (172); and like the Christian resurrection, this messianic event has the potential to confer a new life on those faithful to it. As Joe puts it, 'Glimmung [...] told me about life waiting for something to come along and sustain it [...] He said that this Undertaking, this Raising of Heldscalla, was that thing, that event, for me' (56–7). If the transformation brought about by *klesis* involves the 'expropriation of each and every juridical-factical property (circumcised/uncircumcised; free/slave; man/woman)' (Agamben, 2005: 26), this takes place literally, physically, for all those called later in the novel when they physically become part of the Glimmung (159). Yet (more importantly) the transformation is also spiritual, and has already occurred for Joe just through the event of being called: talking about the Glimmung's contacting him, about the possible salvation the Glimmung has offered, 'he felt his conviction grow until it became absolute and powerful, and he felt it change him; it woke him up until, by now, he could say, as Glimmung put it, *I am*' (57). This is a partial reason why, at the novel's close, Joe can ultimately reject the Glimmung's offer to remain with him as part of a corporate entity – to remain part of the saviour – for a thousand years.

Yet the aspect of the Glimmung that is closest to Bergsonian mysticism lies in neither his processual, elemental nature, nor his intuitive appreciation of what Mali Yojez calls the 'basis' of people's lives: it is, rather, in that his salvific purpose is to awaken, as Bergson puts it, 'the mystic dormant within us, merely waiting for an occasion to awake' (MR: 100). Despite the Glimmung's call, it was Joe's own 'conviction' that 'woke him up'. Indeed, as Bergson suggests, the person aroused by the true mystic may be responding, 'in certain circumstances', to his own personality (MR: 100).

This suggestion, that a response to a mystic personality might ultimately be a response, in some sense, to oneself, is a further hint that some form of self-salvation may be essential to the possibility of immanent salvation. We touched on this possibility in the last chapter in considering the projection of self on to the object, which becomes, in certain contexts, a condition encouraging the production of the divine. The suggestion in *Pot-Healer* that the saviour-figure may awaken the mystic in others not simply through calling them, or becoming a model to follow, but by placing them in a position to become their own saviours, furthers the emerging Dickian logic of self-salvation by pointing to the likelihood that the saviour-figure must ultimately efface itself. At the same time, it reminds us that immanent self-salvation must actually or apparently (in either case with the help of fabulation) take place through the involvement of a third party. There must, at least at some level, be belief in the saviour's existence for it to be effective; yet as I have tried to emphasize, an immanent notion of salvation depends on the acceptance that actually transcendent (in the sense of divine or supernatural) figures probably do not exist. Thus the most effective immanent saviour-figure is the one that takes itself out of the picture while leaving behind the effects – traces or intimations – of its fabulated transcendence.

The saviour in need

The Glimmung is not only attempting to awaken in others a capacity for self-salvation, but is genuinely engaged in a desperate attempt to save himself. Mali Yojez is both right and wrong when she suggests that the Glimmung 'planned this Undertaking to save us. [...] The Raising of Heldscalla is only a pretext' (53, original italics). Yet although all those he has brought to Plowman's Planet had 'intended to destroy yourselves, and were in the process of so doing when I found you' (87), he really does need them.[1] The dynamic fabulation at work in *Galactic Pot-Healer* primarily consists in increasingly rendering the apparently all-powerful Glimmung as fallible, ultimately to a critical, life-threatening extent, such that his own salvation is as much at stake as those he ostensibly comes to save. Joe receives information early on (albeit from a dubious source) that the Glimmung is fragile and senile. Though this is counter to his and the other recruits' experiences of the Glimmung's vitality, it causes him to begin to have doubts. As he learns more about his putative saviour, strong parallels between their situations emerge. Far from being all-powerful, the Glimmung is at times deeply pessimistic about his chances of success in the great Undertaking. He spends much of his time inhabiting the lonely, murky depths of the ocean on Plowman's Planet, just as Joe in his earthly environment returned each night to his depressing, subterranean apartment. Likewise, where Joe does not take advantage of the possibility of having pleasant surroundings faked for him via a 3D projection, so the Glimmung eschews available artificially fabulated enhancements to his environment: 'Where I dwell there are no lights. I could of course manufacture life, light, and activity around me, but they would be extensions of myself alone' (85–6). The Glimmung refuses the strategy used by Palmer Eldritch, of seeking to overcome his own isolation by producing a world consisting only of projections of himself.

The Glimmung is also threatened by a metaphysical set of forces of mechanization, represented by the 'Black Glimmung' and the strange, quasi-mystical Kalends, which mirror the physical threats experienced by Joe on Earth. The Black Glimmung is a kind of dark mirror-image of the Glimmung, his supposed nemesis, a living, or at least, moving – Joe refers to it as 'the synthesis of life only' (125) – apostrophe of decay which manifests mechanization in its most general, entropic form. Where the negentropic Glimmung sees his purpose as the Raising of Heldscalla, the Black Glimmung exists to keep the cathedral in its submerged, ruined state, in which it will gradually decay into nothingness. In his struggle against such an opponent, the Glimmung needs not only the talents of those he has brought to Plowman's Planet, but their energy, their living force, to the extent that he wants them to bond with him physically and 'live, as separate entities, within my one somatic presence' (159).

The figure of somatic bonding in effect (corpo)realizes a state in which most of the characters, including the Glimmung, have already been for some time: each has already become part of a corporate entity seeking self-salvation through their mutual dependence on one another, before the Glimmung made this literal by absorbing them into his body. However, when the characters first become aware of the Glimmung's fallibility, the fact that he is not the all-powerful being they had believed, they initially lose faith in the project, preferring to return to their miserable but familiar former lives. Their doubts have been strengthened by a peculiar aspect of Plowman's Planet, the Book of the Kalends, a mystical, perpetually updated text, which purports to record in advance the planet's history. It appears to chronicle the Glimmung's defeat and the failure of his Undertaking (77). Yet, as with the Black Iron Prison, the Nazi war machine, and indeed most ideologically dependent institutions, it seems that much of the power of the Kalends' mysticism derives from the belief that is conferred upon it. It comes down again to a question of assenting to 'reality'.

The Glimmung engages in a mortal struggle with his nemesis deep in the ocean. His team hurries to the space-port to leave the planet, fearing the wrath of the victorious Black Glimmung, with only Joe electing to remain, watching in a melancholic state from the water's edge (138-9). It is at this point, when the saviour's transcendent qualities are most in doubt, that Joe's own salvific potential is most fully realized. Having placed his faith in the Glimmung *despite* the disappearance of his transcendent qualities – in other words, placing faith in his immanent capacity, deriving from his biological strength and will to survive – Joe inadvertently puts himself in a position to be able to save the others. The Glimmung finally routs his opponent, triumphing not only over the mechanizing force embodied by his foe, but over the Kalends' attempt to mechanize both history and the future. When the defeated, dying Black Glimmung hurtles towards the space-port to destroy the others, Joe is able to get a message to them, letting them know of the battle's unexpected outcome, so that they are able to disembark the ship before it is obliterated.

The elements that associate *Galactic Pot-Healer* with a process of dynamic fabulation, making it something more than a story of certain living entities being saved, are crystallized in Joe's ultimate rejection of the Glimmung's offer to take part in the Undertaking. With his enemy defeated, the Glimmung is free to carry out the raising of Heldscalla, though this remains an immense, arduous task. The destruction of the Black Glimmung, one embodiment of mechanization, does not mean the removal of the forces of mechanization and entropy from the world, but constitutes an event affirming the ability of the living to go on countering these forces. The Glimmung invites the others to combine with him as a corporate entity. This way, he says, 'we can function for a thousand years, *and none of us will be alone*' (173, original italics). Joe is well aware of what he would gain in accepting this offer. The sources of his suffering – mechanization, isolation, depression – would almost certainly be overcome; he would be able to spend a massively extended life engaging in the activity that he loves; and he would be with Mali Yojez, with whom he has the chance to experience 'the most tender love possible' (66).

Knowing all this, the one the Glimmung most expected and hoped would join him (174) ultimately elects to remain alone. Why should someone turn down a virtually guaranteed offer of a long, happy and fulfilled life? In light of the struggle against determinism that has allowed Joe to reach this point, it may be that it is the guarantee itself – rather than the chance of happiness – that he is unwilling to accept. Those of Dick's characters who embrace the possibility of a desirable future programmed in advance – such as Floyd Jones, Arnie Kott, Reese Verrick – do not tend to fare well. Joe's decision can be interpreted as an indication of the intimations of determinism that still reside in the Glimmung's project. Despite the clear difference between this and the mechanistic future represented by the Book of the Kalends, there is still an element of closure in the Undertaking – not least in the physical closure within a single entity it necessitates, but also in its consigning of those involved to an entire lifetime spent working towards a single task, however soul-enriching this task may be. Once they accept his offer, the Glimmung tells them, they will not be able to separate from him again: even this life-affirming endeavour would mean closing off certain aspects of the future, of the potential for further creative evolution.

By the end of the novel, the possibility of salvation which the Glimmung represents for Joe has already been actualized: its potential (*dynamis*) *is* its realization (*energeia*). He was awakened by the call of the Glimmung, and is committed to that event, to the renewed anti-mechanistic subjectivity it has conferred on him, amounting to a capacity for self-salvation, rather than to the specific, worldly project to which the call ostensibly related. Accordingly he determines to move on from healing pots – from restoring the past – to creating his own – forging the future. In this he echoes Frank Frink's decision in *High Castle* to cease making antique replicas and begin producing his own new creations. Since this is an attempt to turn away from closure, rather than to select the objectively better of two possible paths, there must be no certainty of success. The outcomes of the endeavour must remain open, and it is appropriate in this regard that the first pot Joe makes, in which he looks for 'his justification [...] for leaving Glimmung and all the others', is 'awful' (177). In this further use of the device of undercutting at the very close of the novel, Dick highlights the fact that any adequate notion of salvation must be without guarantee.

Furthermore, it would seem reasonable to suggest, especially in light of Dick's relentless interrogation of the nature of salvation in relation to his own mystical visions a few years later in the *Exegesis*, that he himself might have considered the Glimmung's corporate entity too easy a way out. The Glimmung remains in several respects a typical sci-fi alien, too fantastical to offer much in the way of practical salvation to Dick or his readers. Thus we can see in Joe's turning away from the alien god, Dick's own turning away from the easy answers that science fiction can sometimes feign; this would be in keeping with the subversion of generic science fiction elements that, as we have seen, many commentators have pointed to as the key to Dick's mature approach (e.g. Pagetti 1992; Fitting 1992a). With the closure of the narrative, the fabulated saviour it contains begins to become static. The one in need of salvation, to keep its possibility open, must move on and start the search again, even if this will only entail constructing – fabulating – new transcendent figures and notions of salvation, and, like Tagomi with his silver triangle, testing them against the exigencies of immanence to see what salvific potential' they might yield. It is almost as though, at the last moment, having apparently found the path to true salvation, near-eternal bliss, Joe realizes that it is pure fantasy – that *any* absolute salvation would have to be considered an illusion – anticipating Dick's own dialectic movement in the *Exegesis* between belief and scepticism, faith and doubt, transcendence and immanence. Joe's acceptance of the Glimmung's call to self-salvation, coupled with the rejection of his offer of a guaranteed happy future, reflects such a movement, which never absolutely abandons either immanence or transcendence, but likewise will not allow either to become absolute.

This is the only way the future possibility of salvation (and the future itself) may remain open. It is what remains after the superposition of the transcendent figure of eternal bliss upon the immanent realm – a remainder taking the form of a badly made, ugly clay pot, which nevertheless marks the vast openness of the future.

Robot theology

Thus far I have focused on the relationship between the human and the alien saviour in *Galactic Pot-Healer*. The novel gradually undermines both as stable, bounded figures (or fictions), through a fictionalizing process which increases the reader's sense that the apparently transcendent saviour-figure is himself in dire need of salvation, while simultaneously developing an awareness of the salvific potential of the immanent human protagonist. If the reader shares Joe's disbelief in and mistrust of the Glimmung at the outset of the novel, and his rejection of him at the end – she may also grasp the value of the intimations of transcendence encountered along the trajectory from one point to the other, and so realize at least something of the potential for self-salvation within the immanent human world. Thus a division is introduced within the division human/god in the manner of the Pauline division of the division flesh/spirit. The human is divided into the capacity for a mechanizing/mechanized (closed) existence and the capacity for creative (open) evolution; the saviour is likewise divided into open and closed – symbolically, in the juxtaposition of the Glimmung against the rival Black Glimmung, and literally, in the way the Glimmung's chances of success or failure in his struggle are made genuinely open, uncertain, in opposition to the Kalends' attempt to impose closure upon them, and the future in general.

Yet the division of the division also takes place in *Galactic Pot-Healer* in the site of the mysticism/mechanism opposition, in the juxtaposition of the Kalends against the robot Willis. As seemingly immortal (98) entities able to foretell the future (72) and to come and go as they please on Plowman's Planet (96–8), the Kalends are in direct contrast to Willis, a robotic servant who exists only to work for others. Initially Willis appears to share mechanistic traits with the array of stubborn devices Joe had left behind on Earth, such as a seemingly rigid refusal to deviate from pre-designated procedures, even when they are pointless. However, it soon becomes clear that the Kalends are in fact on the side of decay and destruction, while Willis possesses distinctly living, creative, empathic and even mystical qualities. His apparent mechanization masks a sophisticated, free-willed personality, as revealed when he gives up on the protocol of responding to questions or instructions only when addressed by name, saying 'aw, the hell with it' (100).

When Joe encounters a Kalend, it appears 'like a negative of life itself' (96). The neutrality of the Kalends' apparent recording of the future has already been called into question: the spiddles, a native life-form of Plowman's Planet, believe that the Book *causes* the things it declares to take effect – including the eradication of the Fog-Things, once the planet's dominant species (72). The emphasis placed on the connection between the mechanistic worldview and the actual rendering-mechanical of life is particularly evident when Joe looks for his own name in the Book, and finds the following statement: 'Joseph Fernwright learns that Glimmung considers the Kalends and their Book his antagonist, and is said to be plotting to undermine the Kalends' (77). In the process of being read, this becomes a performative statement, enacting that which it describes. Later a Kalend points him to a passage which predicts that he will discover something in the cathedral at the bottom of the ocean that 'will cause him to kill Glimmung' and lead to the failure of the Undertaking (98). Again, the passage functions to bring about the events it describes, prompting Joe to make a submarine trip to view the sunken cathedral during which he awakens the Black Glimmung and forces the Glimmung into battle prematurely, which almost leads to his death.

This performative technique is employed again when Joe encounters his own decaying corpse (113), a vision of his future fate that is intended to fulfil itself by causing Joe to abandon faith in the Glimmung. As Joe later puts it, when waiting almost hopelessly for the outcome of the Glimmung's underwater battle: 'the Book made a pool ball out of me, an object set in motion, as in Aristotle's view of the world. One moving pool ball hits the next; it hits a third; that is the essence of life' (139). The Kalends have used their mechanistic outlook to reduce Joe to the status of the mechanical – carrying out what they willed because he believed it to be inevitable, even though he himself did not wish it to happen; and when he makes this statement, believing he has indeed brought about the Glimmung's death, he has come to see all life through the lens of mechanism.

Yet as we have seen, these pessimistic thoughts do not consume Joe entirely, since this also turns out to be the moment at which his salvific potential is most fully realized. His appreciation of the fact that mechanism (the Book) mechanizes, that a deterministic perspective renders things deterministic, is at the same time a realization of the non-inevitability of what it proclaims: if it enacts what it says only on the basis of one's belief in it, one can choose to believe otherwise, and contribute to the production of an alternative reality. One reality field may then begin to seem less solid, as another begins to materialize. Joe's experience of the Kalends' use of fabulation to bring about closure has effectively awakened his awareness of the transformative potential that can be accessed through a dynamic use of fabulation.

In its simplest form, dynamic fabulation describes (or imagines, conceives, depicts) that which has become mechanical (including the fabulator) as not so, and by this description renders it 'open' – which essentially does *not* mean saved from mechanization, but indicates a state of being such that its future is no longer determined. In battling not only the Black Glimmung, but simultaneously the mechanizing determinism that attempts to predestine his defeat, the Glimmung's uncertainty regarding his chances of success becomes essential: 'It may work; it may not. I don't claim to *know*; I am only hoping. I have no certitude about the future – *nor does anyone else, including the Kalends*. That is the basis of my entire position. And my intent' (86, original italics). This further underlines the importance of Joe's ultimate rejection of the Glimmung's offer of guaranteed future happiness: in maintaining uncertainty about what is to come, he is actually adopting the Glimmung's outlook and strategy.

The supposedly mystical Kalends are thus shown to be mechanistic and mechanizing entities which are antithetical to, and have no real understanding of life: 'with them, Joe Fernwright thought, there is not life but merely a synopsis of life. We are a thread that passes through their hands; always in motion, always flowing, we slip by and are never fully grasped' (97). In contrast, the robot Willis, supposedly a mere machine, has a deeper understanding of life and what Bergson calls *true* mysticism than most humans. Beyond citing poetry and writing pamphlets on the mythology of the deities of Plowman's Planet, he declares the same antipathy as Joe and other living creatures towards the forces embodied by the Black Glimmung and the Kalends: '[n]o structure, even an artificial one, enjoys the process of entropy. It is the ultimate fate of everything, and everything resists it' (101). When debating the question of the Glimmung's fallibility with Joe, he points to Christ as 'an interesting deity' due to his 'limited power' (105). The robot theologian explains, 'Christ stands empty handed; he can save no one, not even himself. And yet, by his concern, his esteem, for others, he transcends' (105). He is interrupted before he can fully explain, yet it is clear to Joe that the robot possesses an understanding of the importance of *caritas* where others present do not (107). Furthermore, Willis makes several gestures which demonstrate his *caritas*, in particular through unprompted displays of concern for Joe's well-being, including the practical gift of a plastic carton in which to bring up shards of damaged pots, and the impractical offering of a religious charm or symbol to take with him to the sunken cathedral, which he himself admits will be of no practical help (110). That these gifts are unsought, and that Willis has to explain them to Joe, emphasizes that he is reducible to neither machine nor servant (roles in which he would be able to show 'concern' only as a form of labour). As if to confirm Willis' inclusion in the category of the living, he is engulfed along with the others when the Glimmung draws them into its 'magnasoma' (158).

Willis is an immanent soteriologist, or at least, theologian: in posing the question of how Christ, with all his limitations, can be considered a deity and saviour, he reflects a question posed by his own existence – how can a mechanical being possess *caritas*, or be concerned with salvation? The dynamic fabulation of *Galactic Pot-Healer* addresses these questions, supplying with regard to the Glimmung the answer that Willis is prevented from completing with regard to Christ: the Glimmung's *caritas* combines with his fundamental fallibility to awaken in Joe the capacity for salvation and self-salvation; without this fallibility, there would be no possibility of identification with the saviour, and no openness with regard to the future. This is an enacting of Badiou's life–death chiasmus, a dividing of the life/death division. By the same token, the capacity of a robot servant to display open morality, to become mystical in the Bergsonian sense of valuing life and resisting mechanization – while the ostensibly mystical Kalends turn out to be a force of mechanization – emphasizes that such potential is within even the most seemingly mechanical modes of existence.

Humans: The cosmic bourgeoisie

Some of the ways in which the human commonly imagines its relationship to certain kinds of nonhuman other – such as gods, androids, animals, aliens – could be mapped on to the broad delineation of classes within many human societies: that is, into the three categories of those who work for others, those who work for themselves, and those who do not work. In various early cosmogonies, such as Hesiod's *Works and Days* (2008 [c. 700 BCE]), or the ancient Mesopotamian myth *Atrahasis* (Ipiq-aya 1998 [c. 1700 BCE]), the gods create humans to carry out manual labour they do not wish to perform themselves. Following a period of unrest, with or without the help of a Promethean figure (a rogue dissident turning traitor to his own divine upper class), the humans establish for themselves a degree of autonomy. In modern science fiction, robots and androids are usually created for the same purpose, to carry out work on behalf of their creators, an act which relocates humans in the position occupied by gods in their own cosmogonies (although, as in a capitalist system, it remains uncertain whether they acquire their divine attributes by creating workers, or simply by not working).

By virtue of the others it creates, the human is thus able to position itself as both inferior and superior, the fallen god and the spiritual animal – a kind of cosmic middle-class. Where in *Galactic Pot-Healer* those recruited for the Glimmung's great Undertaking situate themselves towards the lower ends of the various species to which they belong, as the wretched, those in need of salvation, the protagonist of *Do Androids Dream of Electric Sheep?* (1993a [1968]), a bounty hunter of fugitive androids, sees himself as effectively already-saved. In Rick Deckard's worldview or reality field he is automatically, as human, radically superior to nonhumans, his sense of the absolute difference between himself and the androids he hunts being reflected in the way he prizes living animals over externally identical replicas (such as electric sheep). Yet once again, the novel's deconstruction of the human/saviour and the human/android divisions, closed cultural fictions which are opened up through dynamic fabulating, is directed towards the awakening of the capacity for self-salvation within the mechanized-mechanizing human.

Deckard's ability to view himself as living a privileged, superior life, despite the fact that he inhabits a world crippled by nuclear war and its aftermath, far from being unusual, is a fairly common human trait. It is integral to the psychology that throughout human history has sustained slavery, class, caste systems, and many other forms of social violence and inequality (e.g. on the basis of race, gender, religion or physical capacity). Those with the power to transform the situation see no need, regarding themselves as already-saved and others as not requiring or not worthy of salvation. This self-perception is therefore just as important a target for dynamic fabulation as the self-perception of those who believe themselves beyond hope: the two positions – that which views salvation as unnecessary, and that which takes it to be impossible – are to be challenged as fabulations maintaining closed morality. As we will see, Deckard's trajectory through the novel encompasses both these positions, as he goes from viewing himself as fully self-sufficient, requiring no support (let alone salvation), to a state of utter despair, in which he believes he is beyond salvation. The modicum of hope the novel offers – its own soteriological trajectory – lies in the way it subtly encourages us to conclude that he is wrong in both cases.

By all appearances, Deckard's world is as threatened by mechanization as any other of Dick's scenarios. A global nuclear war has left Earth depopulated, and those who remain inhabit a decaying urban infrastructure, their health under constant threat from radioactive dust: 'The legacy of World War Terminus had diminished in potency; those who could not survive the dust had passed into oblivion years ago, and the dust, weaker now and confronting the strong survivors, only deranged minds and genetic properties' (11). As one of these 'strong survivors', Deckard is surprisingly, almost unnaturally upbeat at the beginning of the novel. This is suggested in the very first paragraph, as he jumps eagerly out of bed in his multi-coloured pyjamas, ready to start his working day, very much resembling the 'super-everyman' typical of the pulp science fiction tradition (Russ 1975; see Chapter 2). *Androids* can be read, in a manner paralleling Petter Fitting's (1992b) reading of *Ubik*, as a systematic deconstruction of the conventional science fiction protagonist, culminating in his mental, physical and spiritual near-collapse.

We are led to believe initially that Deckard's positive early morning outlook is brought about by the Penfield mood organ, a device which can be set to create different affective states through 'artificial brain stimulation' (10) and whose 'merry little surge of electricity' (7) is what wakes him; yet we are soon told that he 'hardly needed' its help, since 'a creative and fresh attitude to his job' is his 'habitual, innate approach' (10). The merry little surge of electricity is thus more a reflection than a cause of his positive attitude – a hint in the very first line of the novel that he is, in some sense at least, already on the side of mechanism and mechanization.

Yet the process of Deckard's destabilization, charted across the novel, is also begun right here on the first page. His cheery demeanour is immediately contrasted against his wife Iran's 'grey, unmerry eyes' and her desire to remain asleep (7). Deckard is irritated to find that she has deliberately set her mood organ to encourage this state. Their subsequent exchange is both comic and unsettling in its exploration of the paradoxes involved in having a machine that programmes human moods: how can you ever objectively judge the best mood to programme, when the mood you are in while programming has previously been determined by an earlier iteration of the same process? Deckard seems able to ignore the flaw in his reasoning that his wife, who wants to go back to sleep, should programme herself to want to be awake. Similarly, when she asks him to turn off the television, he responds by suggesting that she dial 'the desire to watch TV, no matter what's on it' (9). When she tells him she does not want to dial anything, his response that she should dial a setting that will make her want to dial leads to the following outburst:

> I can't dial a setting that stimulates my cerebral cortex into wanting to dial! If I don't want to dial, I don't want to dial that most of all, because then I will want to dial, and wanting to dial is right now the most alien drive I can imagine; I just want to sit here on the bed and stare at the floor. (10)

The exchange encapsulates the whole problem of the inadequacy of closed fabulation in the modern era of mechanization. When the artificiality of a means of coping with life, of stimulating the cerebral cortex to bring about a positive mood, whether through religion, television or a(nother) little electrical device wired into the brain, is revealed, it becomes effectively useless for its primary function. When the fictional nature of God and gods is widely accepted in a secular society, most do not respond favourably to the suggestion that, if they believe in these fictions, they will be happier (though the mind is certainly capable of obscuring this fictionality from itself for just such a purpose, under the right circumstances). Dynamic fabulation addresses this problem by refusing any easy distinction between fiction and reality, between authentic and artificial. It attempts to allow the saving power of fabulation to function, as it were, in full view. The Penfield mood organ, however, is unable to perform such a task, being nothing more than a tool for effecting a particular kind of closed fabulation. It can only fulfil its function for those who do not need it: Iran, whose mood is naturally low, has programmed for herself 'a six-hour self-accusatory depression' (8); while Rick has programmed himself a positive mood only because this accords with his 'habitual, innate' disposition. It is the closed fabulation sustaining this disposition, his sense of his innate superiority, which the mood organ can only reinforce, that is opened up or challenged through dynamic fabulation in the course of the novel. Deckard's self-perception as already-saved is based first on the sense of supremacy that comes from awareness of his survivor status; and second on his non-mechanized, living status in contrast to the androids which/whom it is his job, as bounty hunter, to 'retire'.

At the start of the novel, along with his optimistic outlook, Deckard has absolute faith in the androids' mechanistic, non-living status. As the android Rachael Rosen observes, '"You have no difficulty viewing an android as inert [...] So you can 'retire' it, as they say"' (35). In one of the lines that survived with only slight alterations the long process of transforming the novel into the film *Blade Runner* (1982), Deckard makes clear his pragmatic, uncomplicated approach: for him, an android 'is like any other machine, it can fluctuate between being a benefit and a hazard very rapidly. As a benefit it's not our problem' (35). The gradual blurring of the distinction between human and android which is one of the key dimensions of the rest of the story, central to many critical discussions of both the novel and the film (Francavilla 1991: 9; Barlow 1991; Fitting 1992a: 134), is simultaneously the occasion for Deckard's loss of self-certainty and thus his self-discovery as in need of salvation.

The paradoxes Deckard is able to ignore when arguing with his wife over her use of the Penfield mood organ are also inherent – and necessarily bypassed – in his understanding of the opposition between human and android. Carlo Pagetti has suggested that Dick 'challenges the narrative and cultural values of SF', in this case, the man/machine distinction and the self-confident, bourgeois hero, 'not by denying them flatly, but by exploiting them to their extreme formal and ideological consequences' (1992: 25). The deconstruction of Deckard's self-certainty largely takes place through the gradual revealing or forcing into view of such logical inconsistencies. This is a challenge not only to Deckard, or to the conventional science fiction protagonist, but also to the self-conception as 'already-saved' which I suggested in discussing *High Castle* is arguably an implicit aspect of the post-war Western psyche, and its corresponding humanist ethics.

The logical contradictions involved in trying to sustain a rigid human/android distinction are already implicit in Deckard's situation, needing only the right catalysing situations to make them directly observable. He is required to display the very lack of empathy that is supposedly the defining trait of the androids he destroys. Every encounter he has with an android (and virtually with any entity) involves some version of this difficulty. Initially he displays the capacity to ignore the inconsistencies and maintain a pragmatic approach, but the unprecedented intensity of having to retire six androids within twenty-four hours – his previous record being four in one month (15) – gradually wears down his psychological defence mechanisms.

The six androids Deckard is to retire on the day the novel's action takes place have recently escaped from Mars, where they had worked as slaves for human colonists. The first encounter poses little or no challenge to Deckard's self-confidence – largely because his life is directly threatened. When he is attacked by the android Polokov, there is little opportunity for moral dilemma; Deckard's actions would presumably be the same if he considered Polokov to be alive, just as a human Polokov could be expected to react violently to a bounty hunter sent to kill him. This practical indistinction, whereby the biological/metaphysical status of the two characters has no effect on their actions, hints at the destabilization of the division between android and human that is to come. There is a further hint in the brief moment of confusion when Deckard realizes that he is talking to an android rather than a human: '"You're not Polokov, you're Kaladyi" […] "I mean you're Polokov, the android"' (73).

The second assignment, though less physically confrontational, proves more difficult morally and emotionally. Being, like Dick, a lover of opera, Deckard is pleased to find his next target Luba Luft, who is posing as an opera singer, rehearsing *The Magic Flute*. He is 'surprised at the quality of her voice', causing him, momentarily, to see himself as a negative, destructive force, 'part of the form-destroying process of entropy' (77). Indeed, by his own logic, a machine that is a benefit to society – as he clearly considers someone with such talent to be – should not be his problem. A further contradiction arises when he administers the Voigt-Kampff test, designed to distinguish androids from humans, and which he is legally required to employ where there is any possible doubt as to the status of the subject he is about to retire. The test looks for empathy, on the basis that it is a human characteristic which androids are unable to reproduce or mimic accurately. Deckard explains that a clear indication of an android's lack of empathy is that it does not care what happens to another android. Luba Luft reasonably responds that, since his profession requires him to kill androids (and as we already know, he takes a positive attitude to his work), this lack of empathy must be one of his own key traits. When he vaguely counters this by stating that he has taken the test already, a long time ago, she again correctly reasons that, if he were an android, the memory of such a test could easily have been implanted, a possibility that has already been discussed (49), or that an android Deckard might have killed and replaced the human version after the test had been administered (79).

Deckard's disorientation is increased when he is arrested and taken to a Hall of Justice that he did not know existed. There he meets Phil Resch, another bounty hunter, who helps him kill both Luft and the next android on his list, a man named Garland, audaciously posing as the police chief. Deckard has the sense that he has been thrown into a parallel universe, in which Resch is a kind of mirror of himself, which makes it all the more unsettling when he begins to suspect his opposite number of being an android. After seeing the callous way in which Resch kills Luba Luft – without administering the test, just because she is 'needling' him (103) – Deckard voices his suspicion, applying the same logic Luft had earlier used against him: 'I see a pattern. The way you killed Garland and then the way you killed Luba. You don't kill the way I do […] You like to kill. All you need is a pretext' (106).

Deckard reasserts his humanity here by stating that he does not enjoy killing androids. Yet he was unable to resort to this line of defence earlier when Luft challenged his human status. His hesitation, presumably, lies in the fact that this admission produces another dilemma: for Deckard to confirm that he does not like killing androids is to imply that he regards them as something other than 'mere machines' – that there is some aspect of them with which it is possible to empathize, making them entities worthy of emotional and moral concern. Such a view could be disastrous for his ability to go on doing his job, which is dependent on his being able to remain confident regarding the absolute difference between himself as human and the androids as machines. Thus he is caught between this and the equally debilitating counter-position: that he enjoys or feels no remorse about killing the androids, indicating his affiliation with them. Both options force him into a self-identification with the android, one by questioning their nonhuman status, the other by questioning his status as human: a clear affiliation with either would undermine the notion, in which he is deeply invested, that it is acceptable to kill an android.

Android and theoid

Deckard is thus ensnared in the contradictory logic of his situation: his job requires that he not empathize with androids; yet to remain human he must empathize. The effect of the encounter with Resch, redoubled by a romantic liaison with the android Rachael Rosen, is to cause his understanding of the opposition between human and machine, the basis of his entire outlook – his reality field – to undergo a dramatic inversion:

> So much for the distinction between authentic living humans and humanoid constructs. In that elevator in the museum, he said to himself, I rode down with two creatures, one human the other android … and my feelings were the reverse of those intended. Of those I'm accustomed to feel – am *required* to feel. (110)

This realization occurs after the Voigt-Kampff test has shown Resch to be human, despite his displaying what Deckard cannot conceive as anything other than inhuman traits. Meanwhile, Rachael Rosen fails the test but inspires an emotional and empathic response from Deckard, underscored by his sexual involvement with her. Rachael is the property of the Rosen Association, which manufactures the androids that are sent to the colonies; yet she is kept on Earth, apparently for the primary purpose of stopping bounty hunters like Deckard from destroying the company's commodities. After sleeping with him she reveals her role, at which point Deckard tries but finds himself unable to kill her. She declares that she has ended the careers of many bounty hunters this way (152). Yet even as he recognizes 'her victory over him' (153) in that he will now have to give up his career, Deckard's resolve to finish his assignment by retiring the remaining three androids on his list only seems to grow.

A common topic in discussions of the film *Blade Runner* is the question of whether Deckard is actually an android. An often-cited piece of evidence is a scene near the end of the film suggesting that the character Detective Gaff (played by Edward James Olmos) has access to his dreams.[2] There are many equivalent hints in the novel, such as the accusation made by Luba Luft, or in the linguistic subtleties of Deckard's interior monologue. For example, the Voigt-Kampff test identifies androids on the basis of a lack of empathy towards killed or injured animals, looking for reactions of disgust to mentions of calf-skin wallets, butterfly collections, bullfighting (42), even the killing of a wasp (80): yet despite Deckard's desperate desire to own a real animal, he thinks of the fugitives on his list being 'plugged like a file of ducks' (75).

However, in the novel at least, the question of Deckard's ontological or biological status is rendered irrelevant – whereas the process by which this takes place has special significance. Unlike in Dick's short story 'Impostor', where a revelation regarding the human/android status of the main character provides a satisfying 'twist' ending, in *Androids* the distinction between human and android is completely dismantled, such that to ask to which category Deckard belongs becomes meaningless. He is clearly at times capable of displaying what he regards as *both* human *and* android characteristics, just as he is able to regard biological humans as morally, emotionally android, and vice versa.

In the vocabulary of Saint Paul, we may say that the novel undermines the android/human distinction as understood according to the flesh, and replaces it with the android/human division according to the spirit. This would not be a simple exchange of one vocabulary for another, since the question of what defines an android is *already* couched for Dick (and Deckard) in a Pauline ethics. Despite appearances, the Voigt-Kampff test is not undermined by the production of what might be regarded as flawed results. On the contrary, in testing for *caritas*, for love or empathy, it suggests that this is the *only* viable criterion for determining moral worth or responsibility – for demonstrating entitlement to life. This implies that the investigation of the human/android distinction in modern science fiction is actually a continuation of a moral struggle over definitions, rights and treatment that has been at the heart of human social life for most of its history. By the same token, it may prompt us to ask whether the question of the android – literally, of the 'human-like' as opposed to the human – is not also an ancient human question.

In Walter Benjamin's 'On the Mimetic Faculty', written in 1933, he suggests that the 'gift of seeing resemblances is nothing other than a rudiment of the powerful compulsion in former times to become and behave like something else'

(1997: 160). Michael Taussig carefully identifies in this short text what he sees as one of Benjamin's key themes, 'the surfacing of "the primitive" within modernity as a direct result of modernity' (1993: 20). The figure of the artificially produced humanoid in modern science and science fiction, from Descartes' mechanical man (Descartes 1985 [1633]; Descartes 1998 [1637]: 31–2) to Steve Grand's robot orang-utan Lucy (named after a three-million-year-old human ancestor),[3] from Frankenstein's creature to Data in *Star Trek: The Next Generation*, may be another site of such surfacing. The strange relationship between likeness and radical difference, which, far from being opposites, can be understood as deeply intertwined, if not mutually (re)producing ideas, is embedded in some of the most influential archaic Western accounts of the origins of the human. Where an Old Testament God is understood to have created Man in His own image, emphasizing a likeness and a separation between the two beings that only make sense in tandem, modern founding myths of the humanoid robot or android retain this combination of tropes – even down to the masculine bias (*android* literally means manlike – the equivalent feminine term would be *gynoid*). The production of the primitive, whether in image, rhetoric or material form, entails its creator's self-establishment as beyond or above the primitive, yet in a gesture that is always threatening to undermine itself.

An aspect of this relationship which, as I mentioned above, is found both in ancient myths of human origins and in modern science fiction stories of the birth of the android, but which seems strangely absent from the biblical cosmogony, is the notion that the new life-forms (human or android) are essentially created as slaves or instruments, with the sole function of carrying out work. (Perhaps a trace of this idea can still be discerned in the Book of Genesis in God's granting to man of dominion over the earth and the animals, which, though traditionally understood as an assignation of power, might equally be viewed, especially from a contemporary, ecologically aware perspective, as a burden of responsibility.) Mythical presentations of humans as labour-saving devices may reflect an understanding of mechanization as a fundamental human characteristic. However, they also reflect an emancipatory human self-conception in which enslavement is understood as having been overcome at some pre-historical stage: the acquisition of autonomy, rights, freedoms is conceived as accompanying the flight from or overcoming of a primitive mode of existence. The accounts of Hesiod, and the Flood narrative recounted in *Atrahasis*, dramatize the struggle between the humans as guiltless victims, managing (with help) to evade destruction at the hands of the wrathful gods. Though assigning more blame to humans, the Old Testament version retains the theme of a violent negotiation between humanity and divinity, resulting in the establishment of a fragile balance. Whether through resistance to or appeasement of the divine, such myths tell the story of humanity's supervening of its own mechanization (or primitive state) in order to earn a small measure of the autonomy enjoyed by the divine. The human, created as android, becomes *theoid*, godlike.

Thus to a large extent, the dream of the artificial humanoid being created by humans, as found in science fiction, cybernetics, robotics, and other sites of modern culture, is a return to some of humanity's very old mythological views of its own origins. This may be one reason for the commonly expressed fear that contemporary or future androids will pursue a similar path to that which led their theoid creators to their post-android status. Karel Čapek's play *R.U.R.*, which coined the term 'robot' from a Czech word meaning servitude or 'forced labour', epitomizes not only the tendency to situate the robot as subhuman servant, but the fear of slave revolt that runs through the heart of the human relationship with its android others. From Asimov's robot stories to the *Terminator* films and the re-imagined *Battlestar Galactica* series, the anticipated overthrow of the humans, leading either to their eradication or their subjugation as slaves, the robot/android narrative can be said to replay a version of the human conception of its own past emergence from primitivism. This process is conceived as necessarily involving struggles with other forms of life, animal and divine, in which humanity both expresses and conceals its own mechanizing characteristics by transferral on to its nonhuman others.

Dick's staging of the human–android relationship, not only through figures like Deckard and the theological robot Willis, but through a long series of artificial and mechanized humans in his fiction – including the teaching machines of *Martian Time-slip* (1999a [1964]), the demonic, part-mechanical, part-divine Palmer Eldritch, the Abraham Lincoln simulacrum of *We Can Build You* (1977b [1972]), Garson Poole, the eponymous organic robot of 'The Electric Ant' (2000b [1969]), not to mention a string of ethically, psychologically and biologically androidized characters who are supposedly human – re-engages this mechanizing and mechanistic potential that is already at the heart of the human, but which its own origin myths construct as having been overcome. The struggles of androids and other forms of 'artificial' life to forget or suppress these same mechanizing characteristics in themselves become increasingly indistinguishable from those of humans. Patricia Warrick may be correct that Dick fears that, in building machines programmed to kill, 'man will become the machine that kills' (1980: 225). However, in the way he deals with this idea, his fiction suggests that this is what the human has been all along. His dynamic fabulating opens up the closed fabulation, manifest variously in numerous mythological, psychological, political and philosophical discourses, which depicts this mechanizing dimension (often associated with images of animalism or 'brute nature') as belonging to a prehistoric, primitive stage that has long been left behind. In other words, Dick's dynamic fabulations of the human/android figure take the relationship which many ancient and modern mythologies present as binding creators and their creations, and recover its status as the relationship between creators and more creators. The static form of this relationship, as a rigid hierarchy between superior and inferior beings, gives way to an alternative, dynamic conception, which may well have preceded the biological and mythological evolution of creation myths, and which indicates the continuity or potentially endless growth of the creative thrust of life.

Creative destruction

In the course of this discussion of *Androids*, I have not yet mentioned its most explicitly mystical saviour-figure, Wilbur Mercer. While from one perspective he may appear almost incidental to the main plot, Mercer also seems to reflect in symbolic microcosm Deckard's inconclusive (thus never successful, yet never-quite-defeated) quest for immanent salvation. It is significant that Deckard seeks out Mercer – who provides emotional support for 'most people' on the planet (24) – only as a final act of desperation, when the irreconcilability between his mechanizing and anti-mechanistic seems to have left him on the brink of self-destruction. By the time he comes to retire the remaining three androids on his list – Roy and Irma Baty and their friend Pris – Deckard has decided that after this job he can no longer continue as a bounty hunter: 'This is my end, he said to himself [...] After the Batys there won't be any more' (149). Yet he is still able to carry out his task. Indeed, he is if anything by this point more efficient, killing all three androids within a few moments, and with minimal communication – in direct contrast to his encounters with the previous three, of whom he personally killed only one, in defence of his own life, letting Resch kill the other two after lengthy interactions.

Deckard seems therefore to be completely divided in his attitude towards androids by the end of the novel. He has empathy for them as other living beings – having admitted to Rachael, before she revealed her deception, that she is non-living only in a legal, not a biological or moral sense; yet he is still able to destroy them. Though his inability to kill Rachael might be construed as a sign of his (and his recognition of her) humanity, it might just as easily be interpreted as machine-like pragmatism: after all, she is not on his list of targets – killing her is not part of the programme. In this duality, Deckard seems to have been alienated from himself, comprising two separate identities which can neither accept nor excise one another: 'But what I've done, he thought; that's become alien to me. In fact everything about me has become unnatural; I've become an unnatural self' (172). This may be considered the uncanny outcome of a twisting science fiction narrative; yet it is also an expression of a fundamental contradiction of the human as a social animal governed simultaneously by intuition and intellect, and by closed and open morality. Deckard is placed in the archetypal condition of needing salvation, being faced with a seemingly impossible situation which it is simultaneously impossible to accept – needing a way out of a no-way-out situation. This need is explicitly addressed through the figure of Wilbur Mercer.

Deckard is initially quite sceptical about Mercer's saviour status, despite the fact that much of Earth's remaining population appears to be made up of believers. People place themselves in touch with Mercer through what is referred to as the 'black empathy box'. By gripping the handles of this strange device, the user is transported to a barren landscape where they experience 'physical merging – accompanied by mental and spiritual identification – with Wilbur Mercer' (21–2). Mercer is locked in a cyclical process of suffering, death and rebirth that seems to draw on elements of Jesus' crucifixion and resurrection, the myth of Sisyphus, and the *Bardo Thodol* (the text often referred to as *The Tibetan Book of the Dead*). He must engage in an endless climb to the top of a hill, while unseen oppressors referred to as 'the killers' hurl rocks at him. When these rocks strike, the users share Mercer's pain, and may even find themselves cut and bruised after using the empathy box. Each time Mercer reaches the hill's summit, he is cast down into the tomb world, where he has to wait an immeasurable time for the bones and corpses of other dead creatures around him to 'metabolize' back into life (23). When this happens, he finds himself once again climbing the hill, and the cycle repeats.

What do people gain from combining with Mercer in an experience almost entirely characterized by suffering? To begin with, there is the sense of the transcendence of self that comes from merging with him and others, similar to the effect of joining the Glimmung's 'magnasoma' in *Galactic Pot-Healer*: it is not just suffering that is experienced, but *shared* suffering. Another benefit may lie in gaining the awareness users gain that death is not absolute. But beyond this, Mercer's suffering minimizes whatever transcendent, miraculous or other divine qualities he may be perceived to possess. Together, these aspects amount to the enabling of a direct identification with a quasi-divine figure who seems to gain no benefit from his supernatural status, coupled with an experience of near-universal decay, of ineluctable, painful mortality in which life nevertheless endlessly returns. Like Sisyphus, Mercer is being punished for the crime of evading death: in his former life, he had made use of a special 'time-reversal faculty' for bringing the dead back to life (23). The use of this faculty was prohibited by law, and to stop him, the authorities – subsequently transmuted into the killers – had 'bombarded the unique nodule that had formed in his brain [...] with radioactive cobalt, and this had plunged him into a different world' (23) – the tomb world from which he eventually, though only temporarily, arose. Like the punishment of both Christ and Sisyphus, the result is not the absolute death that the killers intend, but a form of eternal life, however much suffering it entails. The killers have attempted to 'mortalize' Mercer through mechanization on a spectrum of levels – through the law, technology, social isolation, and, as if to show they have tried just about everything, throwing rocks at him. Yet still he is not destroyed. Mercer's history can be read as an illustration the capacity of life to go on even after the full range of mechanizing processes have been wrought upon it – and thus as establishing a notion of salvation in which a mere flicker of transcendent potential, an intimation of the immortal, remains, even after the removal of every overt transcendent element.

Until late in the novel, Deckard displays little interest in Mercer. When he does eventually grip the handles of the empathy box, he appears to gain nothing positive or salvific from the experience: in fact, Mercer tells him directly that '[t]*here is no salvation*' (135, original italics), and Deckard reports to his wife that 'Mercer talked to me but it didn't help. He doesn't know any more than I do. He's just an old man climbing a hill to his death' (136). Yet if Mercer's potential for salvation depends in large part upon his becoming-mechanized, his very failure to help, and his banality, may be valuable in themselves. For one thing, he confirms, both by example and in words, that the helplessness of Deckard's situation, his self-alienation, is not unique to him, but constitutes 'the basic condition of life':

> You will be required to do wrong no matter where you go. It is the basic condition of life, to be required to violate your own identity. At some time, every creature which lives must do so. It is the ultimate shadow, the defeat of creation; this is the curse at work, the curse that feeds on all life. Everywhere in the universe. (135)

Though Deckard initially appears to derive no benefit from this reaffirmation of his miserable situation, it may ultimately be the basis for his only hope. For this 'curse that feeds on all life' may also, from another perspective, be seen as a reflection or indicator of life's inherent self-saving ability: the potential for acting against one's nature is, even as it constitutes the mechanism of alienation, also the potential for overcoming mechanization, an equally fundamental human characteristic. Deckard must be placed in a position where his capacity for both is foregrounded, in order to see that he has the power to decide. In acknowledging that by destroying the remaining three androids he is becoming an instrument of destruction, he simultaneously demonstrates his underlying ethical nature: 'What a job to have to do, Rick thought. I'm like a scourge, like famine or plague. Where I go the ancient curse follows. [...] Everything I've done has been wrong from the start' (169). Yet even as this wrong-doing has become his habitual mode of existence, he now demonstrates the ability to go against it and give up killing. In this sense, Deckard embodies the Bergsonian account of the putative movement of humanity from closed to open: intelligence brings with it mechanization and the closed society, in opposition to the openness that is a fundamental trait of life; this mechanization becomes ossified as 'human nature', a fiction taking on such solidity that it becomes difficult to see it as anything but reality; thus a second stage of self-alienation is required, whereby the human is once again set against its basic nature, transcending the war-instinct through the reopening of the soul, a renewed, creative evolution beyond mechanization. Within an immanent ontology, 'transcendence' occurs through the dis-closure of a fictional totality. In the soteriological trajectories that lead in the direction of an ethical posthuman awareness, the human is revealed to have only ever been android, human-*like* – and this shift implies an experience that would necessarily be one of both transcendence and its collapse.

Conclusion

In the two novels considered in this chapter, we see Dick's dynamic fabulation at work upon the traditional science fiction protagonist from two opposing directions: Deckard, regarding himself as 'saved-in-advance' and behaving, at least initially, like the indestructible, no-nonsense hero of an early to-mid-twentieth-century space opera, is set against himself, in the manner of a Pauline *hos me* ('as not'); Joe Fernwright is presented as a near-hopeless loser who nevertheless is ultimately able to demonstrate something like the potential of the saviour-hero, without losing any of his down-to-earth (and down-at-heel) character. In both cases, an immanentizing effect leads to the possibility of salvation operating with the most minimal transcendent associations, by a kind of division of conventional divisions between 'saved' and 'doomed' (or 'damned'). The particular reality fields of both Deckard and Fernwright are eroded as others come into view: the saved are revealed as not-saved; the doomed as not-doomed. Meanwhile, a similar effect is enacted through the more mystical saviour-figures of the Glimmung and Mercer: someone with the apparent power to cheat death has been immanentized; the salvation he offers has been revealed as not-salvation. Yet through the working of this messianic tension, something remains, some intimation of immortality, pointing towards the capacity of even the lowliest creature – of every minimally android entity – for self-transcendence, for overcoming mechanization. It would be possible to trace this process of immanentization through almost any of Dick's novels, discerning in each case the process which sees a figure with some transcendent status gradually having it stripped away, though without the possibility of salvation ever disappearing absolutely. The vehicle or establishing condition for this process is frequently amnesia in some form or other, along with the possibility of an eventual anamnesic recovery – as in *Time Out of Joint* (2003c [1959]), as we have seen, but also, for example, in the case of the gods Ormazd and Ahriman of *The Cosmic Puppets* (2006 [1957]), and the deity Yah in *The Divine Invasion* (1996 [1981]), who must forget his own identity in order to return to Earth in human form. In *A Maze of Death* (2005b [1970]), meanwhile, a self-induced amnesia turns out to be the basis for an artificial and temporary form of salvation that must be renounced by the novel's protagonist in order for a saviour-figure (supposedly constructed by a computer intelligence) to emerge from a virtual reality and intercede in a reality beyond it. Even humans with a special talent for seeing the future, such as Floyd Jones in *The World Jones Made* (1993b [1956]), Manfred Steiner in *Martian Time-slip* (1999a [1964]), or Dave Mutreaux in *The Game-Players of Titan* (1991b [1963]), must have these abilities impaired in order to have any chance of saving themselves or others. In other cases, as with Deckard, or Jason Taverner of *Flow My Tears, the Policeman Said* (2001 [1974]), it is the protagonists' innate superiority, their extra-ordinary talents and corresponding self-confidence, that must be challenged or removed, yet even here various forms of forgetting (or being-forgotten) play crucial roles. Generally, following this immanentizing process, there is a (re)discovery of the barely residual intimation of transcendence, of salvation. Yet even when this appears, it must be kept fragile and unstable, which is why Dick's novels so often seem to end with the success or survival of their main characters still in doubt. It is also why, despite a propensity for re-staging major processes of religious (especially Christian) transcendence within science fiction contexts, Dick always ensures that the soteriological qualities of miraculous events are eroded or undermined: the transubstantiation that occurs in *The Three Stigmata of Palmer Eldritch* (2003b [1964]) becomes a 'diabolical Eucharist' (Dick in Rickman, 1988a: 149), drawing other lives into a prison of isolation constructed by an anti-saviour, rather than manifesting salvation in the mundane world; the resurrection of the Anarch Peak, the popular anti-establishment black religious leader in *Counter-Clock World*, is compromised by his assassination; and Lord Running-Clam, the Ganymedean slime mould of *Clans of the Alphane Moon*, despite undergoing a form of death and rebirth (from his scattered spores), must simultaneously lose the larger part of his former personality and memory. It might have been illuminating to have explored some of these other immanent saviours in detail: but essentially I would have been telling the same story each time, and quite possibly with diminishing returns.

Salvation in all these cases is only ever made possible through fabulation and counter-fabulation, through the opening of the closed. Although, as we have seen in both Bergson and Dick, this activity is fundamentally more than imagination or fictionalizing – is, rather, something more akin to Nelson Goodman's 'worldmaking', which 'always starts from worlds already on hand: the making is a remaking' (1978: 5) – nevertheless by the same token it is always capable of being undone, unmade. Dick's novels are frequently viewed as unsatisfying: yet this may only be a reflection of his underscoring of the fragility of whatever hope or potential for salvation he and his characters have found in fabulation. For this reason, we may see it as important that Deckard is shown neither to attain an ultimate state of salvation, nor to undergo a complete self-transformation. A more straightforward plot might have involved him initially treating androids as worthless sub-humans and gradually coming to learn, through his interaction with them, to treat them as equals – while they would be depicted as maltreated victims awaiting emancipation. Indeed, the novel's 'underlying confusion between androids as wronged lower class and as inhuman menace' is what caused Darko Suvin to regard it as an 'outright failure' (1992: 14). Yet an easier, less ambiguous depiction of the androids as victims would mean a negation of their status as truly equal to that of humans – inserting them directly into the binary which Deckard, as we saw above, uses to characterize machines: they must be a benefit or a hazard – no middle ground, no possibility of representing both at once. Just like humans, androids are shown to have both mechanizing and open tendencies, and the capacity to transcend whichever dominates them, a capacity which, in order to remain, must never be realized absolutely. They are free to move between the lower, middle and upper cosmic classes: the task for a posthuman ethics of openness, as for a soteriology of immanence, is to maintain this freedom of movement while simultaneously abolishing the class distinctions across which it is forced to operate.

6

The Reality of Valis

Many have tried to find ways of salvation. The reports they bring back are always incomplete and apt to mislead even when they are not in words but in music or paint. But they are by no means useless; and not the worst of them are those which speak of oneness with God. But in so far as we become one with him he becomes one with us.

(Wisdom 1975: 177)

For years I've felt I didn't know what I was doing; I had to watch my activities and deduce, like an outsider, what I was up to.

(Dick, E: 22)

If we submit everything to reason our religion will be left with nothing mysterious or supernatural. If we offend the principles of reason our religion will be absurd and ridiculous.

(Pascal 1966 [1669]: 83 [note 273])

Although written science fiction is a particularly effective medium for Dick's fabulations, they ultimately demand to be understood as fictionalizing, reality-building activities which extend across psychological, political, philosophical and ethical registers, and refuse to be restricted to literary categories. This is why Dick has so much in common with Saint Paul, over and beyond their shared placement of love at the heart of their ethics, and their concern with seeing past the distorted view of the world, which comes to us darkened and fragmented as if in an imperfect mirror. It is the extraordinary reach of fabulation which gives it both a critical social value *and* a personal value (for Dick or anyone else) in terms of (immanent) salvation. Salvation is both a public and a private matter, concerning both the survival of the individual and that of the group or species: in fact, the transcending of individuating distinctions, the rediscovery of the potential for open morality within the closed sphere of private or local interests, is, as we have seen, a central concern for an immanent soteriology, as it is more generally for many ethical frameworks.

The experiences of 2-3-74 should themselves be understood as fabulations: the beam of pink light communicating vast amounts of information, Dick's experience of sharing his mind with that of another, seemingly wiser figure, the phrases uttered by the 'AI voice', the various other dreams, visions and mystical experiences which form the dynamic, evolving basis for the *Exegesis*, can be placed in a continuity with the fabulations constituting his written science fiction. Dick himself emphasizes their complementary relationship:

> I never anticipated such a tremendous payoff (breakthrough), despite the fact that the corpus of my writing is a map, an analysis, and a guide. The 26 years of writing, without 3-74, is a map of nothing, and 3-74, without the body of writing, is conceptually inexplicable. (E: 268)

Yet this complementarity lies not simply in the fact that his previous writing and 2-3-74 can be used as lenses to better understand one another, but in that they share the saving function that, as we have been exploring all along, forms the basic context of fabulation. This is most directly recognizable in Dick's frequent acknowledgements, especially in early *Exegesis* entries, of the beneficial, therapeutic effects of 2-3-74, referring to 'the state of agitation and distress and perturbation I was in in 3-74 when it suddenly approached me with aid' (E: 156), describing it as his 'physisican' (E: 195), arriving at the time of 'the midpoint life-crisis (the razor's edge Augenblick)' (E: 204) to transform his life through a 'therapeutic psychosis' (E: 242). Although he went through numerous reversals and reassessments of the status of the 2-3-74 experiences over the eight-year period leading up to his untimely death, even when he eventually came to regard the project of the *Exegesis* as 'futile', a 'delusion' and 'a hell-chore', he was still able to see it as having allowed him to find 'a road to God' (E: 643). Fabulations, as I have tried to suggest throughout this book, are no less effective for being conceivable as delusions, hallucinations, fictions, even with regard to experiences of the divine. Thus, even at a late stage in his exegetic project, Dick was still able to declare that 'everything that has happened and that I have been shown, told, every revelation – it's all one vast soteriological engine/program' (E: 888). As Gabriel McKee suggests in a footnote to this entry, '[w]hatever the reigning theory of the moment, Dick is always concerned with deliverance, liberation, rescue. [...] The Exegesis is a record of a human soul in search of salvation' (E: 888).

Though I am concerned with the diversity of modes in which Dick addresses (or fabulates) Valis, this chapter focuses more attention on the novel *VALIS* than on the pages of the *Exegesis*. This is in part for the practical reason that an in-depth engagement with the *Exegesis* – 900 pages long in its recently published edition (which still represents only a tenth of the total material) – would be a challenging task for an entire book, let alone a single chapter. Nevertheless, it is important to read *VALIS*, so far as possible, in tandem with the *Exegesis*, itself a multiplicity of different fabulative strategies which may represent the culmination of Dick's quest to develop an immanent soteriology. The novel can be considered one of Dick's most focused attempts to draw together the fabulative material that had arisen through and following 2–3–74, drawing together several strands of soteriological thought from the *Exegesis* into a single, concentrated, self-contained fabulation. Thus on the one hand it forms a kind of meta-meta-(…)fiction, fabulating Dick's own fabulative responses to his own fabulated encounter with the divine; and on the other hand, it reveals, more clearly than was generally possible in relation to his pre-2–3–74 work, how his written science fiction forms just one (albeit crucial and diversified) element within the broad range of forms taken by his fabulating activity.

Over the previous chapters we have encountered a variety of different challenges faced by Dick's immanent soteriology, which can generally be summarized in the form of pairs of seemingly contradictory imperatives. At root these are always tied to the basic situation which simultaneously generates the need for and idea of salvation – the situation in which there is no way out, and from which one *must* find a way out: I cannot avoid death, yet *I must not die*; I cannot save my friend, yet I cannot not save my friend. It is the archetypal situation of Gilgamesh (though the ancient Mesopotamians probably had their own much older archetypes).[1] Fabulation is the means by which humans have always coped with this situation, yet in the era of mechanization, in which humanity's own mechanizing tendencies become ever more explicit, many formerly effective such strategies are revealed as defunct. The contradictory imperatives producing the need for salvation are modified and take on a variety of new forms, which the immanent soteriologist attempts to address, and which shape the fabulations they produce in the process. As Dick's fabulations become more overtly and self-consciously soteriological following 2–3–74, these contradictory pairs of imperatives simultaneously constrain and inspire the fabulative evolution of Valis.

One of these pairs consists in the requirement that a given image, path, figure or logic of salvation be fabulated – invented – by the one in need of salvation, coupled with the condition that the saviour, or the saving effect, must be experienced as coming from 'outside'. If the one in need of salvation were fully conscious of their capacity to save themselves, either the need to be saved would disappear, or the fabulated means of salvation would risk losing its power. This contradictory imperative is a direct corollary of the no-way-out scenario in which a desperate soul refuses to accept a lack of viable options. One of the best-known literary depictions of this scenario is arguably the opening of *The Divine Comedy* – in which Dante (simultaneously character, narrator and author, just like Dick in *VALIS*), lost in a dark wood, is threatened by ferocious beasts on all sides, without hope of escape: into this scenario enters the poet-saviour, who points the way through a monumental fabulated construction. In a sense, this is what happens to Dick in 1974, as he emerges from a state of great despair with a fabulated, but powerful saviour-figure – though with an arduous journey through hell, purgatory and heaven still ahead of him. Dick himself likened Dante's 'description of the ascent of the soul' to his own post-2-3-74 experiences (E: 540; E: 541).

Implicit within these constraints is the further condition that Dick must not only fabulate a saviour-figure (or several), he must also, in some sense, erase his own awareness of having done so. While fabulating, and indeed while increasingly recognizing the valuable effects of fabulating, he must continually 'forget' (in a special sense) the act or process of fabulation. This less overt counterpart to the high valuation Dick consciously places on anamnesia throughout the *Exegesis*, a form of (self-)forgetting that 'forgets' itself, a process that eradicates its own traces, is perhaps not as difficult to achieve as it may at first sound. In Bergson's exemplary scene of modern fabulation from the field of psychological research – the woman who saved herself from falling into an open lift shaft – both these conditions were already fulfilled: she imagined a figure pulling her back from the fall that would have killed her, and responded to this figure by allowing herself to be flung backwards to safety. In discussing this example, as when accounting for the functioning of fabulation in general, Bergson posits that the fabulation is produced and elicits a response more quickly than the intellect is able to fully process it. Thus, in a sense, from the perspective of conscious reflection (to the extent that this corresponds to the operations of intellect), the saving figure, or whatever it is that is fabulated, really does come from outside: Bergson's dualisms operate in the gap opened up by a Cartesian self astounded by events that a Spinozan framework of immanent substance (manifesting in different modes) renders fully plausible.

Another such imperative whose functioning we have considered in some of Dick's pre-2-3-74 novels is that any personified or apostrophized figure of salvation must not be all-powerful: like the Glimmung in *Galactic Pot-Healer* (2005a [1969]), or Wilbur Mercer in *Do Androids Dream of Electric Sheep?*

(1993a [1968]), any Dickian saviour appearing to possess transcendent powers must have them severely impeded. Indeed, their capacity to save – even, in fact, or especially, to save themselves – should be radically questioned as part of this process. While an immanent saviour should be able to supervene obstacles that could not be overcome by an ordinary human being according to his or her own self-conception, such a figure must also not be portrayed as beyond all threat of destruction or failure themselves.

All of these problematics are subsumed within the fundamental issue of an immanent soteriology: the question of how to save oneself. How does one fabulate a saviour adequate to one's needs, create a saviour out of oneself, without allowing the knowledge or awareness of this process to undermine its effectiveness? Though this may seem like a question of the salvation of the individual, the logic of fabulation, as Bergson suggests, applies to any 'self' – an individual, a society, a species (perhaps even a god). In fact, the fundamental thrust of the dynamic activity of fabulation (as opposed to the way its products are subsequently intellectualized and allowed to ossify) is to refuse or negate the closing of such categories, both hierarchically and laterally: that is, to prevent the individual from conceiving itself as closed off from the society or species, and from other individuals; likewise to prevent the society and species from closing themselves off from other societies as well as other species. Indeed, across the *Exegesis* in general, it is possible to trace the emergence of something like a Simondonian perspective, in which forms and modes of individuation lead to the emergence and dissipation of various apparent entities and identities, individuals and transindividuals as 'relative realities' (Simondon 1989). Dick (like Bergson) continually finds both ethical and soteriological potential in the activity of undermining the limits and impermanence of entities, reality fields and moral frames otherwise taken to be objective and eternal.

Salvator salvandus

Much of the immanent soteriology of *VALIS* is deployed through a series of creative forms of self-splitting, which offer a variety of creative strategies for negotiating these contradictory imperatives. Dick finds a particularly valuable conceptual resource in this regard in the gnostic idea of the *salvator salvandus*, the saviour saved (or needing salvation) as elaborated by Hans Jonas:

> The fact that in the discharge of his task the eternal messenger must himself assume the lot of incarnation and cosmic exile, and the further fact that, at least

in the Iranian variety of the myth, he is in a sense identical with those he calls – the once lost parts of the divine self – give rise to the moving idea of the 'saved saviour' (*salvator salvandus*). (Jonas, quoted in *VALIS*, 131)

The identity this term expresses between the saviour (*salvator*) and those to-be-saved (*salvandus*) can be seen as encompassing two trajectories, both of which would be important to the possibility of immanent salvation: the saviour is posited as being in need of salvation; and conversely, the one hitherto needing salvation is placed in the role of potential saviour. The notion of the saviour becoming endangered, and of those endangered becoming saviour(s), constitute two different stories or narratives that we have already explored in Dick's novels. Yet the term *salvator salvandus* collapses the two into the saviour/saved couple – the difference in the stories being temporarily neutralized, or held, as it were, in a state of suspended animation, in half-life, by the substitution of grammatical logic for actual chronological development.

This rendering a-temporal of what is by necessity chronological is crucial. The concept of *salvator salvandus*, if it is a concept, describes the necessary conditions for self-salvation – whether this takes the form of action exerted directly upon the individual by that same individual, or the dispersed, chain-like form we observed in *The Man in the High Castle* (1965 [1962]), whereby the possibility of the individual's salvation is ultimately contingent upon that individual's salvation of another, who becomes a saviour in turn, and so on. In either case, the relationship between creator and creation (connoting simultaneously the relationships between subject and object, divine and human, living and non-living) is replaced by a relationship between creator and creator, or a dynamic, de-personalized notion of creativity. This involves an irreducible narrative component, a change of status that must take place over time. Though the saving action is enacted by an individual upon him or herself, a virtual third party is constructed or posited (fabulated) by default if not by active conception, as what comes from within is experienced as coming from without. (Indeed, this necessary placeholder between self as subject and self as object may be the most minimal form of God – convergent with the germinal form of technology – as a basic operation of (self-)differentiation.) This component is what stops a notion of self-salvation from collapsing back into a notion of self-preservation, which can (and archetypally does) take place in an instant. *Salvator salvandus* may thus stand as a figure for the key operation of open or dynamic fabulation, whereby two times, two states or two modes of existence are conflated without being mixed, for the purposes of determining a remnant of actual salvific potential that survives both the immanentization of the transcendent and the transcendentalizing of the immanent.

The *salvator salvandus* theme appears and is problematized on the first page of *VALIS*. Horselover Fat, the central character, receives a phone-call from his friend Gloria. She asks him for some sleeping pills to help her commit suicide. Fat wants to help, indeed, to save her. But what would this entail? If he tells her the truth – that he has no pills – she will hang up and seek them elsewhere, putting herself beyond his reach; if he gets hold of some pills for her, she will use them to kill herself. Thus he decides to do neither: instead, he pretends to have ten, and invites Gloria over to collect them. In other words, he fabulates, rejecting a seemingly totalizing binary by inventing a hitherto unseen third path. Fat provides Gloria with a representation which will convince her to do that which is most likely, at least as he sees it, to keep the possibility of her salvation (her survival of a time of crisis) open.

According to both his psychiatrist and the narrator, Fat's desire to save others constitutes his own pathology. He needs to stop trying to save other people in order to save himself. His awareness of this has no effect on his instinctive and intellectual urge to save Gloria – thus he will not, of his own volition, do what is necessary to save himself. His salvation depends on his undertaking it without intellectually or consciously deciding to do so. Bergsonian fabulation has precisely this function – and the very personage of Horselover Fat, as we learn in the first few pages of the novel, is already a fabulation for just this purpose, being a projection of the narrator Phil Dick.[2] This fabulation is, however, one that has been constructed long before the beginning of the narration (or, one might say, the process of narration, itself already a form of self-splitting, begins long before the novel) – even if the narrator tells us, 'I am Horselover Fat, and I am writing this in the third person to gain some much needed objectivity' (11). The friends of the main character(s) generally treat Fat (at least according to the narrator's reports) as a separate person, accepting the character Phil Dick's alter ego as one of them – except during the period near the end of the novel where Phil Dick becomes a single personality again. This is one among several ways *VALIS* rehearses in a less science-fictional setting the mutual contamination of private and shared fantasies or imaginary worlds that had characterized many of Dick's earlier novels, such as *Eye in the Sky* (2003a [1957]), *The Three Stigmata of Palmer Eldritch* (2003b [1964]), and *Ubik* (2000c [1969]).

Whatever role the fabulation of Horselover Fat is playing for the narrator, the novel itself, including the characters of both Horselover Fat and the narrator Phil Dick, taken together can be understood to be playing a similar role for Philip K. Dick the man. When we read the words 'I am Horselover Fat' there is no way of determining whether it is the narrator (as imagined by Dick) who is writing, or Dick the author. A contiguous chain is thus highlighted between the narrator Phil Dick's fabulation of himself as other than himself, in order, potentially, to save himself (from himself) – and the fabulation of Phil the narrator by the author Philip K. Dick the 'real person' (a category that increasingly loses any stability of meaning).

An attempt to map the structural relations between these figures diagrammatically might result in a series of concentric rings which are simultaneously recursively linked, each contained ring also constituting a reference to or rehearsal of that which encloses it. These multiply infolding layers should be taken as amounting, deliberately or not, to a dynamic or organically evolved metafiction of the kind we found in *The Man in the High Castle* (1965 [1962]), once again emerging from the necessary constraints of an immanent soteriology (e.g. the constraint that the fabulator must obscure the full working of his own fabulations from himself) rather than from a premeditated engagement with literary convention of the type more frequently cited in literary-critical discussions of metafiction. We should note that both madness and speculative fiction perform the same fabulative role here, in making the subject appear other than itself. The separation of Horselover Fat and Phil Dick (character) is both an element of psychological breakdown in the life of the character, and a literary device employed by the novel; but these two statements are effectively reversible, such that the character could be said to be employing a literary device while the novel goes through a psychological breakdown.

In Chapter 2 we learn of Fat's first experience of something like salvation. In the depicted scenario there are two saviours, one immanent and one transcendent – the difference elided by their being rolled together into a single, de-punctuated sentence: 'The first thing that came along to save him took the form of an eighteen-year-old highschool girl living down the street from him and the second was God' (18). The girl, Stephanie, who is also his dope dealer, leads Fat to God by creating and giving him a pot in which, the narrator claims, God slumbered. The actual encounter with God comes in the form of a beam of pink light, which blinds him for several days, but leaves him with a wealth of information he had not previously possessed. Yet it is Stephanie who is credited with being the main agent of this 2–3–74-like event, in shaping and firing the pot, while what God did, we are told, was 'barely enough and virtually too late' (19). The novel thus performs an immanentization of the supposedly transcendent saving power of Valis, both within the plot and, implicitly, in terms of Dick's own experience of the beam of pink light, which he initially discusses in the *Exegesis* with little of the circumspection and irony exhibited by the novel's narrator. This immanentizing effect, which as in his other novels reduces the figure of salvation to a bare but ineradicable minimum, in this case takes place very rapidly, first through the narrator's sceptical discussions of Fat's theories and his 'exegesis', followed by an account of Fat's own research into possible scientific explanations of the experience; the undercutting effect we observed in *Galactic Pot-Healer* recurs here with, for example, Fat's discovery that the particular colour pink he experiences – which it is originally claimed can be generated by God alone (20) – turns out to be the same as the colour of a home-made laser beam he finds some teenagers playing with at the end of his street (21).

The main effect of the beam of pink light is to provide Fat with new knowledge, some of which immediately has literally saving effects. Thus his experience is *gnostic* in at least a broad and etymological sense, bringing (saving) knowledge, as shown by the dia-gnosis of a life-threatening birth defect in his five-year-old son – an event also apparently drawn directly from Dick's life.[3] The fact that one of the first concrete outcomes of Fat's/Dick's encounter with God takes the form of a diagnosis is also significant in that the salvation which comes about through this knowledge is of the most fundamental kind – salvation from mortal illness, the saving of a life.

One of the ways Dick confers a new significance on the *salvator salvandus* theme is by tying it to another idea with gnostic overtones – his theory that the universe is composed of information, which we humans have forgotten to read/hear/understand.[4] This lost access to the universe-as-information implies a loss of something like a primordial interconnectedness, an immanent, pre-social state in which everything is directly interrelated. Our inability to access the information of which the universe is composed, Dick/Fat suggests, renders us 'idiots', in the Heraclitean (and etymological) sense which, as we have seen, was the basis of Dick's distinction between the *idios kosmos* and the *koinos kosmos*: 'idiot' in this sense means 'private', isolated from the rest of the world: 'Each of us has become private, and no longer shares the common thought of the Brain, except at a subliminal level. Thus our real life and purpose are conducted below our threshold of consciousness' (23).

This 'real life and purpose' appears to correspond neither to Durkheim's collective consciousness nor to the Jungian collective unconscious – being neither the result of social/collective living, nor of specifically human experiences, but of having access, as individuals, to the same meaning, being part of a common underlying reality that precedes sociality. It is closer to the continuity between, in Bergson's understanding, the creative tendency in evolution and the joy or openness of true mysticism, which makes the latter an experience of (self-transcending) immanence. The pink beam of light reconnects Dick/Fat with this commonality, whose prior loss Bergson identifies with the fullness of our past as it extends back not just to our individual births, but through history, species, life, ultimately to the bare materiality of the universe itself – a notion Gunter (1999) terms the 'biological unconscious'.[5]

In discussing the incompleteness of the Bergsonian soteriology near the beginning of this book, I suggested that a problem with true mysticism as an adequate route to salvation is that such a connection is almost by definition incompatible with the demands of everyday life – the practical conditions of survival and social interaction that were putatively responsible for its loss in the first place. Dick in his later years, and Fat in *VALIS*, can be seen as constantly grappling with this problem: how to unify the mystical gnosis, which re-activates a deep sense of one's commonality with all life but is paradoxically a quintessentially private, incommunicable experience, with the exigencies of everyday life, which is socialized at every point but pathologically, mortally lacking in the more absolutely, underlying commonality towards which the experience of the true mystic points? In fabulating a situation in which two apparently separate people (Dick and Fat) are, in another sense, the same being, Dick is able to stage the rediscovery of an underlying connectedness that had been lost according to the gnostic (but also the Bergsonian) mythos. As he puts it in a late *Exegesis* entry: 'And this messenger, this salvator salvandus, is of course who and what I saw and experienced as Valis. It is both my own unfallen self, and it is the gnostic Christ' (E: 886).

The believer and the sceptic

The complexity that emerges through all this multiplied self-splitting (along with the new possible modes of reconnection it enables) is encapsulated – and momentarily flattened – in the narrator's ironic response to Fat's idea that we have become separated into private, 'idiot' worlds: 'Speak for yourself, Fat' (23). An imagined narrator who is also the author suggests that his own alter ego is insane or foolish to believe that two people, such as the two of them, might have an underlying unity; the choice of words, 'speak for yourself', reinforces the split between them while reminding us that the speaker is in effect addressing himself, simultaneously supporting and contradicting his own theory. The primary function of this self-splitting is to allow the two opposing perspectives on Valis, and salvation in general, to interact and find ways to combine, without either undermining themselves or cancelling one another out.

Thus the immanent and transcendental requirements which Dick's immanent soteriology places on Valis are reflected in his division of himself into two personalities with divergent perspectives tending towards the credulous and the sceptical respectively. Whereas Horselover Fat is inclined towards transcendent interpretations of his 2–3–74 experiences, the narrator Phil Dick leans towards more scientific and rational explanations. Eventually the apparent mutual exclusivity of these two perspectives gives way to mutual dependence: full acceptance of a transcendent explanation makes its content a part of reality, therefore immanent; conversely, if Fat only *thinks* he is in touch with God, the question of the cause of his hallucination remains mysterious, touching on the other-worldly simply in its abnormality (24).

This dramatization enables Dick to explore critically his own doubts about the 2–3–74 experiences, without giving up on a figure of salvation that he desperately needs to be real. This mirrors (or presents in microcosm) a mode of operation found throughout the *Exegesis*, where, in speculating about the 2–3–74 experiences, Dick frequently proceeds by positing a premise, statement or thesis before subjecting it to a series of challenges, and/or deriving from it further statements, as if by deductive reason. We might refer to this as a process of 'fabulous deduction', in that the data or observations through which it functions are primarily 'facts' emerging from Dick's own fabulated experiences. It is often driven forward by a criticism or expression of doubt regarding some aspect of his own interpretations of the 2–3–74 experiences – sometimes even through the adopted voice of a sceptical challenger or co-investigator – but nearly always seems ultimately to entail equal measures of new speculation or theoretical invention. This is epitomized by a dialogue in Folder 44 (probably from 1979) in which Dick's adopted critical voice attempts to give worldly explanations for each aspect of the 2–3–74 experiences (E: 518–20). A large part of the exchange centres on the diagnosis of his psychological condition – on the implied basis that an explanation of Valis as non-transcendent must account for how the experiences were produced. In the course of the debate, as more and more diagnoses (psychodynamic, pharmacological, pscychiatric) fail to account for all the symptoms, or negate one another, the sceptic-voice gradually begins to question its own position, saying 'It does not compute', and the two become partially aligned. Interestingly, they do not then turn to the certainty of a transcendent explanation, but are only able to recognize the insufficiency of their investigation and the necessity of another: 'This is where the inquiry has led. The ego could not face or solve the crisis problem because of its severity, fled, and in its place another self solved the problem successfully. This leads us to a new frontier which is not mapped' (E: 520). This conclusion is ambiguous, in that it leaves absolutely uncertain the question of whether some other entity entered to take over and help Dick face his 'crisis problem', or whether he fabulated this entity, in the manner in which, according to Bergson, humans have been doing for as long as they have been facing crises.

Such a process can be seen to take place in *VALIS*, as the narrator, who seems continually ready to highlight elements of Fat's unhinged mental state, opines that Fat only 'imagined God had cured him', yet nevertheless comes to accept that 'in all fairness I have to admit that God – or someone calling himself God, a distinction of mere semantics – had fired precious information at Horselover Fat's head by which their son Christopher's life had been saved' (25). The sceptic or doubting perspective immanentizes the transcendental elements of the saviour, yet by the same token allows them to be reconceived and restated on stronger terms following an apparently critical examination. Neither side can ever achieve a total domination of the other, as this would entail the abandoning of either critical reason or openness to the possibility of salvation. This back-and-forth movement is not only a general pattern underpinning Dick's thinking about Valis: as he becomes aware of it, he increasingly identifies this movement of endless self-negation with Valis itself: 'In my case the dialectic shows up by a constant thought (mental) statement generating its negation, which then generates *its* negation ad infinitum. [...] This is not a result of the dialectic (Valis); it *is* Valis; therefore I am Valis' (E: 468).

In the novel, the unstable polarization of Dick and Fat towards positions of rational scepticism (immanence) and mystical faith (transcendence) is further reflected in their friends David and Kevin, with whom they will later form a secret group (or *ekklesia*) called the Rhipidon Society. The group's rambling theological arguments often pursue ideas to absurd extremes in a way that echoes the rambling dialogues of the Substance D addicts in *A Scanner Darkly* (1991c [1977]), a connection the narrator makes explicit: 'By now the epoch of drug-taking had ended, and everyone had begun casting about for a new obsession. For us the new obsession, thanks to Fat, was theology' (29). Fat's qualified credulity with regard to Valis is shadowed by David, the devout Catholic, who attributes all suffering to man's free will and cites C. S. Lewis to back up his arguments. Kevin, who uses the fact that his cat was run over as evidence that the essence of the universe is 'misery and hostility', functions symmetrically as an extreme version of the scepticism of the narrator (and the character Phil Dick). As Warrick writes, the four characters 'are best understood as a dramatization of the inner state of a single mind' (1987: 171) – though this psychological interpretation is again reversible, and can be understood as another way in which Dick repeatedly presents actual individuals as already being 'stations in a single mind' (110).[6]

Another, perhaps less likely parallel may be identified here between the first half of *VALIS* and David Hume's *Dialogues Concerning Natural Religion* (2007 [1779]), which also involves three or four figures debating the existence and nature of God (three if we count only the philosophers Philo, Cleanthes and Demea, four if we include the narrator Pamphilus, who was present and gives us his opinions on whose arguments were strongest). While this text has often been taken as an implicit critical rejection of religious belief by a philosopher renowned for his thorough scepticism, it gives the reader no definitive reason to align one or other viewpoint with that of its author. Contrary to the general perception of his contemporaries, there is today considerable uncertainty over whether Hume was an atheist, with some scholars ascribing to him a theist position that is 'not inconsistent with his empiricist methodology and naturalistic worldview' (Andre 1993: 164). An early twentieth-century investigation of this possibility was made by Charles Hendel, who saw Hume's 'confessed' theism as being *justified by* (rather than contrasting against) his naturalistic view of human life and knowledge. In this light, we can speculate that Hume wrote the *Dialogues*, just as Dick wrote *VALIS*, in order to explore his questions and uncertainties regarding religion: 'He had convictions and he had his doubts. His writing of them took the form of personal conversation' (Hendel 1925: 2). We have already encountered Dick's unconventional relationship to causality, which amounts not just to the Humean problem of its logical justification, but to a professed inability to perceive or grasp causal relations. In a sense, Dick begins with the view of acausal reality that Quentin Meillassoux (2008: 82–111 and *passim*) arrives at through a speculative response to Hume, in which the impossibility of proving the necessity of natural laws becomes simply a reflection of their non-necessity (rather than of the limits of human understanding). Dick effectively remains on the side of Hume in accepting that the lack of logical (or, in Dick's case, perceived) necessity does not preclude the possibility of there being a natural necessity for causality. However, whereas Hume holds on to a putative natural causality that would correspond more or less to the mind's expectations, Dick takes a step towards a speculative materialism in endlessly seeking out, or inventing and giving equal credence to, alternative, non-linear forms of causality that might account for the world's strange appearance (to him) at any particular moment. In this sense, Hendel's description of Hume's *Dialogues* as a set of discussions comprising an 'implicit testimony to a natural religion in the very search for its meaning' (1925: 308) might equally be applied to *VALIS*, and perhaps even more so, the *Exegesis*; for the latter, it could be argued, constructs the very forms of divinity, salvation and religion it is looking for, even in the process of searching for them – though without ever coming to rest on a single version.

Just as neither Dick's nor Fat's position can fully subsume that of the other, neither David's view of Fat's God as a transcendent saviour, nor Kevin's view that he is entirely a product of Fat's insanity, is entirely sustainable. While Kevin repeatedly highlights the inconsistency of a God who saves and condemns abitrarily – 'so God saved your son's life; why didn't he have my cat run out into the street five seconds later?' (26) – his own position is equally fraught with contradiction. Kevin is so passionately anti-God that he cannot help positing the existence of a deity figure in order to blame it for being 'evil, dumb and weak' (27), even as he wants to argue against this figure's existence. As he writes everything the group discusses down in his journal as potentially useful investigative (exegetical) material, it is as though Dick/Fat's polarized self-division is maintained by the gravitational pull of the two extremes represented by David and Kevin. It would be tempting to suspect, with Michael Feehan (1995), that the origin of Dick's interest in split subjects, doubling or reduplication, derives from an obsession with his lost twin sister Jane, who died when he was only a few months old (such is in fact the eventual conclusion of Dick's staged dialogue with himself in Folder 44 of the *Exegesis*, cited above). Certainly, a sense of a lost 'other half' seems to have played a significant role in his psychological and emotional difficulties throughout his life, and shows up repeatedly in his novels – perhaps most strikingly in the character of Edie Keller in *Dr Bloodmoney* (2000a [1965]), who carries her half-dead twin brother within her body and maintains telepathic (or rather *plesio*pathic) contact with him. Dick frequently embeds his instances of twinning within religious or mythic scenarios, as with the twin Zoroastrian gods Ahriman and Ormazd who start out as a young boy and girl in Dick's early novel *The Cosmic Puppets* (2006 [1957]), the twin male and female halves of the Godhead that have become separated in *The Divine Invasion* (1996 [1981]), the Glimmung and his female counterpart, recovered at the end of *Galactic Pot-Healer*, and the twin hyperuniverses I and II in the Two Source Cosmogony at the end of *VALIS*. Hence in reference to an entry in the *Exegesis* describing the experience of World as the attempt at recollection of a lost, dead twin, the narrator states: 'If, in reading this, you cannot see that Fat is writing about himself, then you understand nothing' (37).

Pointing to a psychological basis or source for a recurrent trait in someone's character or thought does not exhaust or even explain the significance of that trait. The experience of the loss of his twin, or more likely, the experience of speculating throughout his life on the possible effects of this loss, becomes the material out of which an array of fabulations and fabulative strategies develop. Whatever the reasons for the entry of twinning or reduplication as a motif into his work, Dick finds in it a transformative and soteriological potential that through fiction far exceeds the reach of psychological or psychoanalytic explanations of its origin, leading him to employ it as part of a wide-ranging, continually redoubling fabulative strategy.

The pharmakonic god

The association of God with drugs, prefigured in *Palmer Eldritch*, is one of the recurring themes of both the *Exegesis* and *VALIS*. The connection lies partly in their shared status as causes and objects of addiction; but it is also in the way God becomes pharmakonic, in Derrida's sense, as simultaneously holding the potential to function as both poison and cure: 'there is no such thing as a harmless remedy. The *pharmakon* can never be simply beneficial' (Derrida, 1981: 99). By the same token, neither can we ever be sure the effects of a supposed poison are entirely negative. Even Palmer Eldritch, effectively an 'anti-saviour' who uses drugs to entrap users in a kind of purgatorial virtual state, is perceived by one of his 'victims' as possessing 'a vast, reliable wisdom' derived from the accumulated experience of having lived many lives (2003b: 212).

For the narrator of *VALIS*, drugs are – or were, in what he calls 'the dope decade' – both the solution to and the cause of life's problems, sometimes literally, sometimes metaphorically. The memorial list of the 'people who were punished entirely too much for what they did' at the end of *A Scanner Darkly* (1991c: 276–8) testifies to Dick's experience of the destructive effects of drugs. Yet as that novel suggested, through the figure of another split character who was both narcotics agent and the drug dealer he was investigating, and as the narrator of *VALIS* explains, those trying to police the drugs, the 'authorities', were at least as deranged as the drug-takers: 'This time in America […] was totally fucked. […] The authorities became as psychotic as those they hunted' (11). The narrator gives an example in which those authorities created mayhem with the local infrastructure – disrupting the very order they exist to preserve – in order to 'baffle radicals who might intend trouble. The elevators got unwired; doors got relabeled with spurious information; the district attorney hid' (12).

In a strange parallel to the police investigator who must behave psychotically, there is a strong suggestion in *VALIS* that, in order to have any chance of being useful in terms of something like salvation, God, must become in some sense the problem. This can be viewed as another means of enabling a process of immanentization. Hence God becomes the source of Fat's mental illness, as drugs supposedly had been previously – even as ultimately there is hope that God may be the cure. What is required to prevent God from failing in effectively the same way as the Californian policing authorities or Bob Arctor is that the saviour become the one in need of salvation without wholly losing his/her transcendent qualities: this would enable compatibility/interaction between *salvator* and *salvandus* (saviour and to-be-saved), while maintaining the potential salvific value of such interaction; simultaneously, it makes it possible for the ones-to-be-saved to identify with the saviour-figure who seems immanent within their reality, yet with residual intimations of transcendence, pointing to the potential for self-transformation.

The flawed or ambiguous nature of the 'God' that Fat encounters is emphasized in its failure to prevent his attempt to kill himself:

> Either he had seen God too soon or he had seen him too late. In any case, it had done him no good at all in terms of survival. Encountering the living God had not helped to equip him for the tasks of ordinary endurance, which ordinary men, not so favored, handle. (46)

The question of why God allows (or fails to prevent) suffering, versions of which have been central to numerous theological enquiries and atheist critiques of religion, challenges the believer and/or theologian to find an alternative to the seemingly exhaustive choice between his being either fallible, (tolerant of) evil, or non-existent. If the value of God is to be preserved for soteriology, fabulation must develop reasons for maintaining faith in the face of such charges as Kevin's 'how does God account for my dead cat?' This may be one reason so much of the teaching and study of religion draws on stories: the problem of evil, or suffering, never goes away, and must be repeatedly addressed in new and inventive ways. It may also hint at why various modern philosophers' responses to the problem continue to employ fabulative elements. Leibniz, for example, like Dick, finds it necessary to imagine other possible worlds in order to account for the problem of evil and suffering. For Pascal, the potential benefits of belief in God outweigh the potential losses should such belief later turn out to be misplaced, while comparatively little is to be gained from taking an atheist position (1966: 150–1). Kant, by a different argument, similarly suggests that practical morality requires that we 'postulate the *existence of God*' (1997 [1788]: 104) while accepting that, purely from the perspective of theoretical reason, this 'presupposition of a supreme intelligence' will remain a '*hypothesis*' (1997: 105). These and similar arguments end up rationally advocating fabulation: both Pascal and Kant are effectively suggesting that we should act *as if* that which has no obvious or intellectually measureable manifestation in reality (God) were fully real. Yet what Dick's immanentizing of God draws our attention to is the possibility that, more than just being the effect of a compromise between traditional religious belief and modern rationalism, the becoming-immanent of God, whether a process dramatized through myth or science fiction, or an effect produced through critical argument and scepticism, may always-already constitute the means by which the potential for salvation arises from the divine.

For this reason, Dick cannot allow himself to imagine or conceive the saviour-figure he and Fat encounter as absolutely real, or absolutely 'here', any more than he can accept its disappearance. A punctual, ever-present God, however well fabulated, ought to result in Fat's absolute salvation, and finding himself in a less-than-blissful state after the encounter would undermine the fabulation. Indeed, it seems likely from all that we know of Dick's life that nothing short of the impossible restoration of his lost twin Jane – coupled with something approaching an end to human suffering in general – would suffice to allow him to consider himself absolutely saved. On the other hand, giving up on Valis entirely would mean accepting himself and the world as being beyond salvation. These exigencies can be understood as already determining the nature of Valis, both as it was fabulated by Dick for himself in the mode of immediate experience, and as it was allowed to grow through the pages of the *Exegesis* and *VALIS*. In writing the novel, Dick articulates – though only through the lens of a fictional narrative – this truth which he cannot conceal from himself and yet cannot allow himself to absolutely accept – that he has created, fabulated Valis to save himself:

> that which came to my rescue in 2-3-74, that supernatural entity Zebra, was me; and Thomas was me, and only when I *actually* understand (and experience this as real) will I really have the answer – but I have not yet reached that point. It is still impossible for me to grasp the AI voice as my own, true, secret voice. (E: 333)

In terms of the logic of fabulation then, it is *necessary* for God to arrive virtually too soon or too late – as the narrator puts it, God did not arrive at the eleventh hour, but 'waited until three minutes before twelve'. This may be how fabulation always works – by finding a moment in between the last moment and the end – which is to say, in the interval between the last moment the intellect is able to register and the event of destruction to be averted (or the moment at which such destruction becomes irreversible). The woman approaching the empty lift shaft in Bergson's example of the modern psychological working of fabulation felt she was seized and thrown back before she could think to verify the existence or not of the lift operator. Her saviour did not exist, but because she could not intellectually work this out before he affected her, she was still saved. Thus when Fat attests to 'the wisdom of my body, which knew not only to defend itself from my mind but specifically how to defend itself' (45) we may detect hints at the continuity between instinctive physical (re)actions (vomiting up the digitalis he has overdosed on, his heart's ability to overcome arrhythmia), and the fabulated encounters with God that have come to perform a wider range of saving functions in his life.

In these senses, an immanent saviour, perhaps any viable notion of salvation, must be pharmakonic. It must therefore be constantly attended to, reformed, re-imagined – subject to, if not identical with, a dynamic fabulating activity, rather than ossifying into a static, fabulated form. We have seen in a variety of ways through both Bergson and Dick how each of the fabulations that prevent society from being destroyed by the anti-social, mechanizing intellect can in turn become a mechanizing destructive force, requiring further singular acts of creativity to continually invent new modes of salvation: Perky Pat, already a fragile substitute for a lonely existence, is never far from turning into Palmer Eldritch.[7] Dick's fabulation of Valis as recounted and continued through the *Exegesis*, redoubled and reworked in the novel *VALIS*, illustrates with great intensity this ongoing struggle to maintain a dynamic mode of fabulation against the constant risk of reverting to mechanization and closure.

Reduplicative paramnesia (time becomes space)

We have seen how the two stories or trajectories encapsulated in the *salvator salvandus* figure can be understood as the key(s) to a possibility of immanent salvation through dynamic fabulation: the saviour becomes the one in need of salvation, moving from transcendent to immanent status, while those in need of salvation take up the position of potential saviour with regard to others or themselves. In every form, a self-splitting is involved, whereby the individual becomes both subject and object, different from him/her/

itself while still identifying with this other. An impossibility is made possible through fabulation. This scenario, in which two incompatible entities or realms (immanent and transcendent, saviour and to-be-saved, present crisis and future salvation) are able to co-exist or at least simultaneously appear, is formally and thematically comparable to the messianic time described by Agamben. As we have seen, in Agamben's Pauline-Benjaminian figure of 'the time of the end', the state of worldly crisis and transcendent state of salvation are superimposed, such that transformation of the present becomes a real – i.e. first conceivable, then potentially material – possibility. The significance of another of *VALIS*'s key motifs – expressed in the refrain, 'here time turns into space' (40) – may be understood in terms of this operation.

This line from Wagner's *Parsifal* is spoken by Gurnemanz to Parsifal, when the forest landscape in which they are standing fades out to be replaced by a wall of rock, and for a moment (at least as Dick envisaged it) the two distinct places are superimposed. Lévi-Strauss has referred to this moment in Wagner as 'probably the most profound definition that anyone has ever offered for myth' (1985: 219). What is normally possible only in a temporal sequence – a body occupying different places, different states, a person becoming someone quite different – fabulation makes possible in space: indeed, dramatic art, and arguably storytelling in general, fundamentally depend on it.

But the scene also mirrors Dick's own experience of existing simultaneously in two locales, ancient Rome and present-day California, which was a spur for the investigation of fabulation in Saint Paul earlier in this book. The phenomenon whereby an individual experiences another environment superimposed on the one they physically inhabit is actually a recognized neurological condition. It is referred to in neuropsychology as 'reduplicative paramnesia', a term coined by Arnold Pick (1903). In documented cases, the 'imaginary' spatial environment, belonging only to the individual's experience, which overlays the environment perceived by everyone else, is frequently one which the subject has previously experienced. The condition can thus be considered a psychological mechanism whereby what is literally possible only temporally (existing in two places) is transmuted by the use of something like fabulation into a spatial mode. Unsurprisingly, since this and other so-called misidentification syndromes are generally found to be the result of some form of brain injury, such conditions are treated as disorders or deficiencies. Yet in the light of the positive effects of fabulation, and of the effects of such experience on Dick, we may ask whether such 'delusions' may not be performing a valuable, positive role in terms of an individual's ability to endure an otherwise unacceptable reality. Dick himself suggested something along these lines in a 1964 essay, arguing that 'the sane man does not know that everything is possible' and that someone with a mental illness may simply be someone who 'at one time or another *knew too much*' (1995: 174). For Bergson, likewise, '[m]ental imbalance [...] is frequently [...] an excess of mental power rather than a deficiency: the usual restrictive role of the brain has been weakened to allow a greater degree of consciousness to flood the subject' (Mullarkey 1999: 101). This does not mean that the psychotic or otherwise mentally abnormal patient is automatically better off, but it does point to the great therapeutic and even socio-political potential in so-called delusional (or, equally, 'mystical') states, which Dick was arguably engaged in a constant struggle to optimize from his 2–3–74 experiences onwards.

Dick was well aware that this effect of reduplicative paramnesia had appeared in several of his novels (though for once he appears not to have come across the relevant *Encyclopedia Britannica* that would have allowed him to so name it):

> *Eye, Joint, 3 Stigmata, Ubik* and *Maze* are the same novel written over and over again. The characters are all out cold and lying around together on the floor mass hallucinating a world. Why have I written this up at least five times?
> Because – as I discovered in 3–74 when I experienced anamnesis, remembered I'm really an apostolic Christian, and saw ancient Rome – *this is our condition:* we're mass hallucinating this 1970s world. (E: 337)

In the narrative examples Dick refers to here, where one spatial environment was superimposed over another, the hallucinated world was a kind of trap, a maze dominated by an insane deity or malicious force – even if they were initiated out of some beneficial intent. Salvation lay in escaping or finding the way out of the hallucinated prison. After 2–3–74, however, when Dick addresses this scenario, the maze *itself* is reduplicated, transformed into something else, such that the notion of 'time becoming space', the basis for the hallucinatory prison, also becomes the means of its transformation. When the *Parsifal* phrase is first cited in *VALIS*, the narrator prefaces it by saying, 'there is no route out of the maze. The maze shifts as you move through it, because it is alive' (40). However, as he reflects on the notion, it is increasingly associated with Fat's mystical encounters with Valis – a figure who, he understands, in order to replace the maze with another reality, must first become it.

Here Dick appears to be blending together the Christian notion of transubstantiation and another central gnostic idea, whose modern significance had been explored by Hans Jonas in *The Gnostic Religion* (1958). According to this particular version of gnosticism, the universe as we experience it, the material world, is a sort of prison for humanity, created and ruled over by powers of a lower order than the true God. These lower powers, the Archons, and/or their leader, who 'is often painted with the distorted features of the Old Testament God' (Jonas 1958: 44), keep humans trapped in the maze, separated from the true divinity, with whom they were originally one. The true (alien) God who must find a way back into this world, bypassing the Archon guards, is central to the plot of *The Divine Invasion*, written directly following *VALIS*. Yet such a process, frequently discussed in the *Exegesis*, is already operative in *VALIS*, where Valis – sometimes referred to in such contexts as Zebra – is presented as first masquerading as part of the visible world, mimicking or camouflaging itself beneath apparent reality, before actually becoming that world, or rather, transforming it into him. The present material of the world is rendered, in a sense, dynamic, self-differentiating, *temporally intensive* at every point in its spatial extension: 'We are being processed along, and as we go we are changed and informed; there is no ontology for us, no concrete being – it is all, as Bergson saw, a becoming. We are, in a way, passing through a Cosmic Car-Wash' (E: 72).

The notion of time turning into space is associated first with the insane Mind, and then with the true God, within a few pages of *VALIS*. This idea and its signifying phrase remain fixed, while their significance or associative context is wholly altered, just as the landscape transforms itself around Parsifal and Gurnemanz while they stand still in what is simultaneously a pragmatic piece of stagecraft and a magical transformation. Athough the idea constitutes a particular trope figuring the structural requirements of a fabulation that would make immanent salvation possible, it is the way it is deployed that exemplifies this capability. We have seen this throughout Dick's work, as he depicts and explores a multiplicity of fabulative strategies, from Preston's writings about Flame Disc to Hawthorne Abendsen's *The Grasshopper Lies Heavy*, from Ragle Gumm's artificial 1950s idyll to the computer-generated worlds of *A Maze of Death*; not to mention the diabolical forms of fabulation deliberately targeting closure, such as the hallucinatory effects of Palmer Eldritch's Chew-Z, or the Book of the Kalends in *Galactic Pot-Healer*. In these and other cases, the novels themselves work to develop their own mode of fabulation as they test the examples they imagine, probing various models of fabulation for their potential and their inadequacies. Always at stake in this testing is the question of how successfully a given form or mode of fabulation is able to break down (or further divide) the immanence/transcendence division, whether this is manifest in the form of the separation between human and machine, present suffering and promised future redemption, worlds within and outside the diegetic boundary, or the saviour and the one in need of salvation. In every case, fabulations which had come to be understood as 'reality', that is, which had become most static, are rendered dynamic, transformative and open to transformation, once again.

Dick's concerns with the artificiality of apparent reality and the importance of its transformation are intrinsically proto-political, proto-ethical, proto-ecological – even when he is most focused on (and submerged within) his own psychological needs and his personal relationship with Valis. It is no surprise to find, for example, towards the end of the *Exegesis*, suggestions that the crisis which Valis, along with putative future saviour-figures (such as the one he refers to as 'Tagore') are required to address is that of ecological or environmental disaster arising from human mechanization. Humanity is destroying itself – and must therefore do something to save itself from itself. The process of its self-destruction takes place over time – the actions of a present 'self' are closing off its future existence, which amounts to destroying a future version of itself; therefore the present self can live under the illusion – which seems to be a rational observation – that it is not destroying itself, its destruction being deferred on to an as-yet non-existent future version of itself. In order for this self (which may be either an individual or humanity as a whole) to clearly perceive what is happening, time must be made into space – in the specific sense encapsulated by the *Parsifal* reference (but also in the manner of the messianic time of Paul, Benjamin, Agamben), whereby two radically segregated times are superimposed, the future upon the present. It is insufficient for this to take the form of a warning, or a prophecy, which (unless articulated by a particularly powerful storyteller) maintain the radical separation between present and distant future. The superposition can take place only through fabulation, through the bringing of the future or the past into the present, as the fantastical becomes reality: the eclipse must be experienced first as impossible, then possible, and finally as both at once. As Fat says of the early Christian whose thoughts he hears after 2-3-74, Thomas is not communicating across time to 1960s California, but 'living in ancient Rome *now*' (109). If the fabulation is successful, not only does self-destruction acquire the character of actuality for the present self, the crisis being recognized as reality, but the possibility of self-transformation – or self-salvation – also appears as a part of the emergent reality field.

Bergson's understanding of the mechanization of life as the crisis of modern humanity comes at the end of a lifetime's investigation of the relationships between ontology, psychology, biology and ethics, one whose roots, and continuity, can be traced back to his early analysis and critique of the human tendency to spatialize time. Having considered Dick through a Bergsonian lens, by using *VALIS* in turn to take a refractory glance back at Bergson, we glimpse the possibility of salvation from the modern crisis whose analysis is the culmination of his work, exactly where he began – where time becomes space.

The fabulative cure

The pharmakonic nature of Valis is reflected in the social mechanisms which exist to save Fat and others like him from psychological collapse. Following a failed suicide attempt, he is incarcerated in a psychiatric institution against his will – and billed for it, which will eventually add to his despair, since if he cannot pay he is in danger of being locked up again, as a criminal (50–1). In this self-perpetuating cycle, whereby the system reproduces that which it is intended to treat, 'the remedy is here but so is the malady' (72).

Fat is, however, offered a more effective saving strategy in this context, at the hands of his psychiatrist Dr Stone, who gets him to discuss the cosmological statements in his *Exegesis*, rather than treating these and his visions as symptoms of madness that must be exorcized. A particular statement Fat makes during these discussions is that time does not exist, an echo of the *Parsifal* refrain. Fat suggests that this is a hermetic secret that has been known to a privileged line of thinkers, including Apollonius, Saint Paul, Simon Magus, Paracelsus, Boehme and Giordano Bruno. Far from setting Dick (or Fat) at odds with a crucial facet of Bergsonian ontology, this can be read as an echo of Bergson's critical account of the habitual understanding of time, that is, of 'clock-time', the measured time of the intellect and of time-keeping mechanisms, which he sees as a spatialized representation of time rather than time itself. Deleuze (1991: 114) similarly observes that the non-existence of time for the Freudian unconscious does not mark an incompatibility with Bergson, but rather a potential affinity.[8]

In a more developed sense, it can be argued that time and space really do cease to have the status of separate categories in Bergson's ontology – the words being retained for the purposes of explanation, but effectively used as if under erasure. As Frédéric Worms puts it, matter and mind in Bergson ultimately turn out to be 'two degrees of the same activity: *tension* in time and *extension* in the extended, or in other words, duration in general' (1999: 90). Bergson replaces the dualism of time and space with something like the proposition: matter endures. Time would then be something like pure spirit, without substance, and space something like inert matter without motion or force. Neither can exist independently of the other, hence the materiality of spirit and the spirituality of matter. In this sense, Fat's experience is quite Bergsonian: 'space and time were revealed to Fat – and to Thomas! – as mere mechanisms of separation' (110).

Nevertheless, Fat seems to be getting at something more than an ontological statement when he tells his psychiatrist that time does not exist. This hermetic 'secret' also forms part of an elaborate fabulation.[9] In discussion with Stone, Fat quotes frequently from his *Exegesis*, explaining that he has been contacted by a being from another star system that is the Logos and which had slumbered at Nag Hammadi until its rediscovery; in the process, he mixes in references to Xenophanes, *yin* and *yang*, and the Dogon people of Sudan – whose mythological egg Deleuze and Guattari use to illustrate their 'body without organs' in *A Thousand Plateaus* (1988 [1980]). More telling than the contents, however, is the facility with which Fat adapts his interpretation in line with both questions and new information brought to his attention by Dr Stone. It is as though any experience or piece of information could form a new and relevant part of the puzzle he is simultaneously trying to construct and solve. Fabulated or gathered 'facts' form the basis for intellectual chains of reasoning, which evolve in a particular direction until they run into contradictions or dissatisfying conclusions. At such moments, new 'facts' are brought in to allow the chain of deductions to set off again in a new direction. The conversations between Fat and Dr Stone in *VALIS* thus echo Dick's conversations with himself regarding 2-3-74 in the *Exegesis*, following the same (il)logic of fabulous deduction. Their reproduction in a mental health framework simultaneously highlights Dick's awareness of how insane he must look to most outsiders, and his need to continue pursuing, developing his fabulations with the help of endlessly generated external figures and voices. As Pamela Jackson suggests, the *Exegesis* is 'a mishmash of external voices' (E: 63, note) – though these are held together, constantly and creatively re-arranged by Dick's relentless, dynamic fabulating, which continually brings out of them new theories and scenarios: Jackson also notes (E: 134) the extent to which Dick would physically rearrange the pages of the *Exegesis*. *VALIS* forms not only another means of extending this process, but also folds it in on itself by representing it and continuing it at the same time.

Dr Stone can be regarded as another one of Dick's endlessly multiplying (or self-splitting) invented voices, another fictionalized means of splitting from himself in order to observe himself as if from the outside. Yet within the diegesis of the novel, however unstable the boundaries of its reality field may be, Stone plays the role of saviour-figure, contrasting against the more authoritarian mode of psychiatric management which threatens to send Fat into a spiral of despair and whose 'therapeutic' methods supposedly drove his friend Sherri to suicide.

(The aggressive, destructive side of psychiatric 'care' is epitomized by the angry, impatient Maurice – a psychiatrist and former assassin – who is infuriated by Fat's schizo-theological ramblings.)

What makes Stone's treatment restorative is that he takes Fat's fabulations seriously, encouraging his theorizing and fuelling it with new material, rather than attempting to cure him of it: 'He adapted his therapy to the individual, not the individual to his therapy' (65). Stone even goes so far as to acquire for his patient a typescript of a recent translation of one of the Nag Hammadi texts (unpublished at the time the novel is set), privately from the translator.[10] This provides Fat with yet more material upon which to work his fabulous deduction, seeming to offer both external verification for certain aspects of the 2–3–74 experiences, and new information for its further interpretation. In developing this interpretation, Fat constructs what he needs in order to feel well again: 'Stone had saved him. [...] Whether the content of Stone's information was correct was not important; his purpose from the beginning had been to restore Fat's faith in himself' (65).

Stone's method reflects an understanding of the power of fabulation, as well as the pharmakonic nature of all fabulations, which requires that they be handled with delicacy. Accordingly, his approach is to help the conditions emerge in which Fat will develop the fabulations he needs to save himself. The therapy culminates in something like the magical-performative speech act Agamben associates with messianism or faith, and which would be one source of fabulation's saving power. The narrator expresses the belief that there is a series of words specific to each person that has the power to heal that person, and that Stone had found the words specific to Fat: 'In that simple sentence, "You're the authority," Stone had given Fat back his soul' (66). Stone, previously the holder of authority, associated with Fat's extended incarceration, has in fact set him free, and at the same time conferred authority upon him: Fat has become the authority over himself, thus free of authority – literally autonomous, in a Pauline fulfilling and ending of the Law.

With Dr Stone having temporarily taken on the mantle of saviour-figure, for a while he becomes the focus of the ongoing immanence/transcendence debate between Dick and Fat (or narrator and character). Fat attributes a 'paranormal' capacity to Stone's use of Bach herbal flower remedies and describes him as a god or a partial manifestation of God, while the narrator simply sees him as a very talented psychiatrist using the Bach remedies as 'a palpable hoax, a pre-text to listen to the patient' (65). In dealing with both Valis and Stone, the point on which Dick and Fat seem most in agreement is that the beneficial (as well as the detrimental) effects of experiencing the saviour at times render the distinction between immanence and transcendence practically insignificant. At such moments, the narrator's scepticism threatens to blend into Fat's credulity – for example, in their responses to the fact that the gnostic text selected by Dr Stone includes a reference to pottery. 'How', the narrator asks, 'had he known the significance of *pot* and *potter* to Fat?' (67). While not going quite as far as Fat, who sees this as further evidence that Stone 'was a micro-form of God' (67), the narrator avers that at least 'Stone would have to be telepathic' to know that Fat associated pots with divinity. Yet there are quite straightforward immanent explanations that neither raises – such as the possibility that Stone could have read one of Dick's novels (there are plenty of references in the novel to the fact that he is a science fiction writer), such as *Galactic Pot-Healer* (2005a [1969]) or *Flow My Tears, the Policeman Said* (2001 [1974]), both of which associate pottery with a divine power of salvation and healing.

Despite such convergences, the question of transcendent and immanent explanations is not permitted a resolution into an either/or. But nor is it, for that matter, in any simple sense a question of both/and. Rather, the possibility of its resolution must be held open, never achieved, yet never abandoned. Fat himself is held in such a state of suspension, having undergone (through his suicide attempt and subsequent recovery with Stone's help) a sort of resurrection that is not quite divine, but not completely without intimations of transcendence, even if these belong only to the experience of coming close to death: 'Fat had to die, or nearly die, in order to be cured. Or nearly cured' (66). The unresolvable nature of the question of divinity, the impossibility of either the immanent or the transcendent account of religious phenomena banishing the other, seems to be at the core of Horselover Fat's pathology. Yet central to the logic of the implicit soteriology of *VALIS* is that it constructs or reveals this apparently insurmountable obstacle as an essential strength. This is not in the mode of the theologian who makes the unknowability of God a necessary requirement for true faith. Rather, it is a response to the impossibility – and ultimate undesirability – of absolute (transcendent) salvation. In both the Christian logic of Judgement and the medical logic of crisis, the soul, the body, the subject, is held at the point of discernment (crisis-point) between two paths appearing as mutually exclusive and totalizing: salvation or damnation, recovery or death.[11] Where the perceived impossibility of salvation seems to herald an inevitable collapse into death, the Dickian open or dynamic fabulation finds or creates another possibility within this dichotomy, not simply carving out a space for a previously excluded middle, but introducing a 'division within the division'.

Between saved and damned, cured and mortally wounded, there is the division between the almost-cured and the almost-lost, which opens up the potential for saving and becoming-saved as processes rather than accomplished events or future-oriented fantasies.

Recursion: Valis as limitlessly iterative soteriology

In the more autobiographical first half of VALIS, which has been my primary focus here, Fat's fabulative attempts at self-salvation can be considered convergent with Dick's. In the second half, the fabulating shifts into a more speculative or science-fictional mode – though one which, especially towards the novel's close, continues to pursue soteriological ends. Importantly, this shift allows Dick to reconnect the fabulative approach to salvation developed thus far in a private psychological and bodily register with the other major challenge for an immanent soteriology – the problem of avoiding reversion to closure at the social and biological levels. It also illustrates a key, recurrent (and recursive) aspect of Dick's fabulation in general.

The reader may well have the growing feeling by the middle third of the novel that something has to give in all this theological-psychological speculation. The chain of fabulative deduction is straining: one or either of the two broad categories of explanation of Fat's experiences – that he is being contacted by a transcendent God, or that he is simply insane – needs a new order of confirmation. Just as the reader of the *Exegesis* may get the sense that Dick undertakes the writing of VALIS to give new impetus to his exegetic endeavour – draft early pages of the novel, as Jackson notes (E: 451, note), are included among the papers of the *Exegesis* as if part of it, yet this necessarily produces a dramatic shift in voice and tone – here the novelistic narrativization of the 2–3–74 experiences seems as though it may be about to stall in turn, as its characters find themselves going round in circles in their search for answers.

It seems that every time a particular fabulation of Valis threatens to run out of steam, Dick fabulates it again, in a new way which overcomes or escapes whatever insufficient element had become most visible. If, prior to 2–3–74, his science fiction offered the opportunity to repeatedly create new versions of the saviour and new modes of salvation, we might speculate that over time, the unavoidable *fictionality* of these saviour-figures rendered them increasingly inadequate for his soteriological needs, even as he became more dependent on his fabulating in his pursuit of personal salvation. The experiences of 2–3–74 might then be understood as fabulations of a new order, in which Dick was able to conceal his own productive role in the construction (or fictionalization) of the saviour-figure from himself – giving it a new air of reality. This pattern recurs, almost fractally, at every level of fabulation, as the *Exegesis* takes over from the waning memories of 2–3–74, the novel *VALIS* offers new creative impetus when he feels his exegetical activity beginning to lose steam, and within the narrative the pattern is replicated again as Fat and Dick, along with their friends, seemingly having exhausted the possibility of understanding Valis, draw new inspiration from a *film* called *Valis*.

The film contains many elements of Fat's mystical experiences – including the pink beam of light, the pot in which god slumbers, subliminal references to the early Christians – and tells a similar story to that which has been revealed to him, of a prison world dominated by illusion, and the struggle to break free through anamnesis.[12] Many elements in the film which connect with the contents of Fat's visions are discernible only by picking up subliminal messages, through symbolic imagery, 'flash-cut' frames, and the sub-conscious effects of its strange soundtrack, produced using innovative techniques referred to as 'Synchronicity Music' (147). It is only at this point that Fat adopts the name Valis for the 2–3–74 entity, although the reader has already been informed by the novel's epigram that it is an acronym standing for Vast Active Living Intelligence System.

Fat and his friends find in the film a confirmation that his visions have some basis in a reality beyond his own mind, since the filmmakers seem independently to have had similar experiences. It is Kevin, the cynic, who brings the film to the attention of David, Fat and Phil Dick. Until this point, Kevin's view had been that in 1974, following a protracted descent into misery and despair, 'Fat had begun a lurid schizophrenic episode to liven up his drab life' (153). Even this materialist/sceptical position recognizes the (limited) saving or at least therapeutic power of Fat's so-called madness, in staving off depression and a suicidal tendency: 'For Fat, total psychosis was a mercy' (153). Converted by the film, Kevin enthusiastically pursues further external verification of the existence of the superior being manifest in Fat's visions. In an extension of Stone's cure, the others begin to see Fat's apparent mental illness as the basis of authority: 'A total reversal had in fact taken place: instead of mollifying Fat we now had to turn to him for advice' (161). The group agrees to join Fat in a quest to find the true Saviour that, as emphasized by the discussion of Wagner's *Parsifal*, has overtones of the Grail legend – especially in that, as Fat establishes in conversation with Phil, the quest must succeed or they will both die (130).

What unites a devout Catholic, a cynical atheist, a suicidal junkie and his slightly more rational alter ego, is primarily the material evidence they believe they have acquired in the form of the matching information shared by the film and Fat's visions. Yet they also share a certain ethical outlook, the core of which is reflected in their decision to call themselves 'the Rhipidon Society'. The name is based on one of Fat's dreams, in which he was a large fish trying to hold an M-16 rifle; his fan-like fins (an anatomical feature designated by the Greek term *rhipidos*) made it impossible to hold the gun (171). In identifying themselves with this scene, and choosing as their motto 'Fish cannot carry guns', the group effectively enact an absolute refusal of what Bergson refers to as the war-instinct. That is, they position themselves not just as pacifist by choice, but fundamentally, biologically incapable of violence – in the manner of the open soul. Yet the group they are to encounter in their quest to find the saviour, those responsible for the film, despite their shared knowledge of Valis, will turn out to be a manifestation of virtually the opposite tendency. The parallel between the two thus provides us with one more opportunity to consider the dangerous ease with which open morality may revert to closure.

Befriending god

Once contact has been made, the stars of the film *Valis*, Eric and Linda Lampton, and its music producer Brent Mini, invite the Rhipidons to come and visit them in their country mansion. There are ominous signs from the moment they arrive, as the narrator associates the mansion, 'set in the middle of grape vines', with Dionysos, god of wine, madness and intoxication (179). There are further reasons for concern when the Lamptons identify themselves as the 'Friends of God' (*Gottesfreunde*), referring to a fourteenth-century German mystic society, but stating that their lineage goes much further back, to the race of Ikhnaton, 'the ugly builders with clawlike hands', to Hephaistos and the Kyklopes (175–6). The association with Hephaistos, god of technology and metallurgy, has connotations of mechanization and instrumentality, and perhaps the Black Iron Prison, while Kevin suggests that it identifies them as the killers of Asklepios: according to Pindar, Zeus killed Asklepios with a thunderbolt borrowed from the Kyklopes for attempting to raise the dead.[13]

At the mansion, Fat and his friends are introduced to Brent Mini and told that he has become terminally ill after suffering the equivalent of radiation exposure due to excessive contact with Valis. Unlike Fat, Mini begged Valis to resume contact following the initial experiences: 'It didn't want to; it knew the effect it would have on me if it returned. But it did what I asked. I'm not sorry. It was worth it to experience VALIS again' (185–6). Mini and the Lamptons are addicted to God. The ambiguity of the *pharmakon* in their case seems to have been resolved in favour of the negative, poisonous side, as the narrator suggests: 'Too much medication, I said to myself, remembering Paracelsus, is a poison. This man has been healed to death' (185). Thus whereas Fat was healed and educated by Valis, the Lamptons have willingly become possessed by God – and 'if your god takes you over, it is likely that no matter what name he goes by he is actually a form of the mad god Dionysos' (179). At one level, the encounter with Mini and the Lamptons can be read as an extended warning or parable about the dangers of such addiction. In forming an elite society, regarding themselves as privileged members of a chosen few Friends of God who are to welcome the Saviour, they have come to exhibit the defining characteristics of the closed society. Accordingly, when the Rhipidons decide to leave, the Lamptons attempt to convince them to stay using a logic of exclusion – of closure rather than openness:

> 'Look at it this way,' Eric had said, backed up by Mini who seemed genuinely crestfallen that the Rhipidon Society, small as it was, had decided to depart. 'This is the most important event in human history; you don't want to be left out, do you? And after all, VALIS picked you out. We get literally thousands of letters on the film, and only a few people here and there seem to have been contacted by VALIS, as you were. *We are a privileged group.*' (206, original italics)

It is precisely this kind of thinking, however, that has convinced the Rhipidons to leave in the first place. As the narrator observes of Mini: 'Your god has killed you and yet you're happy [...] *We have to get out of here. These people court death*' (185, original italics). The Rhipidon Society and the Friends of God do appear to have been contacted by the same entity, and to have developed soteriological frameworks with many overlapping elements. Yet they differ fundamentally and crucially in that the Rhipidons have adopted an open morality while the *Gottesfreunde* are attempting to restrict salvation to an elite group with themselves at the core, in the way every closed society extends its morality only to its own members. The difference between the soteriological speculations of the Rhipidons, as detailed in the first half of *VALIS*, and the perspective of the Lamptons is that the Rhipidons assume the precariousness of their own fabulations, questioning and interrogating them endlessly, whereas the Lamptons have developed a deep self-certainty regarding theirs: the former is a dynamic process of fabulation, the latter a collection of static results derived from a fabulating activity whose creative aspects have disappeared with their formation.

These differences are also reflected in the groups' responses to one another's perspectives. The Rhipidons are open to the Lamptons' cosmology, ready to accept and integrate with their own perspective the stories about the Kyklopes and their ancient role in the construction of the universe. In contrast, the Lamptons' approach to soteriology is corrective and exclusive, rejecting various elements of the Rhipidons' account of their understanding of salvation, smiling archly at their 'mistakes' and speaking constantly in riddles in order to maintain the illusion that they possess a deep 'secret knowledge' that the Rhipidons have yet to learn.

These differences between the two groups are encapsulated in Fat's final memory of Linda Lampton, who kisses him on the mouth 'with intensity and a certain amount, in fact a great amount, of erotic fervour', whispering in his ear that 'this is our future; it belongs to a very few, a very, very few' (206). The Lamptons' love is erotic love, the love of desire, based on feelings towards particular, like-minded individuals within the same closed group – a love which simultaneously constitutes the objectification – the mechanization – of both the desired and the desiring subject. It is in absolute contrast to the love of open morality, the Pauline *caritas* that is automatically extended unconditionally to all others, including those one has yet to encounter. The Lamptons do not seek an open future for all, but a limited, closed future, with survival restricted to 'a very, very few' – the antithesis of an adequate notion of immanent salvation based on open morality.

Despite their disappointment with the path taken by Mini and the Lamptons – 'it constitutes bad news if the people who agree with you are buggier than batshit' (212) – the Rhipidon Society is granted the encounter with the Saviour that is the ultimate purpose of their trip. That is, they are permitted an audience with the two-year-old, Sophia, who according to Linda Lampton is the child of herself and Valis (189). The name Sophia (meaning 'wisdom') is a relief to Dick/Fat, since it distinguishes her from the God he is afraid of finding – 'a deity which slew with one hand while healing with another [...] that deity was not the Savior' (190). Sophia expresses anger with the narrator for his suicide attempt. Not only does she refuse to allow him to defer responsibility on to Fat, she abolishes his alter ego, by declaring that the Rhipidon Society has only three, not four members. Phil (the narrator-bound character) feels himself become whole once again as Fat, his fabulated alter ego, disappears (or is reabsorbed)

(191). The function of the fabulation of Fat, it seems, had been to allow Phil to stay in touch with an aspect of himself that he needed but could not directly, intellectually accept; in losing the fabulation, he regains this dimension. Sophia informs Phil of the importance of self-transformation:

> 'Unless your past perishes,' Sophia said to me, 'you are doomed. Do you know that?'
> 'Yes,' I said.
> Sophia said, 'Your future must differ from your past. The future must always differ from the past.' (191)

Sophia thus appears to reject Fat's understanding that time is irrelevant or non-existent. She also states that the now-deceased Gloria will never return to life, contradicting the Lamptons' assertion that humans are immortal. Sophia differentiates herself from the Friends of God in the manner that Paul and the early gnostic Christians can be distinguished from an orthodox Christian perspective, in treating the Resurrection as symbolic, indicating the possibility of recreating oneself anew, rather than literal, signifying the actual reanimation of a corpse. Sophia also situates herself firmly on the side of the open, by making it clear that the role of the saviour cannot overlap with any force that destroys life: '"I am the injured and the slain," Sophia said. "But I am not the slayer. I am the healer and the healed"' (192). The Rhipidons subsequently re-affirm the absolute difference between the Friends of God, governed by a principle of death masquerading as life, and Sophia, an embodied principle of life: '"It's a paradox; two totally whacked out people – three, if you count Mini – have created a totally sane offspring"' (194). Given the possibility (already raised) that Sophia is herself an 'artificial intelligence in a human body' (193), the full life–death chiasmus has taken place: the supposedly mystic Friends of God, seeing themselves as on the side of life, have been revealed, like the Kalends, to operate according to a principle of closure, of mechanization; while the supposedly mechanistic entity is, like the robot Willis, shown to be on the side of life.

During a second meeting, Sophia confirms the Rhipidons' view that there is an essential difference between their outlook and that of the Lamptons, informing them that it was she who provided them with their motto 'Fish cannot carry guns', aligning their non-violent outlook with herself, with Wisdom. In contrast to the project into which the Lamptons would like to recruit them – that of extending and empowering a secret society – Sophia now gives them another mission: 'What you teach is the word of man. Man is holy, and the true god, the living god, is man himself. You will have no gods but yourselves; the days in which you believed in other gods end now, they end forever' (198). A god – or at least, a figure which is understood to be speaking for something that has through most of the novel been associated with divine or transcendent properties – tells them to cease believing in gods. Thus the purpose of fabulation is made clear: we fabulate gods, transcendent others, saviour-figures, in order to realize our own potential for transformation, for self-salvation. At the same time, the circumstances of its enunciation expose the paradoxical constraints which come with it: this activity must somehow be knowingly undertaken, and yet understood as something more than fictionalizing in any conventional sense: or rather, fictionalizing, fabulation, must be recognized as a worldmaking activity, rather than as a flight from reality. As much as anything else, Dick's soteriology is an endless, seemingly inexhaustible preparedness to find new, creative ways of fulfilling these apparently impossible conditions.

Conclusion

Just because the Lamptons are mistaken in believing themselves to be the Friends and spokespersons for God, it does not render them less dangerous: 'Evil does not die of its own self because it imagines that it speaks for god. Many claim to speak for god, but there is only one god and that god is man himself' (198). In other words, speaking for God, *regardless of whether God exists*, institutes a morality of closure that is in absolute opposition to the open morality that derives from wisdom: this wisdom – the wisdom of love – does not ultimately require a transcendent god, or at most, allows only a glimpse of one that is always in the process of disappearing, such that its emergence within the human is increasingly revealed as an immanent potential. Sophia declares herself human as opposed to divine, yet simultaneously 'the child of my father, which is Wisdom himself' (199).

The Rhipidons at this point clearly believe that Sophia is what she seems – even if what she seems is slightly different for each of them. Phil, the narrator, sees her as one of the four members of the Rhipidon Society, while David and Kevin reprise their polarized perspectives, but this time in ways that converge in confirming her saviour status: David, the Catholic, declares, 'I believe it. She'll be inside us; we won't be alone' (201); while Kevin, the cynic, is infuriated to realize that he has forgotten to ask Sophia about his dead cat – a regret that still implies a genuine belief that he has encountered the divine and missed his chance (202). Fat, of course, has disappeared on contact with the saviour-figure, whose discovery, arguably, was his fundamental purpose, the reason he (a fabulation of Phil Dick) was created.

On returning home, however, the Rhipidons are shocked when they receive a phone-call from the Lamptons, telling them that Sophia is dead. Mini has killed her with his laser-based equipment, trying, in his excessive enthusiasm, to find new ways of harnessing the living information of Valis. Following this catastrophic news, everything appears to unravel, as the Rhipidon Society dissipates and Fat reappears. If Phil is bitterly disappointed to have lost the Saviour immediately after finding her, he is only more enraged when Fat declares that he still intends to search for the Saviour. Yet within the soteriology of the novel, this disappointment at the end of the quest – as so often with Dick's reputedly 'unsatisfying' endings – may be seen to have a crucial function.

In apparently giving up on Sophia – that is, on Wisdom and salvation – the Rhipidons are failing at the mission they were given. Her salvific message was itself an instruction to them to stop relying on her, and become, effectively, their own gods. Thus her dying, though they seem unable to grasp it, may be understood as establishing precisely the necessary conditions for them to undertake their task. As a fabulated saviour-figure within many infolding or nested soteriological fabulations, Sophia's first function is to prevent the thought of (or hope for) salvation from collapsing into a belief in its impossibility. Yet her second function, equally important, is to become mortal, to disappear, in order that the faith placed in this fiction may be redirected to the power of fabulation itself, which is essentially a serial, recursive, life-prolonging activity. Sophia has furnished the Rhipidons with the opportunity to carry out the Bergsonian task of enabling the universe to realize its true function as a machine for making gods (MR: 317). Whether they will accept this challenge, and give up on soteriology as the quest for an already-existing saviour, while beginning the immanent soteriological work of producing salvation, remains an open question, as it almost certainly always must.

Near the end of the novel, Phil receives via television what he thinks may be a further message announcing a new hope of salvation. A brief overlapping of two pieces of consecutive programming produces, in his perception, the phrase 'KING FELIX', which can be connected to his past soteriological fabulations in a number of ways, yet consequently demands new efforts of creative interpretation. After the disappointment of the Lamptons and the death of Sophia, his fabulative deduction has taken a blow, and Valis has gone quiet. Fat has also departed on a new quest, this time global in scope – seemingly suggesting that Phil needs a break even from the alter ego upon which (or whom) he clearly, to a degree, depends for his sanity. But gradually, the fabulating impulse flickers back into life, or at least, half-life. Through new associations with fabulative material discerned in 'hidden meanings' in television commercials, the epitome of the excess trash produced by modern commercialized media culture, those earlier fabulations around Valis and 2–3–74 that had become stale or static with Sophia's death begin to become dynamic once again. Is Phil actually being sent a new message from or about a transcendent godlike saviour-figure who is 'on the way'? Or is he creating from the raw material at hand a reason to go on believing in the possibility of salvation? Is there, ultimately, a difference? In either case, he is opening himself to hope, and doing something that will render the static dynamic, re-energizing the soteriological potential of older fabulations (which is also, arguably, a key function of the novel as a whole). This uncertainty – but also this openness – hangs over the closing lines of the novel, as Phil Dick sits watching television output in which he has no interest, save for that one anticipated meaningful message or conjunction of random information that will offer a clue, a basis for the next step in his immanent soteriology, his path towards salvation. This soteriology takes on its simplest form in this basic activity of seeking out patterns in noise, creating structures from randomness: though at this level it may be at its furthest remove from what is generally conceived as the absolutely life-transforming event of salvation, it is also here that it finds the form most resistant to all forces that would negate or eradicate it, as it converges with what seems to be a fundamental activity of life.

Epilogue: Soter-ecologies

Dick has as a rule taken over a rubble of building materials from the run-of-the-mill American professionals of SF, frequently adding a true gleam of originality to the already worn-out concepts and, what is surely more important, erecting with such material constructions truly his own.

(Lem 1992: 57)

Since the first short story he sold for publication, in which the menacing 'Roogs' masquerade as garbage collectors in order to acquire the contents of the metal 'offering urns' outside suburban houses, Dick had been discerning the hidden value in trash. Perhaps appropriately, when he was taken to hospital shortly before his death, his friend Tim Powers hid the unpublished pages of the *Exegesis* inside a large ashtray bearing the slogan 'Elvis is King', in order to prevent it being found by unwelcome archons.[1] The unending process of seeking out signs in noise, producing meaning from the literal and figurative trash of contemporary culture, which is all that remains for (whatever remains of) the reflective subject at the end of *VALIS*, could be understood as the degree zero of Dick's soteriology: an open-ended, non-programmed readiness to detect intimations of a saving potential anywhere, which, precisely because of this indeterminacy, its apparent weakness, need never absolutely fail.

At this level, soteriological activity converges with the basic activity of fabulation and arguably thought itself. Here the distinction between finding and producing meaning is itself meaningless, and the process becomes indistinguishable from the primal activity of making distinctions, finding or producing objects, resources, tools, entities. From this basic activity, humans make all manner of tangible and intangible, simple and complex inventions: plans, ideas, gods, stories, wars, clocks, guns, hallucinations, buildings, commodities, ghosts, computers, atoms and every other component of what they come to understand as reality. There is no general or fundamental distinction between the fictional and the real, between dreams and technologies: there is merely the degree to which the reality-fictions that I have been calling fabulations become static or dynamic in our experience. This is not to say that the world is an idealist construct, that it has no material substance beyond thought: rather, that we experience 'things' as more or less 'thing-like', more or less 'real', according to the extent to which we perceive them as changing or unchanging, as autonomous and static or embedded in dynamic flows of matter and energy. This ontological and psychological understanding is both Bergsonian and Dickian, concerned with processes and reality fields rather than, for example, atomistic units of matter in Newtonian space-time. Some elements of our reality fields develop a more concrete appearance of stability than others; many, once the reality-building activity is under way, will give the impression of having preceded it, of having been 'there' before us: and indeed, something is 'there' before we perceive it – 'given' to perception in Whitehead's sense, that is, to a creative activity that is the origin of each occasion of experience, even as the objects with which it is concerned are antecedent to that process (Whitehead 1942 [1933]: 206–10). Only where some form of self-establishing (autopoietic) entity is just beginning to emerge (whether it then begins to take on the shape of an individual human, a group, a society, or another nonhuman form of collectivity), is the reality field fully dynamic. In such a state, we (or something) carve(s) out 'things' and 'images' while allowing others to dissolve back into the continuity of non-specific heterogeneous world (or raw worldmaking material), until we gradually determine or are taught that some such elements are of recurring usefulness or desirability, worth keeping around.

Though we may continue to engage dynamically in this fabulative, reality-building activity throughout our lives, it is likely that for most of us the larger parts of our reality fields become static, especially as the elements of which they are composed are confirmed as established elements in the reality fields of others, as parts of the *koinos kosmos*. Few of us are able to return to the degree zero of fabulation, at which any reality is possible, where every moment of perception or affect produces raw materials for an unplanned ontological architecture. To reach such a state would seem to require either the achievement of some form of mystical enlightenment or the equivalent of a psychotic break. It should therefore be no surprise if the extreme and intense pressure of a critical situation in which salvation is at stake turns out to be its germinal condition. Despite the rarity of cases in which such a condition has identifiably produced such a state, there have nevertheless been, it may be argued, many artistic, psychological, political and philosophical attempts to engineer a mode of engaging with the world along these lines. Most such attempts necessarily begin by taking apart the particular aspects of whatever reality field, with its corresponding subject, they wish to challenge – whether this is the hegemony of the (bourgeois) humanist subject, the capitalist social structure, a dominant aesthetic system, a scientific paradigm or an understanding of the divine.

Whether because he was a 'crisis junkie' (Sutin 1991: 148) or because of some natural aptitude for fabulation, Dick tended to engage in such activity in many different arenas. Stanislaw Lem's statement of Dick's facility for working with the rubble of building materials left behind by more conventional American science fiction writers, in order to construct new edifices of his own, may also be applied to other dimensions of his life and work: for example, as he attempts to produce an alternative to the human subject out of bits and pieces of souls, archetypes, androids, and other broken machines; as he pursues an immanent form of salvation through endlessly working and playing with fragments of formerly unified images of the divine, the remains of older concepts and figures of salvation; or as he seeks to reconstruct a world that he can bear to inhabit, from structures that he finds to have been damaged, shattered or dismantled by other thinkers and writers, or to have simply fallen into disrepair under the pressures of secular industrial modernity and post-war consumer culture. Indeed, we frequently see Dick giving a shaky structure a nudge, or subtly dismantling a load-bearing component in order to produce rubble with which he can work.

The attitude that is required to begin building new reality fields from scratch, whether in political, social, aesthetic, ontological, theological or other contexts, is one that treats every part of one's environment as simultaneously trash (the remnant of some other reality field now in ruins or in the process of collapse) and as potential resource. Dick attempts to produce a saviour or god using found objects, processes and texts, most intensively in the post 2-3-74 years through the *Exegesis* and his late novels. Despite his claims during this period to be seeking out a hidden, revelatory, divine or alien meaning, the *logos* of a mystical communication, he is clearly at the same time experimenting, collecting and arranging the materialized, manageable forms in which he receives ideas and information, putting them together to see if and how they fit, and what they do or are capable of doing. This is further reflected in his recursive approach to the resulting texts, whereby he repeatedly returns to ideas he had previously discussed both within the pages of the *Exegesis* and in his earlier fiction, each time developing a new interpretation in light of some new datum, the whole process in turn becoming the object of further (re-)iterations in the novel *VALIS* and arguably those which followed.

Far from constituting a traditionally exegetic activity – but equally far from the enlightened self-confidence corresponding to a certain widespread image of the visionary mystic – this fabulative work at times comes to seem more like the approach of a Dadaist sculptor or, in Matthew Fuller's sense, a constructor of media ecologies (2007: 1–2).[2] Though what Dick is attempting to construct, rather than a multimedia collage, is ultimately the figure of the saviour – or the system, reasoning, logic of salvation – the ideas, concepts, processes and experiences from which he makes it are materialized as found objects, to the extent that large sections of the *Exegesis* consist of encyclopedia entries copied out in full, their order subsequently subject to repeated rearrangements (E: 134, 234 [Pamela Jackson, footnotes]). In the terminology used throughout this book, such an activity might best be described as dynamic fabulation working upon the static.

Bergson, as we saw early on in this study, never differentiates closed and open or static and dynamic forms of fabulation in the manner that he distinguishes the tendencies producing divergent religious, moral and social forms. The closest he comes is in distinguishing two modes of composition by which the philosopher-writer might attempt to channel the impetus of true mysticism. The first of these, while it may be 'original and rigorous', nevertheless draws on ideas already developed and circulating within society and language. His account of the second is worthy of an extended quotation:

> Now there is another method of composition, more ambitious, less certain, which cannot tell when it will succeed or even if it will succeed at all. It consists in working back from the intellectual and social plane to a point in the soul from which there springs an imperative demand for creation. The soul within which this demand dwells may indeed have felt it fully only once in its lifetime, but it is always there, a unique emotion, an impulse, an impetus received from the very depths of things. To obey it completely new words would have to be coined, new ideas would have to be created, but this would no longer be communicating something, it would not be writing. Yet the writer will attempt to realize the unrealizable. He will revert to the simple emotion, to the form which yearns to create its matter, and will go with it to meet ideas already made, words that already exist, briefly social segments of reality. All along the way he will feel it manifesting itself in signs born of itself, I mean in fragments of its own materialization. (MR: 253–4)

Such a mode might well be exemplified by Dick's fabulations, rooted in an 'imperative demand for creation' which continually inspires him to engage in new attempts to 'realize the unrealizable' through writing that is not (just) writing. Though the goal of salvation may never be reached in any conclusive sense, the very unending nature of this soter-ecological activity, the process of building the way to salvation, in a sense becomes the thing sought – as long as it is never treated as finally having been found. Dick's immanent soteriology in general, and the dynamic fabulation of Valis in particular, allow the possibility of salvation to be experienced purely in and as the continued creative impulse to pursue it in the face of its impossibility, to invent a path where there appears to be an ultimate impasse.

Thus, in the course of his soter-ecological activity, rendering dynamic and changeable those reality fields which have become static, creating new reality fields from fragments of the old, drawing in everything around him but magically transmuting kipple into new building materials for a spontaneous negentropic onto-architecture, Dick finds the possibility of salvation in the search for it – as Bergson puts it, in 'fragments of its own materialization'. In a relatively late entry in the *Exegesis*, dated 17 November 1980, Dick recounts a conversation between himself and God, the latter taking the form of 'the infinite void' (E: 639). In the course of this discussion, the identity between Dick's theoretical explanations of 2-3-74 and the nature of the divinity with which it is communicating is made explicit. Each theory or speculation about Valis gives rise to an infinite series of theses and counter-theses, and each time the chain of reasoning or speculation collapses, God declares that he is present in that infinity. Dick seems by this time to be aware that his search, his exegesis or soteriology, can never reach a conclusion. As Bergson says of the true mystic, '[h]is description is interminable, because what he wants to describe is ineffable' (252). Even in elaborating the impossibility of completing his work of exegesis, his dynamic fabulation, Dick continues to produce it – fictionalizing God even as that same God tells him his quest will never be successfully concluded. Yet at the same time, this infinite fabulating process *is* the answer, as long as it remains infinite, inconclusive. God says: 'Without realizing it, the very infinitude of your theories pointed to the solution; they pointed to me and none but me' (E: 641).

Immediately after this account, Dick concludes that he has been deceived by Satan into working on the *Exegesis* for six and a half years, declaring that it has been futile and a 'hell-chore' (E: 643) – but that it has nevertheless paradoxically led him to God precisely through the recognition of this fact. What Dick calls God, or Valis, *is* the dynamic complex system of exegetical speculating and theorizing he has developed. This seemingly mystical scene points to the immanent nature of Valis as an ecological form: Dick has created such a large body of interlocking, contradicting, enhancing ideas and fictions that they have gone on not only representing, but producing, creating, fabulating, long after his physical death; or rather, they have become part of other ecologies that exist or operate beyond the living time and space of any given so-called human. In this one sense, perhaps, he managed, ultimately, to emulate James Joyce, a writer he greatly admired but would never hope to come close to matching by any literary measure.

To engage with the philosophical and soteriological projects of Bergson and Dick is to be engaged *by* them, to partake in and continue the philosophical fictionalizing activities with which they attempt both to challenge and to change 'reality' – to engage in science fiction, the (re)inventing of the known. As Barlow writes, 'Dick cannot merely be consumed or [...] critically digested. Through his writing career [...] he arises within his critics and readers, forcing them into his conversations, making them consider, in their own lives, the dilemmas of his fictions' (2005: 5–6). I would add, however, that it is not Dick himself that emerges within the worlds of his readers, but something in which he himself was only partially (albeit decisively) involved: he was no more the master of his fictions than are his readers. It may ultimately be in this sense that an immanent saviour becomes conceivable – as the object one attempts to specify and explain increasingly takes on or functions with forms of agency and interaction over which one retains influence, but has no hope of acquiring control.

Bergson suggests, following the passage cited above, that the attempt to realize the unrealizable, if it does in some degree succeed, 'will have enriched humanity with a thought that can take on a fresh aspect for each generation, with a capital yielding ever-renewed dividends, and not just with a sum down to be spent at once' (MR: 254). Dick's immanent soteriology, precisely because it did not reach a conclusive moment of success and therefore come to a halt, precisely because of its constitutive incompleteness, has just such a capacity to continually renew itself, offering endless new resources and impetus to other soter-ecologists, rather than consisting in a collection of theories or ideas about salvation to be archived alongside others. As Bergson puts it, for the philosopher beginning to appreciate the mystic's view, 'creation will appear [...] as God undertaking to create creators' (MR: 255). What is at stake here is not the existence of God, but the choice between two modes of creation: that which produces or merely recirculates finite, static creations, and that which transmits and promotes creation as a dynamic, incomplete process. The former is equivalent to the subject producing objects, the living constructing the non-living (which becomes a form of self-objectification, of auto-mechanization); whereas the latter takes every creating subject to be part-creator, part-created, never autonomous, never fully human, nevery truly 'saved'; but never absolutely lost either. Thus it is dynamic fabulation – with its infinite capacity for challenging the real, for transcending any immediate conditions of (im)possibility – upon which one must draw 'in order to conceive as creative energy the love wherein the mystic sees the very essence of God' (MR: 254).

Notes

Introduction

1. For a range of approaches to the relationship between philosophy and science fiction, conducted in a variety of tones, see Myers (1983); Clark (1995); Alsford (2000); Rowlands (2003); Nichols, Smith and Miller (2008); Sanders (2008); Schneider (2009).
2. Stableford (1987) epitomizes the sociological approach to science fiction. Westfahl (1998) makes one of the most comprehensive cases for Gernsback as the founder of the modern genre.
3. An aspect of the historical emergence of science fiction which is often elided in the contemporary common-sense understanding of the genre, and which I have not attempted to explore here, is the extent to which science fiction as an emergent genre follows relatively distinct trajectories in the US and Europe. For an excellent account of both, which respects their differences and explores the relationship between them, see Luckhurst (2005: 15–75).
4. That this 'predictive' mode of science fiction was not Dick's natural approach is perhaps reflected in the fact that Campbell purchased just one of his short stories for *Astounding Science Fiction* – 'Impostor', in 1953 (Sutin 1991: 76). However, it was editors such as Gernsback and Campbell who established the shape of the science fiction industry and genre as Dick experienced it growing up.
5. An extensive collection of Newton's writing (published and unpublished) on religious and alchemical topics, along with his other works, can be found online at *The Newton Project*: http://www.newtonproject.sussex.ac.uk/ (last accessed 9 November 2012).
6. The far-reaching power and the extreme limitations of the reasoning mind are mutually implicated, such that it appears to be infinitesimally diminished and cosmically extended at the same time. As Howard Caygill notes, the sublime as a 'check on the power of judgement is followed by a realization of the power and extent of the ideas of reason' (1995: 380).
7. Quotations from Antonioli (1999) are translated from the original French text.
8. For the line of influence (as well as extensive parallels) between Bergson and Jung, see Gunter (1982). Sutin reports that, under the guidance of friend and next-door

neighbour Connie Barbour, Dick read 'virtually all of Jung's work available in translation' in his early twenties (1991: 60). For Bergson's influence on British modernist literature see Gillies (1996), which includes a chapter on Joyce. For the formative influence of Joyce on Dick see Rickman (1988a: 85–7).

9   For example, there are several details in *The Two Sources* that are suggestive of an overlap with a Marxist politics, including the recognition of the importance of the money-commodity in commodity exchange (MR, 69); the fundamental importance of exchange relations to concepts of social justice and the class inequality at work in both types of transaction (MR, 70); the location of the source of social conflict in ownership (e.g. of land, resources, slaves) (MR, 284); and the discussion of the role played by industrialization in 'revolutioniz[ing] the relations between employer and employed, between capital and labour' (MR, 307), which calls for an awakening to consciousness of this situation and action against it on the part of humanity.

10 See Sutin (1991: 208–33) for a biographical overview of this period in Dick's life. Many of Dick's own accounts are found throughout the *Exegesis*, a smaller selection of which are collected in the earlier, more compact volume *In Pursuit of Valis: Selections from the Exegesis* (Dick, 1991a: 1–62). See also the interviews in *Philip K. Dick: The Last Testament* (Rickman: 1985).

11 Later, however, Dick would suggest that science fiction and theology 'must be related in some important way' (E: 177). Many of Dick's most emphatic statements can be found negated elsewhere in his writing – though in this case the events of 2-3-74 make the shift in perspective appear as more a development in his thinking than a contradiction.

12 See McKee (2004: v–ix) for a critique and reversal of this stance.

13 I have cited the King James Version rather than more recent scholarly editions of the Bible here, for its use of the 'glass, darkly' vocabulary that is referenced in many of Dick's works, such as *A Scanner Darkly* (1991c [1977]) and *A Glass of Darkness*, the original title of his short early novel, *The Cosmic Puppets* (2006 [1957]).

14 In a sense anticipating Hardt and Negri (2000) – though with a less sociological, more metaphysical inflection – Dick understands 'Empire' as a paradigm of power and domination that goes far beyond the scope of national imperialism. See Chapter 3 of this book for a detailed consideration.

Chapter 1: Counteracting Reality

1   The biographical material on Bergson presented here is based on Soulez and Worms (1997).

2   In *Matter and Memory* Bergson had explored at length the fallacies that arrive from attempting to reconstruct that which is naturally continuous – such as experience

or memory – out of a collection of facts or pieces of information. On Bergson's memory as counter to conventional, archival paradigms, see Cariou (1999) and Burton (2008).

3. Soulez notes that Bergson drew specifically on Schaeffle's and Spencer's presentations of the society–organism analogy in his lectures at the Lycée Clermont and the Lycée Henri-IV during the 1890s (Soulez and Worms 2002: 93). For a wider discussion of the use of the organism metaphor in sociology see Levine (1995).

4. In this sense, Bergson may be said to anticipate the post-war influence of the ecological paradigm on disciplines beyond biology, which in the early twentieth century was already beginning to displace the dominant focus on the organism, shifting it towards a concern with environmental systems.

5. Cf. 'If we examine this point more closely, we shall find that consciousness is the light that plays around the zone of possible actions or potential activity which surrounds the action really performed by the living being. It signifies hesitation or choice' (CE: 144).

6. The theory of symbiogenesis was proposed at the beginning of the twentieth century by Konstantin Merezhkovsky. Lynn Margulis, along with her writing collaborator (and son) Dorion Sagan, is responsible for its gaining widespread contemporary credibility, both through experimental results and theoretical publications (Margulis 1981, 1998; Margulis and Sagan 1987).

7. It may be that the unconventional utopianism of Ernst Bloch, with its blend of messianic and Marxist conceptions of futurity, hope and transformation, consists of a long attempt to face this difficulty of the mutually infecting necessity and danger of prescribing a future world. As such it may be one of the few forms of utopianism adequate to the thought of the open society.

8. We might speculate that, had Bergson gone into a more extended discussion of Buddhism, he might have considered including among his examples of true mystics the figure of the *boddhisatva*, who in some Buddhist traditions refuses Enlightenment to return to the world to help others – although the other examples he gives may suggest that he was primarily interested only in citing historical figures.

9. The New International Version translates the passage as follows: 'Now we see but a poor reflection as in a mirror; then we shall see face to face. Now I know in part; then I shall know fully, even as I am fully known.' References to this passage appear frequently in Dick's novels, for example in *The Cosmic Puppets* (2006; 1956) (originally titled *A Glass of Darkness*), *The Man in the High Castle* (1965; 1962), *A Scanner Darkly* (1991c; 1977) and *VALIS* (1991d [1981]).

Chapter 2: Fabulating Salvation in Four Early Novels

1. *Confessions of a Crap Artist* came close to being taken up by a publisher in 1960, but Dick was unable to supply the requested re-write. It was eventually published in 1975, with the other early mainstream novels following posthumously (Sutin 1991: 104–5; Lord RC 2006: 91–2).
2. For Bergson, memories are not stored on a substrate, in a physical container, since it is only in the act of recall that memory gives the impression of consisting in separate chunks or units. This dimension of Bergson's understanding of memory is discussed in detail in Burton (2008); see also Lawlor (2003: 45–6) and Mullarkey (1999: 48–55).

Chapter 3: The Empire that Never Ended

1. Elsewhere, for instance in *Being and Event* (2007 [1988]), Badiou's most extended elaboration of his philosophical system, he posits that mathematics, in particular set theory, is required to carry out ontological work, for which language is fundamentally inadequate.
2. Pasolini's film, in which New York would stand for Pauline Rome, was never made, but the script/notes were published as *San Paolo* (1977). We can only imagine how, in an alternative world, such a film might have affected Dick, seeming to confirm the veracity of his own visions, in the manner of the imagined film *Valis* for Horselover Fat (itself inspired by Nicholas Roeg's 1976 film *The Man Who Fell to Earth*).
3. What may be termed Badiou's 'immanentizing' of Saint Paul's writing, continuing a tendency made prominent by Jacob Taubes' (2004) political theology of Paul, has arguably already been a major theme in twentieth-century theology. Rudolf Bultmann's influential and controversial call for the 'de-mythologizing' of the New Testament *kerygma* led him to advocate a reading of Saint Paul that often does not seem far from Badiou's non-literal understanding. For example: 'The Spirit does not work like a supernatural force, nor is it the permanent possession of the believer. It is the possibility of a new life which must be appropriated by a deliberate resolve' (Bultmann 1964: 22). In turn, parallels between this and early gnostic approaches to Christian teaching might also be discerned, a subject discussed briefly at the end of this chapter.
4. All biblical quotations in this section are cited in the form in which they appear in the English translation of Agamben's text (except where I have indicated otherwise). The translator (Patricia Dailey) drew on several different versions of the Bible in rendering Agamben's translations in English.

5 Badiou's translator, Ray Brassier, like Agamben's, draws on several versions of the Bible in trying to stay as close as possible to Badiou's biblical citations in French. Patricia Dailey gives an English translation of Agamben's rendering of this passage as follows: 'for with [the] heart it is believed unto justice, with the mouth then it is confessed unto salvation'.
6 Dick's own take on the 'What if …' approach is found in the essay 'Who is an SF Writer?' (1995b: 75).
7 Furthermore, we might see versions of this struggle recurring throughout the history of Western thought – the supposed birth of philosophy, the rise of modern science, of Enlightenment rationality, and twentieth-century materialism, all place much value on the possibility of a clear separation of real and unreal, truth and fiction.

Chapter 4: Objects of Salvation: *The Man in the High Castle*

1 Tagomi's wandering here echoes Stephen Daedalus' intermittent automatism in *Ulysses* (1992 [1922]), for example in the 'Proteus' chapter, where he himself repeatedly seems to notice and reflect on it. Whenever a character becomes aware of their own abandonment of agency in such a way, the metafictional dimensions of storytelling start to come into view, so that the roles of reader and writer in the character's supposedly unconscious activity cannot be ignored.
2 For an unofficial, yet comprehensive and effective demonstration of the extent of post-war destruction of human life, presenting, comparing and cross-referencing estimated statistics, see Matthew White's *Historical Atlas of the 20th Century*: http://users.erols.com/mwhite28/20centry.htm (last accessed 21 June 2012).
3 If the end of the Second World War did indeed establish a sense of moral authority and self-confidence among the political and social elites of Western nations, and a sense of entitlement to global leadership that to a large extent compensated for the loss of their colonial powers, then we might equally see this self-certainty as having been shattered with the terrorist attacks of September 2001. That the 9/11 attacks should have had such a massive impact on global consciousness, despite a death toll that, in comparison with much less widely remembered and referenced atrocities, was relatively low, may be in part a reflection of the degree to which they undermined a moral and military self-confidence that had its roots in the Allied victory of 1945.

Chapter 5: How We Became Post-Android

1 Matthew Englund also explores the mutual dependence between the Glimmung as saviour and those he putatively arrives to save, linking this to the relationship between creator and creation in ways that resonate with what I have referred to elsewhere in this book as Dick's organic or dynamic metafiction (Englund, 2012).
2 In this much-discussed scene, Gaff sets a small origami unicorn on the ground, the implication being that he has access to Deckard's artificially implanted dreams. This effect is only produced in later versions of the film (i.e. the 'Director's Cut' and the 'Final Cut'), since it depends upon an earlier scene in which Deckard is shown to be dreaming of a unicorn, and which was missing from the film's original theatrical release in 1982.
3 Steve Grand's attempt to construct an intelligent anthropoid robot from scratch is detailed in his book *Growing up with Lucy: How to Build an Android in Twenty Easy Steps* (2004).

Chapter 6: The Reality of Valis

1 I have developed elsewhere an account of the role of fictionalizing as a response to this impossibility in the Gilgamesh epic and the Prometheus myth (Burton 2013).
2 The name Horselover Fat is itself a cipher for Philip Dick. 'Phil' becomes 'lover' on the basis that the English suffix '-phil' derives from the Greek *philia* (φιλία), love – as in *philosophia*, love of wisdom, or Astrophil, star-lover, in Philip Sidney's *Astrophil and Stella* sonnets; 'ip' becomes 'Horse', again a Greek-English translation; and 'Dick' is treated as German, becoming 'Fat' in English.
3 Cf. 'My eyes close and I see that strange strawberry ice cream pink. At the same instant knowledge is transferred to me. I go into the bedroom where Tessa is changing Chrissy & I recite what has been conveyed to me: that he has an undetected birth defect & must be taken to the doctor at once & scheduled for surgery. This turns out to be true' (Dick, *Exegesis* entry c. 1977, cited in Sutin 1991: 225).
4 Harold Bloom has suggested that 'Gnosticism was (and is) a kind of information theory' (1992: 30). Erik Davis popularized the association of gnosis with information/technoculture in *TechGnosis* (1998), which also provides valuable insights into their place in Dick's thought.
5 This is not to suggest that Dick's ideas here are directly influenced by Bergson; there would have been myriad other possible sources for such notions of the oneness of life and the universe available to Dick in 1970s California – though it is certainly

plausible that Bergson's work had influenced some of these sources in turn (such as Teilhard de Chardin).

6 The characters were also drawn broadly from real-life figures in Dick's life, though deployed stylistically for the purposes of the novel: Kevin was inspired by K. W. Jeter, David by writer Tim Powers, both writers and friends of Dick (Sutin 1991: 258).

7 The Perky Pat layouts are a kind of virtual world (perhaps anticipating contemporary online platforms like *Second Life*), maintained with the use of dolls and Barbie-esque accessories and inhabited with the help of the hallucinogenic drug Can-D by characters in *The Three Stigmata of Palmer Eldritch* (2003b [1964]). Though only partially effective in staving off the emptiness and boredom of their everyday lives, they are relatively innocuous compared to the nightmarish alternative realities accessed through Palmer Eldritch's drug Chew-Z, which, once entered, may be impossible to escape.

8 Deleuze states that Freud's unconscious does not know time 'because it is never subordinated to the empirical contents of a present which passes in representation, but rather carries out the passive syntheses of an original time' (1991: 114).

9 We might even speculate that fabulation itself could be the 'secret' of many ancient mystery religions and so-called gnostic cults: the secret of fabulation would be that the falsity, or rather, the invented status, of the secret knowledge outwardly proclaimed, makes it no less powerful. In other words, the one who strives to find the transcendental secret behind the mystery will discover that there is no secret; yet for the true 'initiate', this *is* the secret (the initiate being defined as such only to the extent that she appreciates this), a fabulative power of transformation that depends on nothing but the imagination to alter material reality.

10 This text can now be found in *The Nag Hammadi Library in English* (1990), titled 'On the Origin of the World'.

11 The ancient Greek *krisis* or *kraisis*, derived from the verb *krinein* (meaning 'to separate' or 'to decide'), referred to both a decisive moment in the development of an illness and the judgement at the end of a trial.

12 The description of the film was inspired by Nicholas Roeg's *The Man Who Fell to Earth* (Sutin, 1991: 258). It also draws on elements of Dick's novel *Radio Free Albemuth* (1999b [1985]), which was written before *VALIS* but only published posthumously.

13 Cf. Kirk (1974: 127) on the fate of Asklepios, and Dick's interpretation in the *Exegesis* (E: 34–7 [4:41]). This would also associate the Lamptons with the 'killers' who assail Mercer in *Do Androids Dream of Electric Sheep?* Mercer was, like Asklepios, punished for raising the dead, the bombardment of his brain with radioactive cobalt echoing the use of the Kyklopes' thunderbolt.

Epilogue: Soter-ecologies

1 Powers has explained the story of his hiding of the *Exegesis* pages in, for example, a panel discussion at UC Irvine on 21 May 2010 ('A County Darkly: Philip K. Dick in the OC'), and in the documentary film 'The Owl in Daylight – Philip K. Dick is here' (Kleijwegt 2010).
2 I explore these aspects of the *Exegesis*, with particular reference to its ecological character, in a forthcoming essay in Dunst and Schlensag (eds), *The World According to Philip K. Dick* (2015).

Bibliography

Adamson, Gregory Dale (2002), *Philosophy in the Age of Science and Capital* (London: Continuum).
Agamben, Giorgio (1998 [1995]), *Homo Sacer: Sovereign Power and Bare Life*, trans. Daniel Heller-Roazen (Stanford, CA: Stanford University Press).
Agamben, Giorgio (2005 [2000]), *The Time That Remains: A Commentary on the Letter to the Romans*, trans. Patricia Dailey (Stanford, CA: Stanford University Press).
Aldiss, Brian W. (1973), *Billion Year Spree: The History of Science Fiction* (London: Weidenfeld & Nicolson).
Aldiss, Brian W. (1992), 'Dick's Maledictory Web: About and around *Martian Time-Slip*', in R. D. Mullen, Istvan Ciceray-Ronay, Jr, Arthur B. Evans and Veronica Hollinger (eds), *On Philip K. Dick: 40 Articles from Science-Fiction Studies* (Greencastle, IN: SF-TH), 37–41.
Aldridge, Alexandra (1983), 'Science Fiction and Emerging Values', in Robert E. Myers (ed.), *The Intersection of Science Fiction and Philosophy* (Westport, CT: Greenwood Press), 15–30.
Alsford, Mike (2000), *What If? Religious Themes in Science Fiction* (London: Darton, Longman and Todd).
Anderson, Benedict (1983), *Imagined Communities* (London: Verso).
Andre, Shane (1993), 'Was Hume an Atheist?', *Hume Studies* 19 (1): 141–66.
Anton, Uwe and Fuchs, Werner (1996), 'So I Don't Write about Heroes: An Interview with Philip K. Dick', transcribed by Frank C. Bertrand, *SF EYE* 14, 37–46. Available from http://2010philipkdickfans.philipkdickfans.com/frank/anton.html (accessed 30 November 2012).
Antonioli, Manola (1999), *Deleuze et l'histoire de la philosophie ou de la philosophie comme science-fiction* (Paris: Editions Kimé).
Apel, D. Scott (1987), *Philip K. Dick: The Dream Connection* (San José, CA: The Permanent Press).
Aristotle (1933), *Metaphysics Books I–IX*, trans. Hugh Trendennick (Cambridge, MA: Harvard University Press).
Badiou, Alain (2000 [1997]), *Deleuze: The Clamor of Being*, trans. Louise Burchill (Minneapolis: University of Minnesota Press).
Badiou, Alain (2003 [1997]), *Saint Paul: The Foundation of Universalism*, trans. Ray Brassier (Stanford, CA: Stanford University Press).
Badiou, Alain (2007 [1988]), *Being and Event*, trans. Oliver Feltham (London: Continuum).

Baehr, Peter (2001), 'The "Iron Cage" and the "Shell as Hard as Steel": Parsons, Weber, and the Stalhartes Gehäuse Metaphor in *The Protestant Ethic and the Spirit of Capitalism*,' *History and Theory* 40 (May): 153–69.

Ballard, J. G. (2005), *Conversations* (San Francisco, CA: RE/Search).

Barlow, Aaron (1991), 'Philip K. Dick's Androids: Victimized Victimizers', in Judith B. Kerman (ed.), *Retrofitting Blade Runner: Issues in Ridley Scott's 'Blade Runner' and Philip K. Dick's 'Do Androids Dream of Electric Sheep?'* (Bowling Green, OH: Bowling Green State University Press), 76–89.

Barlow, Aaron (2005), *How Much Does Chaos Scare You? Politics, Religion, and Philosophy in the Fiction of Philip K. Dick* (Brooklyn, NY: Shakespeare's Sister).

Baudrillard, Jean (1994 [1981]), *Simulacra and Simulations*, trans. Sheila Faria Glaser (Ann Arbor: University of Michigan Press).

Benjamin, Walter (1997 [1933]), 'On the Mimetic Faculty', in *One-Way Street and Other Writings*, trans. Edmund Jephcott and Kingsley Shorter (London: Verso), 160–3.

Benjamin, Walter (1999 [1955]), 'The Storyteller', in *Illuminations*, trans. Harry Zorn (London: Pimlico), 83–107.

Benjamin, Walter (2002 [1982]), *The Arcades Project*, trans. Howard Eiland and Kevin McLaughlin (Cambridge, MA: Harvard University Press).

Bergson, Henri (1960 [1889]), *Time and Free Will*, trans. F. L. Pogson (New York: Harper & Row).

Bergson, Henri (1977 [1932]), *The Two Sources of Morality and Religion*, trans. R. Ashley Audra and Cloudesley Brereton with W. Horsfall Carter (Notre Dame, IN: University of Notre Dame Press).

Bergson, Henri (1988 [1896]), *Matter and Memory*, trans. Nancy Margaret Paul and W. Scott Palmer (New York: Zone).

Bergson, Henri (1998 [1907]), *Creative Evolution*, trans. Arthur Mitchell (Toronto: Dover Publications).

Bergson, Henri (2002 [1934]), *The Creative Mind: An Introduction to Metaphysics* (New York: Citadel).

Bertrand, Frank C. (1995 [1980]), 'Philip K. Dick on Philosophy: A Brief Interview', in Lawrence Sutin (ed.), *The Shifting Realities of Philip K. Dick: Selected Literary and Philosophical Writings* (New York: Vintage Books), 44–7.

Bloom, Harold (1992), *The American Religion* (New York: Simon & Schuster).

Bultmann, Rudolf (1964), 'New Testament and Mythology', in Hans Werner Bartsch (ed.), *Kerygma and Myth: A Theological Debate*, Vol. 1 (London: SPCK), 1–44.

Burton, James (2008), 'Bergson's Non-archival Theory of Memory', *Memory Studies* 1 (3): 321–39.

Burton, James (2013), 'Prometheus and Gilgamesh: The Work of Myth-making', in Claus Leggewie, Ursula Renner and Peter Risthaus (eds), *Prometheische Kultur – Wo kommen unsere Energien her?* (Munich: Wilhelm Fink), 136–54.

Burtt, Edwin A. (2003 [1924]), *The Metaphysical Foundations of Modern Science* (Mineola, NY: Dover).

Butler, Andrew M. (2000), *Philip K. Dick* (Harpenden: Pocket Essentials).

Campbell, Jan (2006), *Psychoanalysis and the Time of Life: Durations of the Unconscious Self* (London: Routledge).

Čapek, Karel (2011 [1920/1936]), *R.U.R. & War with the Newts* (London: Gollancz)

Čapek, Milič (1971), *Bergson and Modern Physics: A Reinterpretation and Re-Evaluation* (Boston, MA: Springer).

Cariou, Marie (1976), *Bergson et le fait mystique* (Paris: Editions Aubier Montaigne).

Cariou, Marie (1990), *Lectures Bergsoniennes* (Paris: Presses Universitaires de France).

Cariou, Marie (1999), 'Bergson: The Keyboards of Forgetting', in John Mullarkey (ed.), *The New Bergson* (Manchester: Manchester University Press), 99–117.

Caygill, Howard (1995), *The Kant Dictionary* (Oxford: Blackwell).

Christianson, Gale E. (1976), 'Kepler's Somnium: Science Fiction and the Renaissance Scientist', *Science Fiction Studies*, 8 (3) http://www.depauw.edu/sfs/backissues/8/christianson8art.htm

Clark, Stephen L. (1995), *How to Live Forever* (London: Routledge).

Clarke, Bruce (2008), *Posthuman Metamorphosis: Narrative and Systems* (New York: Fordham University Press).

Cornford, F. M. (1957), *From Religion to Philosophy* (New York: Harper Brothers).

Currie, Mark (ed.) (1995), *Metafiction* (Harlow: Longman).

Davis, Erik (1998), *TechGnosis: Myth, Magic and Mysticism in the Age of Information* (New York: Harmony).

Deleuze, Gilles (1991 [1966]), *Bergsonism*, trans. Hugh Tomlinson and Barbara Habberjam (New York: Zone).

Deleuze, Gilles (1994 [1968]), *Difference and Repetition* (London: Athlone Press).

Deleuze, Gilles (1998 [1993]), *Essays Critical and Clinical*, trans. Daniel W. Smith and Michael A. Greco (London: Verso).

Deleuze, Gilles (2001 [1995]), *Pure Immanence: Essays on a Life*, trans. Anne Boyman (New York: Zone).

Deleuze, Gilles and Guattari, Félix (1988 [1980]), *A Thousand Plateaus: Capitalism and Schizophrenia*, trans. Brian Massumi (London: Athlone).

Deleuze, Gilles and Guattari, Félix (1994 [1991]), *What is Philosophy?*, trans. Hugh Tomlinson and Graham Burchill (London: Verso).

DePrez, Daniel (1976), 'An Interview with Philip K. Dick', *Science Fiction Review* 19 (5.3): 6–12.

Derrida, Jacques (1976 [1967]), *Of Grammatology*, trans. Gayatri Chakravorty Spivak (Baltimore, MD: Johns Hopkins Press).

Derrida, Jacques (1981 [1972]), *Dissemination*, trans. Barbara Johnson (Chicago: University of Chicago Press).

Derrida, Jacques (2008 [2006]), *The Animal That Therefore I am*, ed. Mary-Luise Mallet, trans. David Wills (New York: Fordham University Press).

Descartes, René (1985 [1633]), 'Treatise on Man', in *The Philosophical Writings of Decartes*, Vol. 1, trans. John Cottingham, Robert Stoothoff and Dugald Murdoch (Cambridge: Cambridge University Press), 99–108.
Descartes, René (1998 [1637/1641]), *Discourse on Method* and *Meditations on First Philosophy*, trans. Donald A. Cress.
Dick, Philip K. (1965 [1962]), *The Man in the High Castle* (Harmondsworth: Penguin/ROC).
Dick, Philip K. (1972 [1955]), *Solar Lottery* (London: Arrow).
Dick, Philip K. (1975 [1964]), *Clans of the Alphane Moon* (St Albans: Panther).
Dick, Philip K. (1976a [1960]), *Dr. Futurity* (London: Methuen).
Dick, Philip K. (1976b [1970]), *Our Friends from Frolix 8* (London: Grafton).
Dick, Philip K. (1976c [1960]), *Vulcan's Hammer* (London: Arrow Books).
Dick, Philip K. (1977a) [1967], *Counter-Clock World* (London: Hodder & Stoughton).
Dick, Philip K. (1977b [1972]), *We Can Build You* (Glasgow: Fontana/Collins).
Dick, Philip K. (1978 [1964]), *The Penultimate Truth* (London: Grafton).
Dick, Philip K. (1991a), *In Pursuit of Valis: Selections from the Exegesis*, ed. Lawrence Sutin (Novato, CA: Underwood-Miller).
Dick, Philip K. (1991b [1963]), *The Game-Players of Titan* (London: Grafton).
Dick, Philip K. (1991c [1977]), *A Scanner Darkly* (New York: Vintage).
Dick, Philip K. (1991d [1981]), *VALIS* (New York: Vintage Books).
Dick, Philip K. (1993a [1968]), *Do Androids Dream of Electric Sheep?* (London: HarperCollins).
Dick, Philip K. (1993b [1956]), *The World Jones Made* (New York: Vintage).
Dick, Philip K. (1995a [1965]), 'Schizophrenia & the *The Book of Changes*', in Lawrence Sutin (ed.), *The Shifting Realities of Philip K. Dick: Selected Literary and Philosophical Writings* (New York: Vintage Books), 175–182.
Dick, Philip K. (1995b [1974]), 'Who is an SF Writer?', in Lawrence Sutin (ed.), *Shifting Realities* (New York: Vintage Books), 69–78.
Dick, Philip K. (1995c [1972]), 'The Android and the Human', in Lawrence Sutin (ed.), *Shifting Realities* (New York: Vintage Books), 183–210.
Dick, Philip K. (1995d [1978]), 'How to Build a Universe That Doesn't Fall Apart Two Days Later', in Lawrence Sutin (ed.), *Shifting Realities* (New York: Vintage Books), 259–80.
Dick, Philip K. (1996 [1981]), *The Divine Invasion* (London: HarperCollins).
Dick, Philip K. (1999a [1964]), *Martian Time-Slip* (London: Gollancz).
Dick, Philip K. (1999b [1985]), *Radio Free Albemuth* (London: HarperCollins).
Dick, Philip K. (2000a [1965]), *Dr Bloodmoney* (London: Gollancz).
Dick, Philip K. (2000b), 'The Electric Ant', in *We Can Remember It for You Wholesale*, The Collected Stories of Philip K. Dick, Vol. 5 (London: Millennium), 225–39.
Dick, Philip K. (2000c [1969]), *Ubik* (London: Gollancz).
Dick, Philip K. (2001 [1974]), *Flow My Tears, the Policeman Said* (London: Gollancz).
Dick, Philip K. (2003a [1957]), *Eye in the Sky* (London: Gollancz).

Dick, Philip K. (2003b [1964]), *The Three Stigmata of Palmer Eldritch* (London: Gollancz).
Dick, Philip K. (2003c [1959]), *Time Out of Joint* (London: Gollancz).
Dick, Philip K. (2004 [1964]), *The Simulacra* (London: Gollancz).
Dick, Philip K. (2005a [1969]), *Galactic Pot-Healer* (London: Gollancz).
Dick, Philip K. (2005b [1970]), *A Maze of Death* (London: Gollancz).
Dick, Philip K. (2006 [1957]), *The Cosmic Puppets* (London: Gollancz).
Dick, Philip K. (2011), *The Exegesis of Philip K. Dick*, ed. Pamela Jackson and Jonathan Lethem (Boston and New York: Houghton Mifflin Company).
Dunst, Alexander and Schlensag, Stefan (eds) (2015), *The World According to Philip K. Dick* (London: Palgrave Macmillan).
Englund, Matthew (2012), 'The Raising of Heldscalla: Reevaluating *Galactic Pot-Healer*' (presentation at 'Worlds out of Joint: Re-imagining Philip K. Dick', TU Dortmund University, Germany, November 2012).
Evans, Christopher (1988), *Writing Science Fiction* (New York: St Martin's Press).
Feehan, Michael (1995), 'Chinese Finger-Traps Or "A Perturbation in the Reality Field": Paradox as Conversion in Philip K. Dick's Fiction', in Samuel J. Umland (ed.), *Philip K. Dick: Contemporary Critical Interpretations* (London: Greenwood Press), 197–206.
Fitting, Peter (1992a [1987]), 'Futurecop: The Neutralization of Revolt in *Blade Runner*', in Mullen et al. (eds), *On Philip K. Dick: 40 Articles from Science-Fiction Studies* (Greencastle, IN: SF-TH), 132–44.
Fitting, Peter (1992b [1975]), 'Ubik: The Deconstruction of Bourgeois SF', in Mullen et al. (eds), *On Philip K. Dick: 40 Articles from Science-Fiction Studies* (Greencastle, IN: SF-TH), 41–9.
Foucault, Michel (1991 [1975]), *Discipline and Punish: The Birth of the Prison*, trans. Alan Sheridan (London: Penguin).
Francavilla, Joseph (1991), 'The Android as Doppelgänger', in Judith B. Kerman (ed.), *Retrofitting Blade Runner* (Bowling Green, OH: Bowling Green State University Press), 4–15.
Freud, Sigmund (2004 [1927]), *The Future of an Illusion*, trans. J. A. Underwood (London: Penguin).
Freud, Sigmund (2008 [1930]), *Civilization and its Discontents*, trans. David McLintock (London: Penguin).
Fuller, Matthew (2007), *Media Ecologies* (Cambridge, MA: MIT Press).
Gillies, Mary Ann (1996), *Henri Bergson and British Modernism* (Montreal: McGill-Queen's University Press).
Goodman, Nelson (1978), *Ways of Worldmaking* (Indianapolis: Hackett).
Grand, Steve (2004), *Growing up with Lucy: How to Build an Android in Twenty Easy Steps* (London: Phoenix).
Grosz, Elizabeth (2004), *The Nick of Time: Politics, Evolution, and the Untimely* (Durham, NC: Duke University Press).

Guerlac, Suzanne (2006), *Thinking in Time: An Introduction to Henri Bergson* (Ithaca: Cornell University Press).
Gunter, P. A. Y. (ed.) (1969), *Bergson and the Evolution of Physics* (Knoxville, TN: University of Tenessee Press).
Gunter, P. A. Y. (1982), 'Bergson and Jung', *Journal of the History of Ideas* 43 (4), 635–52.
Gunter, P. A. Y. (1991), 'Bergson and Non-linear Non-equilibrium Thermodynamics: An Application of Method', *Revue International de Philosophie* 45: 108–21.
Gunter, P. A. Y. (1999), 'Bergson and the War against Nature', in John Mullarkey (ed.), *The New Bergson* (Manchester: Manchester University Press), 168–82.
Hansen, Mark B. N. (2004), *New Philosophy for New Media* (Cambridge, MA: MIT Press).
Hardt, Michael and Negri, Antonio (2001), *Empire* (Cambridge, MA: Harvard University Press).
Hayles, Katherine N. (1999), *How We Became Posthuman: Virtual Bodies in Cybernetics, Literature and Informatics* (Chicago: University of Chicago Press).
Heidegger, Martin (1993 [1954]), 'The Question Concerning Technology', in David Farrell Krell (ed.), *Martin Heidegger: Basic Writings* (London: Routledge), 311–41.
Hendel, Charles (1925), *Studies in the Philosophy of David Hume* (Princeton: Princeton University Press).
Herodotus (2007), *The Landmark Herodotus: The Histories*, ed. Robert B. Strassler, trans. Andrea L. Purvis (New York: Pantheon Books).
Hesiod (2008 [c.700 BCE]), *Theogony and Works and Days*, trans. M. L. West (Oxford: Oxford University Press).
Hume, David (2007 [1779]), *Dialogues Concerning Natural Religion and Other Writings*, ed. Dorothy Coleman (Cambridge: Cambridge University Press).
Hutcheon, Linda (1985), *A Theory of Parody: The Teachings of Twentieth-Century Art Forms* (Methuen: New York).
Hyland, Drew A. (1973), *The Origins of Philosophy: Its Rise in Myth and the Pre-Socratics* (New York: Capricorn Books).
Ipiq-aya (1998 [c.1700 BCE]), 'Atrahasis', in *Myths from Mesopotamia: Creation, The Flood, Gilgamesh, and Others*, trans. Stephanie Dalley (Oxford: Oxford University Press), 9–38.
Irigaray, Luce (2002), *The Way of Love*, trans. Heidi Bostic and Stephen Pluháček (London: Continuum).
Jameson, Fredric (1992), 'After Armageddon: Character Systems in *Dr Bloodmoney*', in Mullen et al. (eds), *On Philip K. Dick: 40 Articles from Science-Fiction Studies* (Greencastle, IN: SF-TH), 26–36.
Jameson, Fredric (2005), 'History and Salvation in Philip K. Dick', in *Archaeologies of the Future: The Desire Called Utopia and Other Science Fictions* (London: Verso), 363–83.
Jennings, Jr, Theodore W. (2006), *Reading Derrida / Thinking Paul* (Stanford, CA: Stanford University Press).

Jonas, Hans (1958), *The Gnostic Religion: The Message of the Alien God and the Beginnings of Christianity* (Boston: Beacon Press).
Joyce, James (1992 [1922]), *Ulysses* (London: Penguin).
Kafka, Franz (1997 [1926]), *The Castle*, trans. J. A. Underwood (London: Penguin).
Kant, Immanuel (1973 [1790]), *Critique of Judgement*, trans. James Creed Meredith (Oxford: Oxford University Press).
Kant, Immanuel (1978 [1781/1787]), *Critique of Pure Reason*, trans. Norman Kemp Smith (London: Macmillan).
Kant, Immanuel (1997 [1788]), *Critique of Practical Reason*, trans. Mary Gregor (Cambridge: Cambridge University Press).
Kepler, Johannes (1967 [1634]), *Somnium: The Dream, or Posthumous Work on Lunar Astronomy* (Madison, WI: University of Wisconsin Press).
Kirk, G. S. (1974), *The Nature of Greek Myths* (London: Penguin).
Kleijwegt, David (dir.) (2010), *The Owl In Daylight – Philip K. Dick Is Here* [documentary] (The Netherlands).
Kolesnikoff, Nina (1993), 'Story/Plot', in *Encyclopedia of Contemporary Literary Theory*, (ed.) Irena R. Makaryk (Toronto: Toronto University Press), 631–2.
Koyré, Alexandre (2008 [1957]), *From the Closed World to the Infinite Universe* (Radford, VA: Wilder).
Kwinter, Sanford (2002), *Architectures of Time: Toward a Theory of the Event in Modernist Culture* (Cambridge, MA: MIT Press).
La Mettrie, Julien Offray de (2009 [1748]), *L'homme machine* (Charleston, SC: BiblioBazaar).
Lash, Scott (2010), 'Information Theology: Philip K. Dick's Will to Knowledge', in Lash, *Intensive Culture* (London: Sage), 185–214.
Lawlor, Leonard (2003), *The Challenge of Bergsonism: Phenomenology, Ontology, Ethics* (London: Continuum).
Lem, Stanislaw (1986), 'Science Fiction: A Hopeless Case – with Exceptions', trans. Werner Koopmann, in Stanislaw Lem, *Microworlds*, (ed.) Franz Rottensteiner (San Diego: Harvest/Harcourt Brace Jovanovich), 45–105.
Lem, Stanislaw (1992 [1975]), 'Philip K. Dick: A Visionary Among the Charlatans', in Mullen et al. (eds), *On Philip K. Dick: 40 Articles from Science-Fiction Studies* (Greencastle, IN: SF-TH), 49–62.
Lesher, James H. (ed.) (1992), *Xenophanes: Fragments* (Toronto: University of Toronto Press).
Levine, Donald N. (1995), 'The Organism Metaphor in Sociology', *Social Research* 62 (2): 239–65.
Levi-Strauss, Claude (1985), *The View from Afar* (Oxford: Basil Blackwell).
Link, Eric Carl (2009), *Understanding Philip K. Dick* (Columbia, SC: University of South Carolina Press).
Luckhurst, Roger (2005), *Science Fiction* (Cambridge: Polity Press).

Lucretius (1969 [1st century BCE]), *On the Nature of Things*, trans. Martin Ferguson Smith (London: Sphere).
Lyotard, Jean-François (1991 [1988]), *The Inhuman: Reflections on Time*, trans. Geoffrey Bennington and Rachel Bowlby (Cambridge: Polity Press).
Mackey, Douglas A. (1988), *Philip K. Dick* (Boston, MA: Twayne).
Margulis, Lynn (1981), *Symbiosis in Cell Evolution* (New York: W. H. Freeman).
Margulis, Lynn (1998), *Symbiotic Planet: A New Look at Evolution* (Amherst, MA: Basic Books).
Margulis, Lynn and Sagan, Dorion (1987), *Microcosmos: Four Billion Years of Microbial Evolution* (London: Allen and Unwin).
Marx, Karl (1976 [1867]), *Capital. A Critique of Political Economy*, Vol. 1, trans. Ben Fowkes (Harmondsworth: Penguin).
Massumi, Brian (2002), *Parables for the Virtual: Movement, Affect, Sensation* (Durham, NC: Duke University Press).
Maturana, Humberto R. and Varela, Francisco J. (1980 [1972]), *Autopoiesis and Cognition: The Realization of the Living* (Dordrecht: Holland).
Maturana, Humberto R. and Varela, Francisco J. (1987), *The Tree of Knowledge: The Biological Roots of Human Understanding* (Boston, MA: Shambhala).
Mayr, Otto (1986), *Authority, Liberty and Automatic Machinery in Early Modern Europe* (Baltimore, MD: Johns Hopkins University Press).
McKee, Gabriel (2004), *Pink Beams of Light from the God in the Gutter: The Science-Fictional Religion of Philip K. Dick* (Dallas: University Press of America).
Meillassoux, Quentin (2008), *After Finitude: An Essay on the Contingency of Necessity*, trans. Ray Brassier (London: Continuum).
Milbank, John (2008), 'Paul against Biopolitics', *Theory, Culture & Society* 25 (7–8): 125–72.
Moore, F. C. T. (1996), *Bergson: Thinking Backwards* (Cambridge: Cambridge University Press).
Mullarkey, John (1999), *Bergson and Philosophy* (Edinburgh: Edinburgh University Press).
Myers, Robert E. (ed.) (1983), *The Intersection of Science Fiction and Philosophy* (Westport, CT: Greenwood Press).
Nakagaki, T., Yamada, H. and Tóth, A. (2000), 'Intelligence: Maze-solving by an Amoeboid Organism', *Nature* 407 (6803): 470.
Nietzsche, Friedrich (1968), *Twighlight of the Idols and the Anti-Christ*, trans. R. J. Hollingdale (Harmondsworth: Penguin).
Nolan, Christopher (director) (2010), *Inception* [motion picture] (USA: Warner Brothers).
Pagels, Elaine (1992 [1975]), *The Gnostic Paul: Gnostic Exegesis of the Pauline Letters* (London: Continuum).
Pagels, Elaine (2006 [1979]), *The Gnostic Gospels* (London: Phoenix).

Pagetti, Carlo (1992 [1975]), 'Dick and Meta-SF', in Mullen et al. (eds), *On Philip K. Dick: 40 Articles from Science-Fiction Studies* (Greencastle, IN: SF-TH), 18–25.

Palmer, Christopher (2003), *Philip K. Dick: Exhilaration and Terror of the Postmodern* (Liverpool: Liverpool University Press).

Pascal, Blaise (1966 [1669]), *Pensées*, trans. A. J. Krailsheimer (Harmondsworth: Penguin).

Pasolini, Pier Paolo (1977), *San Paolo* (Torino: Einaudi).

Pearson, Keith Ansell (2002), *Philosophy and the Adventure of the Virtual: Bergson and the Time of Life* (London: Routledge).

Pick, Arnold (1903), 'On Reduplicative Paramnesia', *Brain* 6: 242–67.

Prigogine, Ilya and Stengers, Isobel (1984), *Order Out of Chaos: Man's New Dialogue with Nature* (New York: Bantam Books).

RC [Running-Clam], Lord (aka David Hyde) (2006), *Pink Beam: A Philip K. Dick Companion* (Ward, CO: Ganymedean Slime Mold Pubs).

Rickels, Laurence (2010), *I Think I Am: Philip K. Dick* (Minneapolis: University of Minnesota Press).

Rickman, Gregg (1985), *Philip K. Dick: The Last Testament* (Long Beach, CA: Fragments West/Valentine).

Rickman, Gregg (1988a), *Philip K. Dick: In His Own Words* (Long Beach, CA: Fragments West/Valentine).

Rickman, Gregg (1988b), 'Philip K. Dick and the Search for Caritas', in *Philip K. Dick: In His Own Words* (Long Beach, CA: Fragments West).

Rieder, John (1992 [1975]), 'The Metafictive World of the Man in the High Castle: Hermeneutics, Ethics, and Political Ideology', in Mullen et al. (eds), *On Philip K. Dick: 40 Articles from Science-Fiction Studies* (Greencastle, IN: SF-TH), 223–32.

Roberts, Adam (2002), 'The Man in the High Castle by Philip K. Dick', online review, *Infinity Plus*. http://www.infinityplus.co.uk/nonfiction/highcastle.htm

Robinson, James M. (ed.) (1990), *The Nag Hammadi Library in English*, 3rd edn (San Francisco: HarperCollins).

Robinson, Kim Stanley (1984), *The Novels of Philip K. Dick* (Ann Arbor, MI: UMI Research Press).

Roeg, Nicolas (director) (1976), *The Man Who Fell to Earth* [motion picture] (USA: Cinema V).

Rossi, Paolo (1984), *The Dark Abyss of Time: History of the Earth and the History of Nations from Hooke to Vico*, trans. Lydia G. Cochrane (Chicago: University of Chicago Press).

Rossi, Paolo (2000), *Logic and the Art of Memory: The Quest for a Universal Language* (London: Athlone Press).

Rossi, Umberto (2011), *The Twisted Worlds of Philip K. Dick: A Reading of Twenty Ontologically Uncertain Novels* (Jefferson, NC: McFarland and Company).

Roth, Philip (2004), *The Plot Against America* (London: Cape).

Rowlands, Mark C. (2003), *The Philosopher at the End of the Universe: Philosophy Explained through Science Fiction Films* (London: Random House).

Russ, Joanna (1975), 'Towards an Aesthetic of Science Fiction', *Science Fiction Studies* #6 2 (2). http://www.depauw.edu/sfs/backissues/6/russ6art.htm

Russell, Bertrand (1912), 'The Philosophy of Bergson', *The Monist* 22: 321–47.

Russell, Bertrand (2004 [1946]), *History of Western Philosophy* (London: Routledge).

Ryan Nichols, Nicholas D. Smith and Fred Miller (eds) (2008), *Philosophy Through Science Fiction: A Coursebook with Readings* (London: Routledge).

Sanders, Steven M. (ed.) (2008), *The Philosophy of Science Fiction Film* (Lexington: University Press of Kentucky).

Schneider, Susan (ed.) (2009), *Science Fiction and Philosophy: From Time Travel to Superintelligence* (Oxford: Blackwell).

Scholes, Robert (1979), *Fabulation and Metafiction* (Urbana: University of Illinois Press).

Scott, Ridley (dir.) (1982), *Blade Runner* [motion picture] (USA: Warner Brothers).

Segundo, Juan Luis (1974), *Our Idea of God* (Maryknoll, NY: Orbis Books).

Simondon, Gilbert (1989), *L'Individuation Psychique et Collective* (Paris: Editions Aubier).

Simondon, Gilbert (1995 [1964]), *L'individu et sa genèse physico-biologique (l'individuation à la lumière des notions de forme et d'information)* (Paris: Presses Universitaires de France).

Sladek, John (1973), 'Solar Shoe-salesman', in *The Steam Driven Boy and other Strangers* (St Albans: Panther Books), 172–9.

Sorel, Georges (2004 [1908]), *Reflections on Violence*, trans. T. E. Hulme (Mineola, NY: Dover).

Soulez, Philippe and Worms, Frédéric (2002), *Bergson: Biographie* (Paris: Quadrige / Presses Universitaires de France).

Stableford, Brian (1987), *The Sociology of Science Fiction* (San Bernardino, CA: Borgo Press).

Stathis, Lou (1984), 'Afterword', in Philip Dick, *Time Out of Joint* (London: Gollancz), 213–20.

Sutin, Lawrence (1991), *Divine Invasions: A Life of Philip K. Dick* (London: HarperCollins).

Sutin, Lawrence (1995), 'Introduction', in *The Shifting Realities of Philip K. Dick* (New York: Vintage), ix–xxix.

Suvin, Darko (1979), *Metamorphoses of Science Fiction: On the Poetics and History of a Literary Genre* (New Haven, CT: Yale University Press).

Suvin, Darko (1992), 'The Opus: Artifice as Refuge and World View (Introductory Reflections)', in Mullen et al. (eds), *On Philip K. Dick: 40 Articles from Science-Fiction Studies* (Greencastle, IN: SF-TH), 2–15.

Taubes, Jacob (2004 [1993]), *The Political Theology of Paul*, trans. Dana Hollander (Stanford, CA: Stanford University Press).

Taussig, Michael (1993), *Mimesis and Alterity* (London: Routledge).

Taylor, Angus (1975), *Philip K. Dick and the Umbrella of Light* (Baltimore, MD: T-K Graphics).

Vest, Jason P. (2009), *The Postmodern Humanism of Philip K. Dick* (Lanham, MD: The Scarecrow Press).

Voltaire (2002 [1752]), *Micromégas and Other Short Fictions*, trans. Theo Cuffe (London: Penguin).

Wachowski, Andy and Wachowski, Larry (directors) (1999), *The Matrix* [motion picture] (USA: Warner Brothers).

Warrick, Patricia S. (1980), *The Cybernetic Imagination in Science Fiction* (Cambridge, MA: MIT Press).

Warrick, Patricia S. (1987), *Mind in Motion: The Fiction of Philip K. Dick* (Carbondale, IL: Southern Illinois University Press).

Watts, Alan (1975), *Tao: The Watercourse Way* (New York: Pantheon Books).

Waugh, Patricia (1984), *Metafiction: The Theory and Practice of Self-Conscious Fiction* (London: Routledge).

Westfahl, Gary (1998), *The Mechanics of Wonder: The Creation of the Idea of Science Fiction* (Liverpool: Liverpool University Press).

Whitehead, Alfred North (1942 [1933]), *Adventures of Ideas* (Harmondsworth: Penguin).

Wilson, William (1851), *A Little Earnest Book Upon a Great Old Subject* (London: Darton and Co.). http://archive.org/details/alittleearnestb00wilsgoog

Wisdom, John (1975), 'Gods', in Malcolm L. Diamond Jr and Thomas V. Litzenburg (eds), *The Logic of God: Theology and Verification* (Indianapolis: Bobbs-Merrill), 158–77.

Worms, Frédéric (1997), *Introduction à 'Matière et Mémoire' de Bergson: suivie d'une brève introduction aux autres livres de Bergson* (Paris: Presses Universitaires de France).

Worms, Frédéric (1999), 'Matter and Memory on Mind and Body: Final Statements and New Perspectives', in John Mullarkey (ed.), *The New Bergson* (Manchester: Manchester University Press), 88–98.

Worthen, Thomas (1997), 'Herodotos's Report on Thales' Eclipse', *Electronic Antiquity: Communicating the Classics*. http://scholar.lib.vt.edu/ejournals/ElAnt/V3N7/worthen.html

Wright, N. T. (2005), *Paul: Fresh Perspectives* (London: SPCK).

Yates, Frances A. (1984), *The Art of Memory* (London: Ark).

Žižek, Slavoj (2010), 'Paul and the Truth Event', in *Paul's New Moment: Continental Philosophy and the Future of Christian Theology* (Grand Rapids, MI: Brazos Press), 74–99.

Index

alchemy 7
alternative history 113
Amazing Stories 5
anamnesia *see under* memory
androidization 18, 19–20, 26, 64
androids/robots 61, 132, 137, 148–52, 154–61, 164, 166–7, 207
animism 39–40, 64
antiques 120–3, 126
Aristotle 5, 9, 149
Asklepios 197
as not (*hos me*) 98–9, 102, 105–7, 113–16, 127, 134, 164–5
astrology 7

Badiou, Alain 52, 87–97, 103, 107, 151
balking *see* ethics
Ballard, J. G. 119
Bardo Thodol 162
Baudrillard, Jean 22
Benjamin, Walter 1, 43, 97, 158
Berth, Edouard 30
biological unconscious 178
biopower 139
Black Iron Prison 18, 87, 126, 130, 135, 197
Buck Rogers 81
Butler, Octavia 53

Campbell, John W. 6
capitalism 15, 21–2, 86, 94, 115, 139, 151
caritas 19–20, 107, 141, 150–1, 158, 199
causality 37, 65, 72, 149, 181
chiasmus (life-death) 95, 98, 103, 108, 151, 200
commodity fetishism 18, 94
computers (intelligent) 73–5, 165
creation (e.g. of life) 53, 132, 151, 159–61, 163, 174, 210
creative activity (e.g. artistic) 109–10, 147, 174, 206, 209–10
creative tendency 33, 46, 51–2, 68–9, 89, 91, 142, 161, 164, 177

crisis 40, 104, 130, 170, 179–80, 187, 190, 194, 207

Dante 172
Davis, Erik 23–4, 48, 109
Deleuze, Gilles 11–15, 88, 90, 135, 191
Dionysos 16, 197, 198
Dogon egg 192
Durkheim, Émile 36, 39, 64, 177

eclipse 1–3, 8, 190
ecology 190, 208–10
Einstein, Albert 31
élan vital 33 *see also* creative tendency
Embarcadero Freeway 125
empire 18, 22, 85–9, 93–4
energy 34, 48–9, 211
entropy 18, 144, 150, 156
Erasmus 16, 85
ethics
    of balking 20, 37, 92, 125, 135
    humanist 32, 155
    and ontology 14, 17–19, 27, 129
    and openness 60, 69, 167
    posthumanist 75, 164, 167
evil 119, 182, 184
evolution 33–6, 38, 44, 46, 148
evolutionary sublime 53

factitious unity 79–80, 140
Flash Gordon 82
formalism (Russian) 27
Foucault, Michel 18, 31
Freud, Sigmund 30, 39, 191
Friends of God 197–8

Gernsback, Hugo 5–6
Gilgamesh 5, 171
gnosis/gnosticism 24, 28, 107–10, 173, 177, 178, 188–9
Goodman, Nelson 131, 166
Guattari, Félix 135

Hamlet 77
Hayles, Katherine N. 22–3, 48
Heidegger, Martin 32, 97, 119
Heraclitus 12
hermeticism 191–2
Herodotus 1–2
hero(ism) 81–3, 155, 164–5
hesitation 37, 92
hos me see as not
Hume, David 181
hymenoptera 36, 39

I Ching 65, 116, 128–9, 133
idios kosmos and *koinos kosmos* 12, 25, 42, 177, 206
imagined communities 46
immortality 5, 163, 200
information
    and biology 53, 65
    culture 24
    universe as 177
instinct *see also* war-instinct (*under* war)
    and intellect 33, 36–41, 44
    virtual 40, 46
intuition 33, 37, 54, 79–80, 109
Irigaray, Luce 28
iron cage 18

Jameson, Fredric 16, 21, 115
John Carter 82
Joyce, James 14, 115, 210
Jung, Carl 14, 117

Kafka, Franz 18, 102
Kant, Immanuel 10, 184–5
Kepler, Johannes 6–7
klesis see vocation
Koyré, Alexandre 7

Lash, Scott 21, 24
law (as principle) 91–6, 100, 193
League of Nations 31, 73
Leibniz, Gottfried Wilhelm 184
Lem, Stanislaw 21, 205, 207
Lévi-Strauss, Claude 187
love 19, 28, 44, 50, 107, 140–1, 158, 199, 201, 211 *see also caritas*
Lucretius 6
Lyotard, Jean-François 32

magic 7, 39, 105
McKee, Gabriel 20, 23–4, 170
Malinowski, Bronisław 39
Mann, Thomas 31
Margulis, Lynn 44, 53
Marx, Karl 18, 94, 97
Mayr, Otto 32
Meillassoux, Quentin, 181
memory
    as anamnesia 165, 172
    artificial 83, 156
    mechanization of 13, 32–3, 79
metafiction 27–8, 103–4, 124, 176
Modern Electrics 5
morality (closed vs open) 44–50, 55, 57–8, 90, 94, 100–1, 152, 162, 197–9
More, Thomas 5
mortality 26, 38–9, 96, 163, 202
Mullarkey, John 15, 59
Murphy's Law 39

Nazism 35, 49, 114–20, 126–31
Newton, Isaac 7
Nietzsche, Friedrich 88

ontology 14, 92, 108, 124, 134, 164, 189, 191, 206 *see also* ethics

panopticism 18
Parsifal (Wagner) 187–9
Pascal, Blaise 169, 184–5
Pasolini, Pier Paolo 94
Péguy, Charles 30–1
pharmakon 183–6, 191, 198
Pike, James (Bishop) 16, 85
Plato 5, 9, 109
Poe, Edgar Allan 5
posthumanism 22, 48, 53, 91, 164
postmodernism 21–3, 27
prediction 1–2, 6, 8, 67, 70–1, 77, 149
Prigogine, Ilya 15
process philosophy 11–12, 13, 117, 206
Pythagoras 5

reality
    artificial 61, 76–81, 144, 175
    breakdown of 12
    reality fields 134–5, 165, 205–6, 209

and the 'tyranny of the concrete' 116, 129–30
recursion 33, 195–6, 202
reduplicative paramnesia 186–91
remnant 99–103, 126, 174
resurrection 88, 95–7, 108, 142, 166
Rickels, Laurence 22, 26
robots *see* androids
Rossi, Paolo 7, 10–11
Rossi, Umberto 19, 24–5, 42, 120
Roth, Philip 114
Russell, Bertrand 8, 15, 52

Saint Paul 16, 19, 24, 52, 85–111, 158, 169, 191
salvator salvandus 138, 173–8, 184, 186
Santayana, George 129
Scholes, Robert 27
Science Fiction Studies 31
scientifiction 5
Shelley, Mary 5
Simondon, Gilbert 32, 135, 173
Sisyphus 162–3
Sophia (Wisdom) 16, 199–201
Sorel, Georges 30–1
Spinoza, Baruch de 172
SS (*Schutzstaffel*) 19–20
Suvin, Darko 5, 16, 21, 106, 166
Swift, Jonathan 5

Thales 1–2, 4, 8–9
theodicy 22
Tibetan Book of the Dead, The see *Bardo Thodol*
transubstantiation 24, 166, 188

United Nations Educational, Scientific and Cultural Organization (UNESCO) 31
universal and particular 49, 90–1, 93, 99–100

Valéry, Paul 31
Verne, Jules 5
visions
  2-3-74 in general 16, 130, 170–2, 179, 185, 195, 209
  of ancient Rome 18, 85–87, 110–11, 187–8, 190
  of lift operators 41, 172, 186
  pink beam of light 16, 170, 176–8, 196
vocation 55, 97–9, 140, 142
Voltaire 5

war
  civil war 77, 120
  First World War 30–1, 38
  in general 2–3, 16, 17, 31
  nuclear 35, 63, 70, 72, 152
  Second World War 35, 63, 114, 116, 128–9
  war-instinct 34–5, 43, 47, 59, 67, 73, 164, 197
Weber, Max 18
Wells, H. G. 5
Whitehead, Alfred North 14, 109, 206
Wilson, William 6
Wilson, Woodrow 31
wonder (as beginning of philosophy) 9–11, 13
wu (emptiness) 127

Xenophanes 5, 192

www.ingramcontent.com/pod-product-compliance
Lightning Source LLC
Chambersburg PA
CBHW071827300426
44116CB00009B/1471